CLICKER TRAINING

FOR

YOUR HORSE

CLICKER TRAINING
FOR
YOUR HORSE

ALEXANDRA KURLAND

Sunshine Books, Inc.
Waltham, Massachusetts 02453

CONTENTS

Foreword

By Karen Pryor, author of *Don't Shoot the Dog!*

Clicker training is a technology, based on behavioral science, that first came into general use in the training of dolphins and whales. Beginning in 1992, clicker training has been sweeping the dog training world. Now it's time for the horses.

To learn anything new, it helps to have a friend to teach you. Alexandra Kurland is just such a friend. She is an experienced rider, teacher, and trainer. As a horse owner herself, she has looked constantly for better ways to communicate with her horses. She studied round-pen training under John Lyons, and incorporates many of his methods in her own teaching. She is a graduate and teacher of Linda Tellington-Jones' Ttouch™, a system of using manual contact to ameliorate both physical and behavioral problems in horses.

When Alex discovered operant conditioning, the basis of clicker training, her inventive mind found dozens of new ways of applying it, ways she could immediately share with her horses, pupils, and clients. As a developer of clicker training, with some experience of horses, I've been absolutely dazzled by Alex's fertile imagination and creative new uses of the technology.

Clicker training is named for the acoustic "marker signal," whether mechanical or vocal, which identifies the behavior that is being reinforced, during the instant that the behavior is occurring. Horses are wonderful learners, but they are not very good guessers. Without a marker signal, it takes many repetitions to identify for a horse what action is being reinforced, whether the reinforcer is negative (an easing of pressure, as in the round pen or "horse whisperer" approach) or positive (a piece of carrot.)

For the horse, the click means, "Treats are coming—because I made my person click." The treat might be food, initially, or a pat, or just a chance to try again. But it's the click that counts. Instead of nosing into pockets for treats, the clicker-trained horse tries to do what you want, while it keeps its ears active, listening for the click. It is learning to learn.

Clicker training is a very forgiving system. When you are using positive reinforcement it's hard to make a serious mistake. Kids can clicker train; so can non-riding parents. In fact, people with no formal training experience often learn clicker training faster than the "experts" with years of force-based training habits to unlearn.

In this remarkable book, Alexandra Kurland shows you how and why to use the techniques of positive reinforcement and shaping, with a horse. She leads you through the methodology step by step, over and over, so that you can do it for yourself. And she makes the biggest benefit crystal clear: Clicker training is not just effective: it's fun!

Horses think clicker training is fun, too. These horses like to learn. They actively try to learn new ways to get reinforced. They want to make their owners click! Look at the facial expressions and body postures of the horses in this book. They are happy horses. And the relaxed, confident, happy horse is a safe horse, too.

Clicker trainers rigorously avoid using physical force and punishment; for many people that's a primary reason for learning clicker training. We clicker trainers avoid punishment for scientific reasons as well as out of humaneness: research shows that learning proceeds much faster if pain and fear are avoided. Furthermore, with horses especially, it's easier on the trainer. If you are using only positive reinforcement, you don't need the physical skills required for dealing with an upset, frightened, or pushy horse. If the horse begins by behaving that way, you can even start your clicker training at a distance, or with a fence or a stall door between you and your new pupil. Alex describes this in detail in the wonderful story of rehabilitating a dangerously aggressive mare named Fig, in Chapter 22.

Back in the 1960's, when I was training dolphins at Hawaii's Sea Life Park, I also raised Welsh ponies. My ponies were trained with shaping, a marker signal, and treats. It was unconventional and therefore, in the eyes of traditionalists, incorrect. Once, at a horse show, while I was inside a stall braiding a pony's mane before its class, I was amused to overhear a woman in the next stall saying to a friend, "Mrs. Pryor doesn't know a thing about horses; but she has the smartest ponies!"

Well, Ms. Kurland knows a great deal about horses AND she also has the 'smartest' horses—and owners. Furthermore, she's an engaging and colorful writer. You'll read this book for the sheer fascinating maverick joy of it. But try the methods, too. No matter where you begin, or what happened in the past, you and your horse can learn to work more smoothly together and enjoy each other more. You may even find, with clicker training, that you and your 'clicker horse' develop the kind of mutual trust and friendship most owners only dream of having.

Karen Pryor
July 4, 1998

For your **FREE** clicker
Call **1-800-47-CLICK**
(1-800-472-5425)
or
Send your name and address to
Sunshine Books, Inc. • 49 River Street • Waltham, MA 02453
e-mail: *clicker@clickertraining.com*

Dr. Dolittle, I Presume:
An Introduction to Clicker Training

IF I COULD TALK TO THE ANIMALS

When I was little, I read Dr. Dolittle and dreamed of talking to animals. When I grew up I found a way to do it. It's not magic. In fact it's completely the opposite. I simply discovered the scientific principles of training and learned how to apply them to horses. My guides for this came from an unlikely source. Dr. Dolittle, I discovered, was really a dolphin trainer.

Imagine yourself back in the early 1960's. You have just been hired by an oceanarium to train their dolphins. No one else has ever done this before. If you get stuck, there are no experts around who can guide you through the process. Swimming in the tank in front of you is a wild-caught dolphin. Your assignment is to get it to jump through a hoop suspended five feet above the water. How are you going to do it?

If this were a horse, any good circus trainer could get you started. Circus trainers have a long tradition of teaching animals to jump through hoops. In fact, the oceanariums relied on them in the beginning to train their dolphins.

The circus trainers did manage to get the dolphins to perform a few simple tricks, but basically they discovered that their methods didn't work on animals that could just swim away.

The circus trainers gave way to a new breed of trainers, people who understood the behavioral science of operant conditioning, first described by B. F. Skinner. Among these early trainers was Karen Pryor, whose landmark book, *Don't Shoot the Dog*, has been the standard guide for clicker trainers since it was first published in 1984. Pryor, more than anyone else, is responsible for bringing clicker training out of the behavior labs and putting it into the hands of real-world trainers.

Clicker training refers to a new method of teaching behavior using a "yes" signal, or conditioned reinforcer, to tell the animal precisely when it has done something right. Instead of the high-frequency whistle used by dolphin trainers, most trainers of land mammals use a toy clicker, hence the name. The sound of the clicker tells the animal that whatever it was doing at the exact moment it heard the clicker has earned it a reward.

Clicker training is a little like the genie in the bottle. Once it gets out, there's no shoving it back in. At first it was just the marine mammal trainers who were interested in applying Skinner's work. Then the word started to spread. Zoo trainers became curious. At the marine parks they didn't just teach the dolphins to jump through hoops. They also taught them to accept handling and to swim onto stretchers so they could be lifted out of the water for medical treatment. If you could do that with a dolphin, why couldn't you do it with a baboon, or a tiger? Clicker training gave the zoos an alternative to squeeze chutes and tranquilizer guns.

In 1992, Pryor teamed up with a canine behaviorist, Gary Wilkes, to present a series of seminars on clicker training for dogs. These services started a revolution in dog training. Nowadays, when you mention clicker training to a group of dog people, there's a good chance that not only will they know what you're talking about, but many of them will even be using it with their dogs.

The one great void in all this was the horse world. I learned about Karen Pryor and clicker training from a friend who trained wolfhounds. When I first read *Don't Shoot the Dog*, no one I knew of in the horse world was talking about clicker training. That's not to say that there weren't people out there using it with horses, but it wasn't part of any mainstream training discussions. When I started clicker training my horse, I felt like an isolated pioneer blazing my own trail.

I learned the early steps of clicker training by reading Pryor's books, *Don't Shoot the Dog* and *Lads Before the Wind*. I watched her videos, and learned from the dog trainers. I might not want my horse to sit down on his haunches, but the principles these trainers used were universal. They could be applied to any species and any behavior. So I went out to the barn and started treating my horse like a dog.

Please don't toss the book aside when you read that. It's not as crazy as it sounds. I didn't teach my horse to roll over and play dead, but I did experiment with some other "doggy" behaviors. I used the clicker to teach my horse to follow a target, to "heel off leash," and to come when called. My first experiences convinced me that I had found the missing piece in my training, the one element that would tie everything else together to create the consistent, solid performance I was looking for.

The clicker acts as a "right answer" cue. It lets me tell my horse very precisely when he has done something I want, and it gives him a reason to want to go on producing more of that behavior. This tiny plastic box and the principles it represents expanded my training beyond anything I had achieved before (Fig. 1).

I introduced clicker training to my clients, and in horse after horse, we discovered the same results.

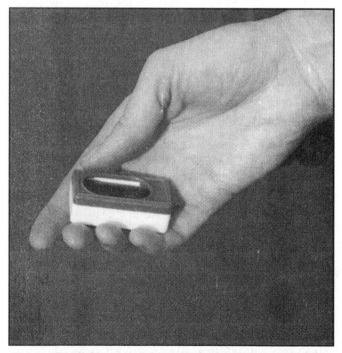

Fig. 1: The clicker.

The horses loved it. Resistances melted away. We experienced quantum leaps forward in the quality of their work. In 1996 I began writing about clicker training for horses, and created a web site for it on the Internet. That's how my work first came to the attention of Karen Pryor. She e-mailed me asking me if I would be interested in writing a book on clicker training. Interested! I jumped at the opportunity. Here was a way to bring this wonderful new technology to the horse world.

BE CAREFUL WHAT YOU WISH FOR

I suggested to Karen that we do a short training booklet outlining the basic principles of shaping, and detailing the beginning steps of conditioning horses to the clicker.

Karen e-mailed me back that she wanted something longer. It's the old story of be careful what you wish for, you may get it. Little did she know, when she first said that, the floodgate she was opening. This book is packed with fifteen years of teaching and riding experience. It's an intensive course on training, problem solving, riding, and, oh yes, that funny new stuff, clicker training.

I had begun teaching in the early 1980's. My own personal horse at that time was a Thoroughbred mare I had raised. When she was two, she was diagnosed as a wobbler. The term is descriptive. She had spinal-cord damage that left her with limited feeling in her hindquarters. She had full muscle control; she just couldn't tell where her feet were. Without sensation she had trouble keeping her balance. It wasn't just that she wobbled from side to side; any sudden change could send her crashing to the ground.

Her neurological condition led me to TTEAM, Linda Tellington-Jones's holistic therapy and training system, and I became a TTEAM practitioner. At the same time I became interested in dressage. The marriage of the two disciplines was the perfect combination for my horse. As her balance improved, I started to ride her, something that had been unthinkable at the time of her diagnosis. I used my dressage training to rebuild her damaged gaits. I introduced her to lateral work, and, to stabilize her hindquarters, I taught her piaffe, or trotting in place. Just as a blind person does, she was learning to compensate for the loss of sensation.

At this point people were getting curious. How was I getting my horse to do all these things their own horses couldn't? They started asking questions, and I began to teach. Over the years I've had a number of instructors and trainers as clients, but for the most part the people I work with are private owners. They range from novice, first-time horse owners and beginner riders to advanced trainers with years of horse-owning experience behind them.

I don't maintain a training facility. Most of my clients keep their horses at home and I travel to them. That means that I am dealing with real-world problems in situations that are often far from ideal. Most of the horses I work with come to me because the owners are having serious problems with them. What I often find is a confused, belligerent horse with a rider who is in way over her head. If I'm lucky, we'll have a ring to work in, but more often than not the only work space is a muddy paddock with unsafe fencing.

The real answer for many of these situations is to send the horse out for training while the person gets some riding lessons, but that isn't always possible. Even where money is not an issue, people are often reluctant to do this. They've all heard horror stories of horses that have gone off for training and come back a wreck. So, we muddle through. We unravel the tangled knots of confusion, and in the process people reconnect with their horse and discover how much fun training their own horse can be.

BACK TO BASICS

A common problem I've found is that many people simply don't know where to begin with their horses. They've got a horse who has bolted off with the last six people who tried to ride it, and they haven't a clue what to do about it. It's not unusual for a training session to begin with the following exchange:

A: "So what do you want to work on this week?"

Client: "Oh, I don't know. Anything you want."
That's the first variation on the theme. The second is:

Client: "I want to work on cantering" (piaffe, jumping, or some other piece that is way beyond the current training level for this particular horse/ rider combination).

Over the years I've learned how to deal with both answers. I say okay, and then I sit back and watch while the person gets the horse ready. The horses always tell me where I need to begin. Sometimes the lesson starts out in the pasture. The horse is working on cantering all right, straight away from the owner. Never mind riding, it takes her half an hour just to catch the horse. Here's a good candidate for clicker training and the round pen (Ch. 21, Crossing the Line into Aggression, and Ch. 26, The Rest of the Barnyard).

Another horse may barge over his owner when she brings him out of his stall. She wanted to work on his tendency to pull and run away out on the trails. We're going to work on trail riding, beginning right here in the barn aisle. This horse is telling me he needs some basic leading lessons. We're going to use the clicker to teach him to respect our space and to respond to our signals. In the process we'll be solving the issues his rider is encountering with him out on the trails (see Ch. 5, The Power of Goal Setting, and Ch. 8, Foal Training).

Another horse may be fine until you try to put the bridle on, or bring out the fly spray. His owner complains that the horse spooks a lot under saddle. She can only ride in one end of her corral because her horse is so afraid of the far corner. She's afraid to take him out on the trails. The last time she did, her horse spooked at a bird and dumped her.

What she's missing are all the signs of fear her horse is showing her right here in the barn. I don't need to take the horse out on the trails to watch him spook. I can see it every time he flinches at the curry comb, or jumps at the sound of a car pulling up. I see his owner dancing around him, trying to soothe him, but never really solving the problem. This horse needs to have a good dose of clicker training and lots of gentle "sacking out" (Ch. 8).

NEVER START WITH YOUR GOAL

The common theme here is, never start with your goal. It doesn't matter what specific job we're going to ask a horse to do, whether it's riding down a trail, working cows, jumping, dressage, or anything else we may dream up, we all want the same thing: a fun, responsive riding horse. I get that by paying attention to what my horse is telling me. Resistance of any kind, whether it's as subtle as a tight jaw or as obvious as a runaway, is just the horse's way of signaling to me what he needs to work on. If I ignore him, I shouldn't blame him if we get in a wreck.

If I have a crack in the plaster wall of my house, I don't want a builder to come in and try to hide it under a coat of paint. I want him to go down in the basement and check the foundation. This book is about rebuilding foundations, brick by brick.

I've written this book for both beginners and advanced riders alike, and I've packed it full, like an overstuffed suitcase. If you try to read it from cover to cover, you may be overwhelmed by the details. I'd suggest instead that you read Part I, The Rules of the Game, and then go out to the barn and introduce your horse to the clicker. When your horse first catches on to the clicker, you can almost see a light bulb go on over his head. This is a truly magical moment. As many times as I've witnessed this, I never get tired of watching the lights go on.

Once you've got the first few steps down, you'll be ready for more. Training is not a linear process. Just as I don't always start every horse in the same place, you don't have to read this book in the order in which it was written. Maybe you just bought a yearling, and the section on raising young horses has caught your eye. By all means skip ahead and read through those chapters. Or maybe you've got a trailer loading problem, or you're struggling with an aggressive horse. Each section contains references that will loop you back to the appropriate discussions and exercises that will prepare your horse for the next layer in his training. So, inevitably, wherever you begin, you're going to find you cover all the material in this book.

THE TOOLBOX

I think of my training as a giant toolbox. When I started out with my first horse, I had only three tools: patience, perseverance, and a great love of horses. What I needed to add were the nuts-and-bolts tools. I've been accumulating tools for years.

Some of the first things I learned are now packed away in the bottom of my box. I've found other training tools to replace them that work better for me. I'm a pack rat by nature, so I never throw anything away. I still keep those early tools in the box, because, you never know, they still might come in handy. It's like those blunt scissors we all used in kindergarten. Every now and then we can still find a use for them.

Some tools I've never included in my box. That doesn't mean they aren't good tools, and you might want to put them in your box. For example, my mare's physical problems ruled out the use of cavallettis and jumping gymnastics. That's a whole area of training for which I had to find alternatives; but your horse might benefit from this kind of work.

Other tools never made it in my box for reasons of philosophy. I tend to use a minimum of gadgets.

I know some of these tools can produce reliable horses who do what they're told without any argument, but for the most part I choose not to use them. Hobbles, martingales, leverage bits, they're all designed to give us more control, and many trainers know how to use them well. I prefer to leave them hanging in the tack shop. The clicker takes up less room in my tool box, and it gets the job done for me.

That doesn't necessarily mean that I think these tools are universally bad and should never be used. If someone feels safer out on a trail in a curb bit rather than a snaffle, then that's the bit that person should use. I may think some of these tools are dangerous, but I don't have to stand on a soapbox and protest against them. If I don't like hobbles, or tie downs, or any of these other restraint devices, I don't have to use them. I don't have to eliminate them, or make someone feel stupid for using them. I know they can't jump in my toolbox unless I put them in there, so I don't need to be afraid of them.

PAYCHECKS

The same can be said of clicker training. It's something new, and that means that there will be people who will push against it. Feeding horses treats during training is something most of us have been taught not to do. "Horses get distracted. They get pushy. You'll just be teaching them to bite."

We've all heard these arguments. And they're right. Without the rules imposed by the clicker, horses can get out of control. It's just that we've learned the wrong lesson from our horses' rude behavior. The horses are trying to tell us what a good motivator food is. Instead of avoiding treats, we should be trying to find a way to use them. If I can harness them into my training program, I'm going to gain a very powerful tool, one I'd be foolish not to use.

It's like using an old-fashioned typewriter in the age of computers. Yes, I can get the job done using outdated technology, but not nearly as well. That, in a nutshell, is what clicker training represents. It gives us the technology to take one of the most powerful positive motivators in a horse's life and put it to work for us.

Conventional trainers never learned how to do this. Without a "right answer" cue, such as the clicker, linking performance to reward, food becomes a distraction instead of a motivator. If you can't enhance performance with positive reinforcement, the alternative is to suppress behavior with pain. Historically, this was the answer people chose to control horses.

Modern training has come a long way from the early days of breaking horses in by hobbling them and pulling their legs out from under them. Most trainers no longer sack horses out by blindfolding them and snubbing them up tight to a post. We don't use ginger under their tails, or chains around their legs. When we hear about methods like this being used, we're horrified. We want to be good to our horses, and we've found better ways to get the job done; but there is still a general reluctance to use food.

If you can get good results and keep your horse happy without giving him a paycheck, my hat is off to you; but I know you can't. Even the most hard-nosed trainers reward their horses. They let go of the reins. They pet them. They let them rest after a hard workout. These are all things a horse finds reinforcing and will work for.

The principles described in this book apply just as much to these reinforcers as they do for food. Even if you don't want to add sugar cubes and chopped carrots to your toolbox, I think you will find in the pages of this book much that you can agree with and use. At the very least I hope you can appreciate the principles and not feel the need to push against those people who want to experiment with this new technology.

For those of you who do decide to add the clicker to your toolbox, I know you're going to have a lot of fun with it. We are all trailblazers and pioneers exploring a new way to communicate with our horses. I've cut a path I hope many of you will want to follow. Together let's turn it into a wide, well-traveled road.

Part I:

THE RULES OF THE GAME

CHAPTER ONE

Click! Dolphin Training for Your Horse

Everyone who works around horses is a trainer. You may not think of yourself like that. To you a horse trainer is someone with years of experience and a string of lesson horses. You may still be struggling with the basics, but the title of horse trainer belongs to you as well. Whenever we are with our horses, we are training them. You may think you are just leading your horse out to his paddock or tossing his hay to him, but every interaction has training implications.

If you want to bring out the best performance your horse has to offer, it's worth taking some time to learn about training. I am not referring here to any particular style of riding. Dressage horses, jumpers, halter horses, working ranch horses, trail horses, driving horses, foals, green horses, the works: the principles I'm talking about apply to all of them.

Training is more than knowing which aids to apply for a canter depart. Training is teaching. It is both a science and an art. Very often what riders want is a cookbook: How do I get my horse to ___? They are looking for detailed steps or recipes to take them through the training process. This book includes many recipes, but before you can test them out, you need to understand the basic principles behind them.

TRAINING AND BEHAVIOR MODIFICATION

You may already have lots of people trying to give you advice. One person is telling you to put side reins on, and the next is telling you take them off. They can't both be right, so what should you do? The answer lies in first asking yourself what you are really trying to get your horse to do.

Do you want him to accept restraints, to follow a feel, to answer a cue? To understand what all this means I need to introduce you to some terms that aren't commonly used in horse training. Bear with me. Some of this may sound like jargon to you at first, but the language will become clearer with use.

Let's begin by looking at a behavior we've all had to deal with—head position. Your young horse is too high-headed. You want him to lower his head and relax his back.

Molding

You could put a martingale on to hold his head down. This kind of training is known as *molding:* the horse learns to allow his body to be placed in certain positions. When a riding instructor takes your hands and places them where she wants them, she is using molding. Side reins and a lunge line are other examples of molding. Think of a fancy bundt cake. The cake is molded into shape by the pan. The question is, does the cake hold its shape when the pan is removed? Is our horse in self-carriage, or has he simply agreed to be molded?

Negative Reinforcement

Suppose your horse doesn't really understand that you want his head down. What happens to you if you are riding and your martingale breaks? Do you have a way to communicate to your horse that you would like him to keep his head down? If the answer is no, you might want to learn how to use negative reinforcement to alter your horse's behavior.

A negative reinforcer is any stimulus in the environment that a horse will change its behavior to avoid or escape. Horses do not like to feel the pressure of the bit against their jaws. If you apply pressure by taking the slack out of the rein whenever the horse's head is up and release it every time he starts to lower his head, the horse will very quickly learn to keep his head down. You don't need to depend on a mechanical device. Now you have a cue that can communicate what you want to the horse.

Targeting

Another way you could lower the horse's head is through targeting. Suppose you show the horse a carrot. You could make him reach down for the carrot, thereby lowering his head. The horse is targeting on or matching his movements to the movements of the carrot. Chiropractors make frequent use of this technique to ask horses to bend and supple their necks.

Leading a horse is another form of targeting. You want the horse to stop when you stop, to turn when you turn, to move when you move. In other words, you want him to target on your body. But how do you teach targeting in the first place? Using food may work, but most of us don't want to run around waving carrots at our horses. So what else can we do?

Shaping

This brings us to shaping and clicker training. In shaping, the animal exhibits a small tendency to perform in a desired way. By using positive reinforcement the trainer increases the tendency for that behavior to occur.

Suppose you want your horse to walk around you on a circle to the left. He's turned out in a paddock so he's free to do what he wants. But imagine what would happen if every time he moved to the left, you rewarded him with a carrot. It wouldn't be long before he'd be moving exclusively to the left.

I can see you shaking your head in disgust. You are saying this is worse than targeting with a carrot. You can't run around the paddock shoving carrots at your horse; you'd be the laughing stock of the barn.

In training horses, shaping rarely is used by itself. We combine it in subtle ways with molding, negative reinforcement, and targeting. You're already using shaping with your horse, though you may not know that's what you're doing. That's really the point of this book. How effectively shaping is used depends on how well you understand how it works.

To give you a clear picture of this, let me describe a system in which only shaping is used: dolphin training.

Consider a dolphin swimming in a pool. A dolphin can't be trained in the same way a horse can. You can't mold it with martingales; you can't restrain it with ropes or a halter. So how do you communicate with it?

Suppose you want the dolphin to jump through a hoop. You could begin by lowering the hoop into the water and hoping the dolphin swims through it. When it does, you'll reward it. The problem is that an untrained animal might never swim through the hoop.

You could nudge the process along by throwing the dolphin a fish every time it swims in the direction of the hoop. If your timing and your aim are good, pretty soon you'll have the dolphin swimming through the hoop to get to its food reward. If you now slowly raise the hoop, you might even be able to get the dolphin to leap out of the water and through the hoop. The dolphin will do this in preference to some other behavior, all for the sake of a food reward.

To the dolphin, the fish is a *primary reinforcer*. A primary reinforcer is the actual reward the animal is working for. The challenge with this type of training is delivering the fish at exactly the right moment. Even if you throw the fish just as the dolphin swims through the hoop, it may not become aware of it until much later. The dolphin might begin to think it gets a fish for swimming away from the hoop, completely the opposite result from the one you are trying to get.

You can solve the problem by introducing a *secondary reinforcer or bridging signal*. A secondary reinforcer is a signal that tells the dolphin that a fish is coming. If the trainer blows a whistle just before he tosses a fish into the water, the dolphin will learn to associate the sound of the whistle with the fish. At first, the whistle is not connected to any other behavior. The dolphin has simply learned to start expecting a fish every time it hears the whistle.

When the dolphin has clearly made the connection, the trainer begins to link the signal to a particular behavior. Now he isn't just randomly blowing the whistle and throwing a fish out to the dolphin. Instead he waits until the dolphin is swimming toward the hoop.

In this method, the process is repeated until the dolphin makes the connection between a particular behavior and the sound of the whistle. In effect, the trainer becomes a giant vending machine that only certain behaviors will unlock. From the dolphin's point of view, it is in control of the training session. In fact, that's one of the major advantages this type of training has over other methods. It's fun for the animal. The dolphins become enthusiastic overachievers who love to show off their skills.

THE EQUINE CONNECTION

How can these methods help you to train your horse? Most training techniques rely on a combination of negative reinforcement, molding, and targeting. You use whips and leg aids to tell the horse to move away from pressure. You close your hand on the reins to mold his head carriage. You teach him to target on your body to lead him.

In addition, you practice positive reinforcement, You pat your horse after a good jump; you tell him he's good when he picks up the correct lead. These are "right answer" cues, but how well do you use them? Can you clearly reinforce individual criteria such as the height a shoulder is lifted in lateral work? Do you use secondary reinforcers well? Do you know what your primary reinforcers are?

Before I started clicker training, my horse was trying to tell me that the answer to those questions was, no, I wasn't being clear enough. He didn't always understand what I wanted him to do, and even when he did, he wasn't sure he wanted to do what I was asking.

That's where I was in 1993. My personal horse, Peregrine, was an eight-year-old Thoroughbred gelding out of my mare. A difficult foaling had left him with a damaged back and stifles that locked hard. The stifle is the joint in a horse's hind leg that is equivalent to our knee. It's designed to lock when a horse is at rest, and then to release when the horse takes a step forward. In Peregrine the joint didn't always release. He would try to take a step, and the leg would remain rigid and unbendable.

Peregrine's stifle problems had haunted us throughout his training. It made him far and away the hardest horse I have ever had to train. The stifles didn't just lock up his body, they locked up his brain as well. When Peregrine was six, I added John Lyons's training to my ever expanding toolbox. John's no-nonsense approach suited Peregrine's temperament, and we began to make good progress together.

Two years later our training was abruptly interrupted by a freak shoeing accident. My blacksmith fitted Peregrine with a pair of rim pads to keep snow from balling up in his feet over the winter. Pads like these go on thousands of horses every year, but within hours Peregrine was hobbling in pain. He looked for all the world like a horse who was foundering. The shoes were on for less than a day, but the damage was already done. Sole pressure from the pads had so badly bruised his feet that he was laid up for over seven weeks with a series of abscesses.

You can create good things even out of bad circumstances. Peregrine couldn't walk, but he could still learn. I had just ordered one of Karen Pryor's early videos on clicker training. If I had been riding, I might not have taken the time to experiment with the clicker, but now I could do nothing else.

I wasn't sure exactly how to begin. In her books Karen had described how she first paired the secondary reinforcer with a food reward by blowing a whistle just before she threw a fish to the dolphins. I tried clicking Peregrine and then giving him a little grain. He liked the grain, but he didn't seem to be making the connection with the clicker.

I was impatient. If this was going to take days, I wasn't interested. The video had shown how you can teach a dog to touch its nose to the end of a target stick. I brought out a whip and held it out in front of Peregrine. Like most horses he was curious. He sniffed it. I clicked and gave him some grain. He nuzzled my pockets, which earned him nothing. He bumped into the whip again, and I responded with a click and more grain.

I remember that session so clearly. At first he was simply curious about the whip. Then he was more distracted by the grain, and what I was hiding in my pockets. Why was I feeding him treats? I didn't normally do that.

I tried to position the whip between his nose and my pockets so he'd bump into it on his way to mugging me. Every time he collided with the whip, I clicked him and gave him a little handful of grain. He started to pay more attention. I watched with pure delight as he reached over and deliberately touched the whip with his nose. I was experiencing that first magical moment in clicker training when the animal makes the connection. Peregrine was discovering that his actions had a direct impact on mine. He was learning how to unlock the cookie jar.

At the time, I wasn't looking for any practical applications for the clicker; I just wanted something that would break up the boredom of stall rest. I didn't know that I was taking the first few steps toward totally transforming the way I train horses.

When Peregrine could hobble a few paces, I got him to target on the whip and follow it around his stall. As his recovery progressed, I reviewed all of his basic training. With the clicker, things that had been almost impossible before became easy. For the first time since he was a small foal, I was no longer fighting against his body. Motivated by the clicker, Peregrine was discovering how to make his own body work.

The clicker was fun, and it certainly made a difference on the ground. The real test came when we went back to work under saddle. Prior to this, if someone had asked me what riding Peregrine was like, I would have said he had the equine version of dyslexia. I often felt as if the messages I was sending him got scrambled on the way to his brain. I'd ask for a turn, and the signals would go into a little black box somewhere in his body and come out all garbled. The clicker gave us the decoder we'd been missing in our training.

After seven weeks of teaching him party tricks and reviewing some ground work, he went back into training further ahead than when he was injured! Everything was different. It wasn't just that he was moving better physically, though that was certainly true. The real change was in his attitude. He was totally focused on me. He was listening, and, more than that, he was deciphering my messages. I remember an early ride where I could almost feel him say, "Oh, that's what you want! Why didn't you say so before?"

Peregrine's stifles made him an unusually difficult horse to train. My next question was, would this benefit other horses? I started to experiment with some of my clients' horses. We conditioned them to the clicker the same way I had Peregrine, by asking them to touch a whip. I discovered it didn't always go as fast as it had with him. Several of the horses took a couple of sessions before they really understood how this new game was played. But, without exception, once they had the idea, they all rocketed forward in their training.

Now, when I work with a horse who isn't trained to the clicker, I feel as though I have one hand tied behind my back. What's the difference? Clicker training is fun for both the horse and the handler. Horses learn incredibly quickly when secondary reinforcers are used. They become enthusiastic, active participants in the learning process.

With the clicker it's almost as though I can talk to my horse. I can single out individual elements of a movement and tell the horse very precisely what I want. With that kind of information, I can reduce both the physical and mental stress of any exercise.

The clicker represents a real shift in thinking on the part of the trainer. The rider is no longer micromanaging the horse's body into a particular movement or "frame." The rider's job is to give a signal, which triggers a response in the horse. It is up to the horse to arrange his body and produce the movements that will generate the reward. He isn't moving away from the negative consequences of a wrong answer. He understands what the right answer is and is working actively to produce it. Training shifts from "what is my horse doing wrong that I need to correct" to "what is he doing right that I can reinforce."

PRACTICAL APPLICATIONS

So how does all this work in the real world? Let's go back to the previous example of your young horse who won't lower his head. Begin by conditioning him to a secondary reinforcer. I often use the exercise of asking the horse to touch his nose to a small plastic cone. (I stopped using whips and shifted to cones instead because I discovered horses can see them better. By the way, I'm not talking about the big highway cones you see at construction sites. What I've use are small six-inch cones that are normally used as lane markers at sporting events.)

When the horse understands the concept, you're ready to apply it to actual training situations. Let's go back to the arena and ask your horse to lower his head using the negative reinforcer of the bit. You're going to cue him exactly the way you did before. The difference will be in how you reinforce correct responses. Originally, the horse learned what not to do—don't put your head up. He dropped his head to avoid pressure. His reward was the release of the bit pressure.

Now, add a secondary reinforcer. When your horse drops his head, make a clicking sound followed by a reward. This enables you to tell the horse "that's what I want," the instant he produces the desired reaction. The negative reinforcer becomes a cue that triggers a response. The difference is that now the horse is working toward a positive goal.

Performance is further enhanced by incorporating a *variable reinforcement schedule* into the reward structure. The horse must keep giving you incrementally more behavior to earn his reward. If you're training him to put his head down, he'll have to leave his head down for longer and longer intervals before you'll click and give him his treat.

If you doubt the power of a variable reinforcement schedule, consider slot machines. Never knowing quite when the reward is coming keeps people pulling the lever. Casino owners use this principle to make money. You can use it to move your horse's performance toward consistent excellence.

What kinds of things can you train with a clicker? The answer is, anything you can imagine your horse doing. I've used it for all kinds of liberty work, including free schooling over a complex course of jumps. I've used it to teach horses to load on a trailer, to ground tie, and to come when they're called. I've used it while riding to teach the piaffe, to introduce the Spanish walk (Fig. 2), and to teach lateral movement (Fig. 3). I've even used it to teach a horse to fetch and to lie down. Secondary reinforcers belong in your program whenever you are teaching something new or when you are encountering a resistance to training.

FINDING THE RIGHT REWARD

Dolphins work for fish. What do horses work for? Food is a powerful primary reinforcer and one that most horses are eager to work for. The secondary reinforcer keeps you from being "mugged." The horses learn that the only time they will be fed in a training situation is when they hear the click. I use food with my own horse, but it's not the only primary reinforcer available. Remember the definition? A primary reinforcer is something the horse finds rewarding. When I'm working my horse in piaffe and he hears a click, he gets a number of things he likes. First, he gets to stop. Piaffe is physically demanding, so a chance to rest is an important reward. He gets food, but he also gets verbal praise and lots of stroking.

If you don't want to use food, you don't have to. The key is to discover things your horse finds rewarding and to link them to a secondary reinforcer.

A common complaint of riders is, "My horse stops whenever I tell him he's good." Secondary reinforcers are not new to the horse world. You use them all the time, and very often you aren't even aware of them. Many of us have encountered horses who stop when you say "good boy." Their trainers didn't intend it, but these horses think "good" is a secondary reinforcer. Secondary reinforcers end behavior. When a dolphin hears the whistle, it's going to scout around for a fish, not continue to jump through hoops.

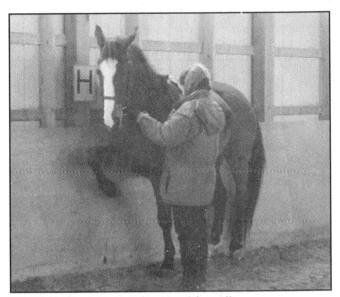
Fig. 2: Clicker training the Spanish Walk.

Does this mean you shouldn't use secondary reinforcers? Not at all. It just means you need to be more aware of what you are teaching. Remember, you are always training. My horse has learned that "good" is an encourager. It means "You're on the right track; keep going." I have several "you got it right" cues. One is the click. Another is the sound "aaah." It doesn't matter what you choose as long as you are clear and consistent.

To sum up, what does dolphin training add to the horse world? Clarity. Consistency. Excellence. And, oh yes, lots of fun.

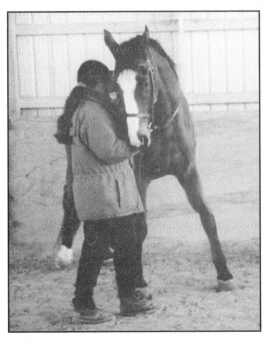
Fig. 3:
Shoulder-In.

CHAPTER TWO

Getting Started with the Clicker: Understanding the Rules of Shaping

Let's begin with a game.* It's played with two people, and it's really very simple. The first person is the one being "trained." This person has a very easy assignment. He is sitting in a chair. The rules of the game say he may move his arms, his head, his legs. He can twist about any way he wants to, but he may not leave the chair.

The second person is the trainer. She is not allowed to speak to her subject. Her job is also very simple. She is to hold an object such as a riding crop or small cone several inches away from the trainee's face.

If you were the trainee, what would you do? You might start by ignoring the crop. You might even look away. But our trainer is very persistent. She continues to hold the crop right in front of your nose. How annoying. After a few minutes you might try brushing it away.

Now a surprising thing happens. You hear a loud distinctive clicking sound, and your "trainer" hands you a sliver of Godiva chocolate. You love chocolate, especially this dark, rich bittersweet chocolate you've just been given. You can see she has more of it. You try grabbing for it, but she whisks it away just out of your reach. If you could get out of the chair, you could snatch it all. Only you can't without breaking the rules, and now that annoying whip is back in your face. You bat it away again. Click. She hands you a creamy sliver of chocolate.

What's going on here? She puts the whip up again. You wish she'd stop that. You want the chocolate. You forgot to have lunch and you're starving. The chocolate has reminded you how hungry you are.

You push the whip away again.

Click. She hands you a third delicious sliver.

Now you are beginning to wonder. Is there a connection here? When she puts the whip up again, you very deliberately touch it.

Click. More chocolate.

Yes! You can get her to give you the whole box, just by touching the whip. You've got her trained. Touch—click—chocolate. How simple. Now all you want is for her to hurry up and present the whip so you can touch it again.

Our simple game has suddenly turned into a very clear illustration of how operant conditioning works.

OPERANT CONDITIONING

Operant conditioning—the very name makes something that is really very simple and fun sound very complex and imposing. When you hear a term like that it makes you think of a university lab, not a horse barn. So first let's review some definitions.

Operant refers to the operator, and, as you can see from our game, it's really the trainee who's in charge. He could have chosen to sit in the chair and sulk. He could even have decided to ignore the rules of the game and leave. (How many of us have ridden horses that have bolted away when they've had enough of our training?)

Conditioning refers to the repeated association of a particular stimulus with a behavior until the presence of that stimulus causes the behavior. Ring a bell every time you flash a bright light in someone's eye, and eventually just the sound of the bell will cause the person's pupils to contract. Say "whoa" often enough just before you make your horse stop, and eventually your horse will stop when you say "whoa." This is an example of respondent conditioning.

In operant conditioning the horse stops on his own, and you reinforce that with the release of the

---

*From *Don't Shoot the Dog! The New Art of Teaching and Training,* by Karen Pryor; Bantam Books rein, or a pat on his neck. The horse associates things he wants with stopping and begins to stop more willingly. We all use operant conditioning to some extent with our horses. How we structure our training depends on how well we understand the rules of shaping.

PUTTING POSITIVES TO WORK FOR US

So why do horses put up with us bouncing around on their backs telling them what to do? The answer is very simple. In fact, all training becomes very easy when you realize that only two things control behavior. It doesn't matter whether you are a horse or a human, we are all motivated by the same two drives. We are all either moving away from pain or toward pleasure.

Traditional horse training relies on teaching horses to move away from discomfort. They learn to move from whips, from our legs, from the bit, from pressure on their halters, and from martingales and side reins. Most of our training relies on some form of negative reinforcement to produce the behavior we want.

Suppose we want to turn the picture around and have the horse learn by linking things he wants to the behavior we want to shape. How would that change our training? First we would have to find things our horse wants. The list would include things like a chance to run and play, a chance to stand still after hard work, time with a favorite pasture mate, a pat, a vigorous neck rub, a chance to roll in a sand pit, and, best of all for many horses, food.

The problem with this list is obvious. It's hard to use these things in a training session. You can't let your horse drop and roll every time he gives you a right answer. Even petting can be a problem. If you give him a massage every time he does something you like, your hand is going to get tired.

Also, for best results rewards need to be delivered exactly when the behavior occurs. That way the horse can clearly mark what he was doing and repeat it again for another reward. Delays between behavior and reward can lead to confusion. You think you're rewarding your horse for dropping his head. He thinks it's for swishing a fly with his tail. So how do you resolve the problem? Very simply. You introduce a secondary reinforcer.

Food, or a pat on the neck, is the primary reinforcer. It's the thing the horse wants. The secondary reinforcer, or bridging signal as it is also called, is a conditioned signal that becomes linked to rewards. It tells the horse, "You are about to get a treat."

Whistle every time you give your horse a carrot, and you'll start to notice that whenever you whistle, he'll be looking around for his treat. If you only give him carrots when you whistle, he won't be checking out your pockets at other times. This is the key. It allows you to use food without it creating problems. The horse learns to expect a treat only when he is presented with a particular signal. I work around clicker-trained horses with my pockets stuffed full of grain, and I am never mugged. Instead, the horses are listening to me and waiting for the magic sound of the clicker.

Once the horse understands that a whistle or a click means food, I can link that sound to behavior. The horse begins to learn that the only time he hears the click is when he presents certain behavior. Now it's the horse who thinks he has me trained. He's aware of the power of his own actions. "Present behavior. Get treat." What a wonderful system!

GETTING STARTED

So how do you actually begin to teach this to a horse? I start by teaching a simple trick. My intent here is to condition the secondary reinforcer and to establish the link between behavior and reward. I'll worry about practical applications after he's learned how the game is played.

I like to start with something that's very simple and easy to understand. I'm going to teach the horse to touch his nose to an object. I've found this works really well in part because it is outside the horse's normal training program. It's so different from anything else he's been asked to do, that he has to pay attention to figure me out.

I like to begin with the horse in his stall (Fig. 4). I put a stall guard up across his open door. That way he can get his head out, but, if he starts to get pushy about the food, I can easily step back out of reach. I begin by holding a small plastic cone between his nose and my body. Don't worry if you don't have a cone. Any handy object will do. I've used whips, hard hats, the lids off of supplement buckets. Anything that's safe, easy to hold, and large enough for him to see will do.

I want my horse to be successful. Without actually pushing the cone at his nose, I want to position it so he's likely to bump into it. Most horses are really curious and will want to check it out. As soon as they touch it, I click and hand them a little grain. About a teaspoonful is all that's needed. The horses are usually really surprised and excited by this. They forget about the cone and everything else except my hands and my pockets. Why am I getting grain? Is there more? They can get very pushy at this stage.

Keep yourself safe, but basically ignore this. Stay focused on your primary intent. If you get distracted by your horse's greed, you'll miss opportunities to reinforce him for good behavior.

One of the rules of shaping states that unreinforced behavior tends to go away. As you reward your horse only when he touches the cone, he will begin to orient away from your pockets. I have seen this take less than five minutes with some horses and several hours or even days with others. Be patient and be creative.

What do I mean by that? You want to create opportunities for your horse to be rewarded. You want him to be successful. For example, if your horse gets distracted and looks away for a moment, take advantage of that. When he swings his head back for another hopeful search of your pockets make sure the cone is positioned so he'll have to bump into it on the way.

He won't understand at first that his bumping into it is the reason he's getting grain. That's not important. As it happens repeatedly you'll see him begin to actually move toward the cone. You can almost see the light bulbs going on as the horse figures it out. Now you have a horse who is clearly touching the cone on purpose. *Click.* You give him grain, and almost faster than you can keep up he's back touching the cone.

At this point you can begin to move the cone around. It's important here to remember four of Karen Pryor's Rules of Shaping.

1. When you improve on a behavior, work on one element of the behavior at a time.

2. When introducing a new element, relax your standards on the old ones.

3. Shift the behavior in small enough steps so that the horse continues to be successful.

4. If behavior deteriorates, return to the previous stage in the training.

All behaviors are made up of many elements. Even something as simple as touching a cone has many different criteria you can reinforce. You could focus

Fig. 4: A safe way to introduce your horse to the clicker is to put him in a stall with a stall guard across the door. If he gets pushy about the food, you can easily step back out of reach. For his first clicker-trained behavior I want this Arabian to touch a target, the plastic cone I'm holding.

on having the horse touch a particular spot on the cone, or on touching it fast, or on tracking it while you move it around.

Suppose you want your horse to touch a cone that's sitting on the ground. You need to focus just on shaping that element (Rules 1 and 2). If you also worked on how fast he responded, or the precision of where he touched the cone, you'd be training too many different elements of the behavior at once. Your horse could easily become confused and discouraged.

If you've been holding the cone at chest height, and you suddenly lower it to the ground, your horse will probably loose track of it and become frustrated. Instead, lower the cone four or five inches at a time. Within minutes your horse will be reaching to the ground to touch it (Rule 3). There's a wonderful proverb that applies here beautifully: Make haste slowly.

You will begin to shift from a fixed to a variable reinforcement schedule. A fixed schedule means that a standard unit of behavior gets a reward. Touch the cone, get a treat. The horse knows exactly how much effort he needs to put out to earn his treat. Fixed schedules create limited results. Variable schedules create excellence.

Fig. 5: *He's consistently touching the cone, so now I'm going to make it a little harder for him. My goal is to be able to set the cone down on the ground and still have him touching it. I'll shape this behavior in small steps, so my horse continues to be successful.*

Fig. 6: *I've taken my hand off the cone for the first time. He's got the idea. He's still touching the cone even though I'm no longer holding onto it. I've successfully shaped this Arab's first clicker-trained behavior.*

If your horse stops strongly touching the cone, move it back to a height where it is easy for him. Reestablish the behavior and then go on to increase the difficulty (Rule 4).

In a variable reinforcement schedule, the reward is unpredictable. Since the horse never knows exactly when his treat will come, he keeps offering more behavior. Touching the cone got a click last time, but now it's not working, so the horse tries bumping the cone harder. By withholding the click, you got the behavior to vary. Some of the touches will be strong, solid ones, and others will be half-hearted brushes. Once the behavior varies you can selectively reinforce any element you choose. Choose movement, and you can get your horse to follow the cone to the ground. (Figs. 5, 6.)

ADDING A CUE

At this point you are ready to put touching the cone on cue. A *cue* is a stimulus that becomes linked to a behavior and eventually causes that behavior. For example, many horses learn to go into a trot on voice command. Horses aren't born speaking English. The first time your horse hears you say "trot" he won't have a clue what is wanted, or even necessarily that he is supposed to respond to the sound. But if you say the word consistently enough just before you know your horse is about to trot, the sound will become linked to the action and can eventually be used to cause the behavior.

The order of training is important here. Create the behavior first, and then present the cue. Many people train in the reverse order, with often confused results. Their inexperienced horse is working on the lunge line. He's ambling along, not paying much attention to them, and they're shouting at him to trot. The horse just keeps walking, so what is he learning "trot" means?

Remember, we know what we intend with our words and signals, but our horse doesn't. Before I say "touch," I want my horse strongly orienting to the cone. I need to know that if I hold it out in front of him at an easy height, within seconds he'll touch it. Until I have the behavior strongly in place, I won't use any verbal cues.

Once he's offering me the behavior consistently, I'll present the cone and say "touch." The word doesn't cause the behavior. It predicts it.

As I repeat this consistently, the signal will become linked to the behavior. Now I can say "touch," and my horse will look around for a cone.

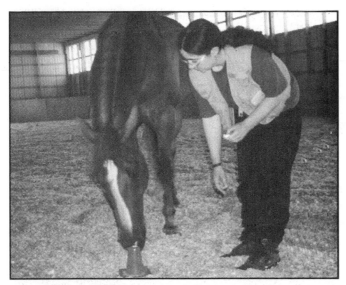

Fig. 7a: Even with the temperatures in the high 90's, I can still do some training. I'm introducing this unbroken half-Arab to the clicker. He could wander off, or he could pester me for grain. Instead he's focused on earning his treats.

Fig. 7b: I'm going to use a variable reinforcement schedule (see text) to get Indy to touch a series of cones to earn one click.

Fig. 7c: Now I've taken Indy outside. He is totally free to leave, but instead he is choosing to walk round my circle of cones touching each one in sequence, just to earn a tablespoon of grain.

Now I can really have fun with the game. I can set the cone further and further away and get my horse to walk, trot, and eventually canter to it. (This can actually be a useful exercise if you ever need to watch your horse move away from you for a lameness exam and you have no one around to lead him for you.)

You can add more cones and get your horse to move around a circle touching each of the cones in turn. You can teach other "tricks." You can teach your horse to kick a ball, to lower his head on command, to ground tie, to bow. Use your imagination and have fun.

GOING BEYOND TRICKS

You can also begin to incorporate the clicker into your horse's regular training. Indy, a six-year-old half-Arabian gelding, came to me in June for training. He was a kind, beautifully mannered horse. His owner/breeder had never had time to saddle-break him, so at six he had a lot of catching up to do.

During the worst of the summer heat when the temperature was creeping toward 100°F and neither of us wanted to work hard, I introduced him to the clicker. He was slow to catch on. It took three sessions before he finally got the connection between touching the cone and getting grain. After that there was no stopping him. He became an enthusiastic overachiever. He needed only minutes to shift from touching one cone to touching a whole circle of cones (Figs. 7a, b, c).

At this point he'd been under saddle for about four weeks. He was proving to be a wonderfully steady horse with lively gaits and an incredibly soft, responsive mouth.

The next step with the clicker was to use it for ground work to teach Indy shoulder-in. The clicker now became linked to movement. Indy had no trouble making the connection. Twenty easy minutes into his first in-hand session he was moving down the track in beautiful shoulder-in (Fig. 8).

The third step in the process was to introduce the clicker under saddle (Fig. 9). I worked Indy in hand for about a week before beginning this process. I used what he was learning with the clicker. Under saddle I asked him to rotate into shoulder-in. As he began to respond correctly, I clicked. Indy startled and came to a full stop (a sure sign that he has clearly understood the clicker). His ears airplaned around as he tried to figure out what was happening.

I scratched Indy just in front of his withers. Normally I use food as the reward. It's so easy to give, and it's usually by far the strongest motivator, but Indy was still at the stage where grain got him excited. Since he was just starting under saddle, I thought he'd do better with a simple scratch.

Indy accepted scratching as his treat, and when I asked for the next step of shoulder-in, he moved easily into it, using what he had learned in-hand to present me with rewardable behavior. He was recognizing cues for a complex pattern of movement, and offering that movement to me under saddle, with no strain or resistance. The clicker bypassed what can be a long and often frustrating stage in training for both the horse and the rider.

The clicker got Indy off to a good start under saddle. It kept his body sound and his mind relaxed while he went beyond basics into the "dance" of lateral work. It let us develop a common language that could lead to an uncommon partnership. With the clicker Indy became incredibly soft and responsive, presenting work that was a thrill to ride.

Even if you never want to take the clicker this far into your everyday training, taking the time to teach simple tricks is a valuable exercise. The principles of good training are the same whether you are teaching a horse to touch a cone, or to jump a fence. Clarity is important in all training, and that is what the clicker and operant conditioning provide.

Fig. 8: Now that Indy understands the clicker, I can use it in his regular training. Here I'm introducing him to shoulder-in.

Fig. 9: Indy had been working under saddle for about two weeks when this picture was taken. The clicker quickly helped him to become comfortable with a rider. Note the lightness of the rein, and the relaxed, soft carriage of his topline.

CHAPTER THREE

Putting the Clicker to Work for You: Training with Positive Reinforcers

I will always remember what the weather was like in the summer of 1994. I have good reason to. That was the year it never seemed to stop raining. The pastures became swamps, and my vaccinated horse contracted Potomac horse fever.

I had the vet out within hours of the first signs of fever. He was in time to stop the most severe complications of the disease, which can include founder and even death, but not to prevent all the aftershocks. I spent the next twelve weeks soaking and wrapping Peregrine's feet as he developed abscess after abscess from a sole laminitis. We'd already gone through one round of abscesses the year before, but this was even worse.

Every day became a struggle to encase his feet in layers of gauze, vet wrap, diapers, and duct tape. Anyone who has had to bandage a horse knows the difficulties the routine can create, especially on an uncooperative horse. His feet hurt so much he was refusing to pick them up. I was by myself, trying to hold up the whole weight of my horse while reaching for gauze pads and strips of duct tape. The routine got old really fast. The solution was to teach Peregrine to hold his own leg up without any support from me.

By this point Peregrine had been clicker trained for about eight months. If I could teach him Spanish walk, I ought to be able to shape something as simple as picking up his feet, even if they did hurt. Shaping means taking a small tendency for a behavior to occur and through selective reinforcement increasing the frequency of that behavior.

SETTING GOALS

My first step was to decide precisely what I wanted. In any training exercise it is important to know your outcome. What exactly was I trying to teach? The clearer you are in understanding what you want, the better you'll be able to teach it.

So, what was my desired outcome? I wanted my horse to pick his foot up easily and quickly on a simple cue, and to hold it up on his own about six to eight inches off the ground without any support from me. He also needed to hold it steady, without jerking it away, for periods up to thirty or forty seconds. And he needed to allow me to medicate and bandage his foot while he did all that.

APPLYING THE RULES OF SHAPING

That was my goal. One of the first rules of training is to put as many steps between you and your goal as you can. That meant at first separating the training from the bandaging. We struggled through a day or two of wrapping while I worked on the cue to pick up his foot. Of course he already knew this from daily foot care, but with abscesses in both front feet he was feeling less than cooperative. Pain was a powerful motivator to keep his feet on the ground. I needed something to counteract this. The clicker and grain solved the problem. He already knew that a gentle squeeze on the back of his tendons was his cue to lift his foot. With grain as a motivator he became a willing participant in what had been a frustrating struggle.

Getting the foot off the ground was only the first step. Next I needed him to hold it up long enough for me to medicate and wrap his foot. To teach this I used my version of Karen Pryor's rules of shaping:

1. Train one criterion at a time.

2. Get a response, get it consistently, then improve on it.

3. Raise your standards in small enough steps that the horse continues to be successful and can be reinforced.

4. Once the behavior is established, shift from a fixed to a variable reinforcement schedule to improve response.

5. When adding a new criterion, temporarily relax the standards of the old.

6. If behavior deteriorates, go back to a previous step in the shaping process.

7. If one shaping procedure is not creating progress, find another. There are always many different ways to build the steps to the desired behavior.

Rule 1 says train one criterion at a time. My two main criteria were the length of time the foot was held up, and the height it was held. I needed to pick one to start with. If I had tried to train both height and time together, I would have ended up with a mess. I chose time to start with.

ADDING A VARIABLE REINFORCEMENT SCHEDULE

At first I reinforced on a *fixed schedule of rewards* to satisfy Rule 2. Every time he lifted his foot even for an instant—*click*—he got a reward.

All behavior is variable. Unlike the android Data, from "Star Trek: The Next Generation," we cannot reproduce exact carbon copies of behavior. The horse is going to hold his foot up for longer or shorter periods on each request. As he begins to realize that lifting his foot is a good thing that leads to a treat, he'll pick it up more and more readily. At this point it's time to move on and improve the behavior. I need to shift from a fixed to a *variable reinforcement schedule,* meaning the reinforcement will be on a random or unpredictable basis.

My horse has learned that he will be rewarded for lifting his foot. If I hesitate just a little before clicking him, I will soon have him holding it up for longer and longer periods. Why should he do this? Why does a person continue to put quarters in a slot machine? They both want the reward. They just don't know when it will come, so they keep offering more behavior. The person thinks: If I put just one more quarter in, that may just be the magic one that wins the jackpot. If I quit, I'll lose everything.

The horse is thinking: My leg is getting heavy, but if I can just hold out for another second or two, she's bound to notice and give me a treat.

Variable reinforcement schedules are the engines that drive behavior toward excellence, but they can also work against you to undermine your entire training program. Think about that annoying horse in your barn who is banging away on his grain bucket. You try to ignore him, but he just keeps on banging even harder. Finally, you give up and throw him some hay to keep him quiet. What you have done is strengthen the variable reinforcement schedule. The next time he will be prepared to bang for hours because he never knows when the reward will come.

Or suppose your horse doesn't want to cross a stream, or load on a trailer, or soften to the inside rein. It doesn't matter what it is. Right before he releases his resistance, you're going to see his worst behavior. That's often when people quit because they don't understand the cycle they are in. They say "He's never going to get it," and they give up moments too soon. What they are doing is reinforcing the length of time the horse will resist the next time.

Extinction bursts

Extinction bursts are an important part of variable reinforcement schedules. Think about the last time you were trying to get that sticky window in your tack room closed. Right before you were ready to quit, what did you do? Bang on it harder? That's an extinction burst—an extra burst of energy before the subject finally quits.

We can use extinction bursts in training. Suppose I want a more energetic canter. My horse is giving me a so-so effort in response to my seat and leg aids. I've rewarded him in the past for a canter of this quality, but now I'm withholding the click. My horse starts to work a little harder trying to get the "vending machine" to work. If I reinforce that extra effort that comes during an extinction burst, I'll get an increasingly consistent, energetic performance. My horse will remain a happy and enthusiastic partner while he's producing exceptional performance.

I used this principle throughout the bandaging process. Once I finished soaking Peregrine's foot, he had to hold it up the entire time I was putting on the bandage. Understanding variable reinforcement schedules and extinction bursts bought me the time I needed.

ADDING A NEW CRITERION

By using a variable reinforcement schedule, I could get my horse to hold his foot up for extended periods. Sometimes the foot was hovering just above the ground, and sometimes it was hitting his belly. It was time now to add a new criterion and reinforce specifically for height.

I needed to remember all the rules of shaping I had followed so far, and I needed to use a new one, Rule 5: When adding a new criterion, temporarily relax the standards on the old. In other words, if I had asked him to maintain the length of time he held the foot up, while I simultaneously pressed for height, I might have ended up with a confused, frustrated horse.

So I began by asking for the foot to lift. When it lifted above a certain height that he was offering consistently, I clicked and rewarded him. It didn't matter how long he held his foot up. If he lifted his foot up high enough after only five seconds, I clicked. If he took thirty seconds to do it, I waited thirty seconds. Height was my criterion, not time. I continued to reinforce this until it became consistent.

Rule 2 says: Get a response. Get it consistently, then improve on it. How could I improve on height? I could put it on a variable reinforcement schedule, and gradually increase the height off the ground the foot was held. Then I could ask him to hold it at that height for longer and longer periods. When I jumped ahead too fast and the behavior broke down, I followed Rules 5 and 6 and rebuilt in smaller steps.

The end product in this was a horse who picked his foot up easily on request and held it up several inches off the ground for extended periods of time.

Now I was ready to bring out my vet wrap and duct tape. I had gone from struggling to hold the foot up on an uncooperative patient, to lightly stabilizing the toe while I applied a time-consuming and awkward bandage.

GETTING MORE THAN YOU BARGAINED FOR

When you train, you never get just one desired result. For every one thing you teach, you're going to get at least three other behaviors. Every goal is just one step in a much larger picture.

I set out to make my life easier during an extended lay up, and ended up improving my horse's performance under saddle. When Peregrine started back into work after twelve weeks of lay-up, I discovered he was much easier to ride. All that time spent holding up his own foot had improved his balance. He had finally figured out how to use his hindquarters to support the weight of his shoulders. His whole front end felt lighter. The reins were softer, he

turned more easily, his lateral work was better than it had ever been, and all I had done was wrap his feet in bandages for twelve weeks! You never know all the good things you are going to get when you first start training.

UNDERSTANDING BASIC PRINCIPLES

Teaching a horse to hold his own foot up may seem like a trivial exercise. I chose it as my example to separate principle from method. Many times we get hung up in the nuts-and-bolts details of how to ride a particular exercise. (Put your left hip half an inch higher, move your right hand further back, tilt your chin, lift your shoulders, etc., etc.) We argue over method, and we get so involved in detail that we forget the basic underlying principles of training.

Suppose I had chosen something much more complex to use as my example. Maybe we want to teach a dressage horse shoulder-in. I might start from the ground and use a clicker. Someone else might start the lesson under saddle, and use conventional reinforcement. One person might teach the horse a seat cue first, another a leg cue. A third might teach a rein cue first.

We can argue which technique works best, but the good trainers will all be applying the principles of shaping, and they'll each end up with something we can recognize as shoulder-in. The trainer who is confused over shaping principles will end up with a mess.

Think of it like baking bread. There may be lots of different recipes, but you have to follow certain rules to produce an eatable result. The order in which you mix the ingredients together matters. The cook who simply throws everything together into a bowl—yeast, flour, water, and all, will just end up with a mess.

In the same way, the trainer who tries to train multiple criteria, who attempts to advance the horse in big steps, who demands excellence in all criteria even while adding new elements, will end up with a muddled mess and a frustrated horse.

Training is easy if you understand the basic steps of shaping. Anyone can produce outstanding performance in a horse. Remember, if you can dream it, you can train it. How far you go simply depends on how consistent and persistent you are.

CHAPTER FOUR

Everything Is Everything Else: Bridling a Head-Shy Horse

In the Practical Uses section (Part II), I'm going to show you how to chunk down all kinds of different training sequences. I'll give you specific steps you can follow to socialize your foal, to handle aggressive horses, to overcome fear issues of all kinds, and to train for upper level performance. Before I do that, I want to give you some practice in developing your own shaping recipes. You'll do this by setting very specific goals for your horse.

To get you started I'm going to give you some common things we all want our horses to do for us. Many of these behaviors will be discussed in the following chapters. Before you read my shaping solutions, I want you to develop your own lesson plan. You may find you come up with something very different from me. That's wonderful. Training isn't a cookbook you follow to the letter. We all train out of our own experiences. Yes, there are underlying principles you need to understand. Good cooks begin with good basic technique, but then they flavor the broth to their own liking.

That's what you're going to do. You're going to teach your horse something new. You're going to begin with the ingredients he already knows, and you're going to develop your training around his personality. A bold horse may not need as many steps as a timid horse. An athletic horse may figure something out a lot faster than a youngster who's just learning where his feet are. Your training goals should be designed for you and your horse.

BRIDLING

Your first shaping assignment will be to bridle your horse. You want to be very specific here. Your goal isn't simply to get the bridle on your horse. That's too vague and would include the horse who puts his nose up in the rafters, or takes you for a dance around his stall. Remember, the clearer your goal is, the easier it is to see the training steps. For each one of your goals, you're going to develop a specific training sequence. If your goals are too general, your horse will tell you. If he has trouble learning a step, you need to be more specific in your lesson plan.

To get you started we'll go through this exercise together. Let's begin by visualizing the following scene: It's a beautiful Saturday afternoon in October, just a perfect day for a trail ride. Your friends are all tacked up waiting for you, only you're not ready because your horse is being an idiot on the cross ties. He's dancing around refusing to let you bridle him. You've had the vet check his teeth. You know there's nothing wrong with his mouth. There's no reason for this. He's just being a jerk. He's got his head up in the rafters like he's some kind of giraffe, and every time you try to get near him he throws his shoulders into you. He's slammed you against the wall twice, and just about knocked the wind out of you. He's such a pig.

Language—the self-fulfilling prophecy

Sound familiar? It may not be your horse, but you've probably seen one just like it. As you read through my description, how does it make you feel? Impatient? Angry? Frustrated? Language is important. How we phrase things will either keep us stuck in the problem, or moving forward toward a solution.

What do I mean by that? Suppose your horse is even worse than the one I've described. How you state your goal is very important. You might find yourself saying, "I don't want my horse dancing around like an idiot."

You might also say, "I want my horse to stand quietly with his head down while I put on the bridle."

In one sense both statements say the same thing, or at least they want the same end product: the bridle on the horse's head. But they create very different pictures. You can't change behavior by looking at the problem. If you tell people your horse is an idiot, chances are that's exactly what he'll be. To find the solution you have to look at the solution. If that sounds a little like Alice through the looking glass, it's really not. It just means you can make major changes in your horse by simply shifting the way you think about him.

Changing your pictures

When you say, "I don't want my horse dancing around, jerking on my arms, and acting like an idiot," what do you see? Don't you picture exactly what you just said you don't want? You see the horse slamming you up against the wall. You can almost feel the force of it. You've got six barking dogs, and the barn cat underfoot, and no room to work. Your six-year-old is whining for attention, and your least favorite boarder just pulled in. How does all this make you feel? Angry? Hostile? Impatient? Frustrated? Tight? Closed? Those are not the emotions associates with effective training.

Now rephrase your goal. "I want my horse to stand relaxed and quiet while I put his bridle on." What images does that conjure up? Don't you see a well-groomed horse standing calmly on a set of cross ties? The aisle is neat with all the tack boxes and equipment stored well out of the way. What are the feelings that match that picture? Friendly? Relaxed? Calm? Patient? Happy? Open? If you were a student, which teacher would you rather have: the one who is feeling angry and hostile, or the one who is friendly and relaxed?

RIDING IN A STATE OF EXCELLENCE

The emotions you feel describe the state you are in. You can be in a happy state. A depressed state. A calm state. Each one of these has many emotions associated with it. What else do you associate with a calm state? Feeling relaxed; peaceful; at ease; centered?

Many of these emotions are also part of what is called a state of excellence. That's an important concept for riding. Maybe you've only been riding for a short while. You didn't start until you were an adult. You're still pretty shaky on the back of a horse, but you know what good riding looks like. You've seen Grand Prix jumping, or maybe you've gone to the Quarter Horse Congress and seen some of the top reining and cutting horses perform. You're still fumbling around with your reins trying to get your horse to go where you want, and these people are doing things you can only dream about.

While it's true your goals might not be to rise to the top ranks of your sport, you can still ride in a state of excellence. Shift your language. Focus on what you want, and it will change not only how you feel, but how you act. When you're in a state of excellence everything flows—you feel inspired, and connected. Whatever you visualize happens. You're calm; you're relaxed; you're focused.

We've all experienced this state at one time or another. It may not have been when we're riding. Maybe it was at work when all the pieces of a project fell into place. Maybe it was playing a sport, or at home working out in the garden, or designing the new extension to the barn. It doesn't matter what you were doing. The key here is: If you can experience that state in one situation, you can transfer it to another. That, in part, is what visualization is about. Your riding skills may not yet be developed enough to take you over a four-foot jump course, but you can still be in a state of excellence that brings out your best performance.

The use of positive visualization

While we're on the subject of visualization, let me ask another question. When you pictured the calm horse taking the bridle, was it your horse? If you've got one of those horses who turns bridling into a daily battle, the answer may have been no. You were visualizing some horse in a magazine. It just isn't possible for you to picture your horse being anything but an idiot. That's great. Let the contrast work for you to help you find your goals. Begin with what you don't want, and then transform it to what you do.

Here's another question for you. How do you describe your horse to your friends? If you call him an idiot, that's what he'll be. No matter what you do, no matter how much training you put into him, as long as you hold that image of him, that's what he'll remain. You need to be able to separate the behavior you don't like from the horse you love. In setting your goals you want to think about what you want to include, not exclude. So let's go through bridling step by step to see how we can develop a set of positive goals.

USING CONTRAST TO STATE YOUR GOALS

Your horse dances around on the cross ties. Even for simple grooming he never stands still, and when you bring the bridle out, he's all over the place. Great contrast. Our first goal is: We want our horse to stand still in a quiet, relaxed manner.

When he sees the bridle, he throws his head up really high. It's a real battle to get the bridle on. Perfect. He's given you your second goal: We want our horse to lower his head within easy reach, and to keep it down.

He refuses to take the bit. He clamps his mouth shut and you all but have to get a crow bar to pry it open. Your horse is a great teacher; he doesn't want you to miss any of the steps. Here's our third goal. We want our horse to open his mouth easily and take the bit.

Your horse is really head-shy. As soon as you start to move your hand up towards his ears, he flings his head up. You need to wear a crash helmet just to be around him. He's really making your job easy; we want him to leave his head down while we lift the headstall up over his face.

Your horse hates having anything near his ears. You have to take the bridle apart just to get it over his head. More great contrast. We want our horse to continue to leave his head down while we take the bridle over his ears.

Your horse hates having his head fussed with. You can't even do a simple thing like fasten the throat latch without him throwing a fit. Fine. We want the horse to continue to stand quietly while we fasten the throat latch and check the bridle.

As soon as the bridle is on, your horse is prancing about like an idiot. He doesn't give you time to get your hard hat, or even check your girth. What a great teacher! We want the horse to continue to stand quietly until we are ready to go.

INCLUDING, NOT EXCLUDING

Now take out the behavior you want to exclude, and rewrite your training goals stating only what you want to include.

1. We want the horse to stand quietly, without moving his feet while he is being bridled.
2. We want the horse to lower his head within easy reach, and to keep it down.
3. We want the horse to take the bit easily.
4. We want the horse to keep his head down while we take the headstall up toward his ears.
5. We want the horse to leave his head down while we take the bridle over his ears.
6. We want the horse to continue to stand quietly while we fasten the throat latch and check the bridle.
7. We want the horse to continue to stand quietly until we are ready to go.

Think about the picture this list creates. How does it make you feel reading this through? Aren't you beginning to see your own horse standing quietly, accepting the bit?

CLEAR GOALS MAKE TRAINING EASY

Our goals create the training steps. Let's begin with Goal 1: We want our horse to stand quietly, without moving his feet while he is being bridled.

In Ch. 7, Nine Easy Steps to the Perfect Horse: Retraining Behavior Problems, we'll see that there isn't just one way we can get our horse to stand still. There are many. If one approach doesn't work, we can try something else. The more different approaches we use, the more solid the behavior will be.

We could begin by using positive reinforcement to shape standing still. Initially we won't even worry about the bridle. Leave it hanging in the tack room for now. We simply want the horse to stand still.

If your horse is nervous, and shifting about for grooming, he isn't ready to be tied. Take him off the cross ties where he could pull back and hurt himself. Put him back in his stall where he's free to move around. Now watch him. Look for any hesitation in his dance. If he pauses even for a second, click and reinforce (C/R). Repeat this several times, and you will begin to see him taking more notice. Now wait another second or two before you click. The key here is to really watch his body language. If you think he's going to move in four seconds click him in three. What will happen is gradually the four seconds will stretch to seven, then nine, then by stages up to a minute or more.

Another way you could shape this would be to have him touch a target. Hang an empty plastic jug up in his stall. If you've already taught him to touch a whip, it's easy to get him to touch the cider jug. Simply hold the whip next to the jug and say "touch." He'll be touching the jug each time you ask him to touch the whip. Repeat this several times, clicking each successful touch. Next take the whip away, and ask him to "touch." Chances are, when he doesn't see the whip, he'll touch the jug. Give him a jackpot, or extra-large reinforcement, and continue. Ask him to touch the jug until he's doing it consistently. Then you can begin to stretch the time out.

One thing you'll notice very early on in this exercise is that you will have all but eliminated stall walking. Even when he's not actually touching the jug, he'll be staying right by the target. His nose will be keeping his feet still (Fig. 10).

Still another approach would be to treat this as a leading problem. (See Ch. 10, Baby's First Steps, and Ch. 15, Ground Manners for the Older Horse.) Review your cues to ask him to back up, step forward, move over. Now if he starts to barge over the top of you, ask him to back up. If he dances sideways, tell him to step forward. It's move, countermove, only you're going to end up leading the dance. As he begins to respond to you, click him for right answers.

You'll end up with a horse who is very light on his feet. He'll move whenever you ask him to. Halts are a byproduct of movement. Just ask him to step

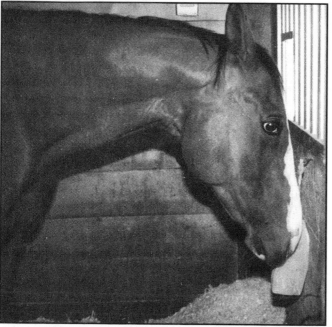

Fig. 10: Peregrine at his target, a plastic cider jug. When a second person leaned in to take his picture, her body language was saying: "Move away from the target," but I was in with him, cleaning his stall, which meant he should stay at his target. The conflict shows clearly in his face.

forward and back, forward and back a few times. A halt comes out of balancing him between these two requests. He's coming forward. Ask him to back, then as he shifts his weight back, ask him to come forward again. You may end up rocking him back and forth several times before he settles into a halt. The instant that he does, C/R. Your reward is twofold. Not only is he getting a treat, but he gets to stand still!

RAISE YOUR STANDARDS

In all three of these methods you now have your horse standing quietly for an extended period of time. It's time to add a new criterion. Remember, the rules of shaping state that when you add a new criterion, you relax your standards on the old. You're going to introduce some new elements so you won't be asking him to stand as long before you click him. Where you begin will depend on your horse.

Bring out your bridle. If your horse immediately falls apart, you need to add some more steps here. Continue to use whatever shaping method you started with, and begin asking him questions. The more questions you can think of to ask him, the better. If the answer to any of these questions is no, go back a step in your training. He's telling you that you need to explain things even more simply to him. What are you going to ask your horse? Let's start with some of these.

"Can I run my hand down your neck and have you stand still? Yes?" C/R.

"Can I brush you and have you stand still? Yes?" C/R.

"Can I bring my hand up to your face and have you stand still? Yes?" C/R.

"Can I leave my hand there a little longer and have you stand still? Yes?" C/R.

"Can I bring a cotton lead rope up to your nose and have you stand still? Yes?" C/R.

"Can I hang the bridle over your stall door and have you stand still? Yes?" C/R.

"Can I walk up to you with the bridle and have you stand still? Yes?" C/R.

HEAD LOWERING

When you reach this step you're ready for Goal 2. We want our horse to lower his head within easy reach, and to keep it down. An easy way to shape this is with a halter and lead rope. Hold the lead a couple of inches below the snap. Take all the slack

 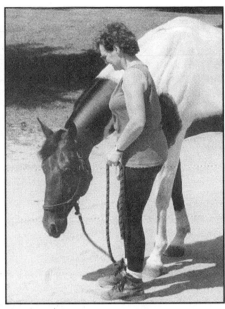 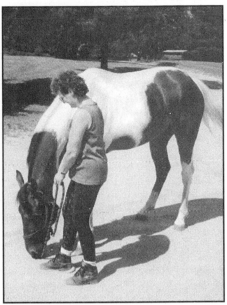

Fig. 11a: This four-year-old paint is learning to drop his head on request. His owner has her right hand resting on his poll. She isn't trying to push his head down. She is just applying steady pressure. She'll take her hand away the instant he drops his head even a little.

Fig. 11b: Horses learn to lower their heads in stages. His nose is almost to the ground, and he's beginning to leave his head down for longer and longer periods. Note how relaxed he looks in all these pictures.

Fig. 11c: This is the result we're after: he's dropped his head all the way to the ground in response to a touch on the poll. His owner will click him and give him an extra treat for this.

out so there is pressure on the halter. Don't try to pull your horse's head down. Wait for him to respond to you. As soon as he even thinks about lowering his head, C/R. Repeat this until he is lowering his head in response to light pressure on the lead (Figs. 11a, b, c). Go through your list of questions: Will you lower your head even when I'm running my hand over your neck, or brushing you, or bringing the bridle out, etc.?

OPEN WIDE

When he's comfortable with that, you're ready for step three, getting the bit in his mouth. This is an easy one, and again something you can shape in several different ways.

We've all gotten a horse to open his mouth by inserting a finger along the bars of his mouth. It's a simple step to add a C/R each time he softens his jaw. Again, you're going to ask a series of questions.

"Will you lower your head and leave it down, when there are no distractions? Yes?" C/R.

"Will you lower your head and leave it down, when I handle your muzzle? Yes?" C/R.

"Will you lower your head and leave it down, when I massage the inside of your lips? Yes?" C/R.

"Will you lower your head and leave it down, when I massage the bars of your mouth with one finger? Yes?" C/R.

"Will you lower your head and leave it down, when I massage the bars of your mouth with two fingers? Yes?" C/R.

"Will you lower your head and leave it down, when I massage the bars of your mouth with three fingers? Yes?" C/R.

"Will you lower your head and leave it down, when I massage the bars of your mouth with four fingers? Yes?" C/R.

"Will you lower your head and leave it down, when I massage the bars of your mouth with my whole hand? Yes?" C/R.

Can you see what we've done? By the time you've gotten to this last step, your horse will be totally relaxed, with his head down on the ground, allowing you to put your entire fist in his mouth. You've taught a very important piece of bridling—open your mouth when I ask.

Now bring out your bridle. You aren't going to put it all the way on, yet. The first step is just to get your horse to open his mouth and take the bit. When he does, click and make a big fuss. Reward him with special treats so he knows he's done something really wonderful. He'll very quickly associate bits with good things.

When I first started with the clicker, I put a handful of grain in my jacket pocket. Now I wear a fishing vest. I have different pockets for different treats. For Peregrine I always have sugar cubes or peppermints in addition to his grain. Sometimes I'll add chopped up carrots, or animal crackers. I can mark a particularly good effort just by increasing the size of the reward or varying my reinforcer.

Surprise is important. If I make a big fuss and give my horse his favorite treat the first time he puts his mouth around the bit, I'll build an instant association between that behavior and the arrival of good things. Instead of being resentful of the bit, he'll eagerly look forward to taking it.

TARGETING

Another way to get your horse to take the bit is to use your whip handle as a target. Hold the bit directly in front of the target. Your horse will have to touch it to get to the target. When he does, C/R. Get him touching the bit consistently, then withhold your click. Your horse will bump the bit trying to get you to click. He may even bite at it. Jackpot! With a few more repetitions you will have a horse who actively seeks out the bit. Your only job will be to position it so he can reach it. He'll do the rest!

THE HEAD-SHY HORSE

Just because he'll take the bit doesn't mean he'll let you take it up over his ears. Goal 4 covers this step. We want the horse to leave his head down while we lift the bridle up over his face. Begin by lifting the headstall up just an inch or two. If he pulls back, don't try to stop him. Say "wrong" in a quiet conversational tone of voice, and offer him the bit again. This time don't lift the headstall quite so high. C/R when he leaves his head still.

Let him drop the bit to take his treat. It just gives you another opportunity to have him practice taking it. Gradually take the headstall a little higher up his face.

Goal 5, taking the bridle over his ears, is just a continuation of this. If your horse is very ear-shy, you can insert a step here. Ask him to lower his head. Now run your hand very fast over his ear, C/R. The key here is to move fast. By the time he has a chance to respond, your hand is already gone.

Gradually slow down your hand movement. He'll very quickly realize you're not going to hurt him, and he gets a click and a treat for letting you play with his ears.

When he is calm about his ears, slip the bridle all the way on, and give him a jackpot. Take the bridle on and off several times, until he's really comfortable with this step.

By the time you've done all this, the last two steps will be easy. Goal 6 asks the horse to leave his head down while we fasten the throat latch, and check the bridle. Goal 7 asks him to stand quietly until we are ready to go.

If your horse is still fidgety while you adjust the bridle, go back and review the preceding steps.

EVERYTHING IS EVERYTHING ELSE

All this may seem like a lot of work just to put a bridle on. How long it takes really depends on your horse. You could run through all these steps in less than five minutes on an easygoing horse that's just gotten a little sticky in his bridling manners, or it could take you hours on a horse with real problems. With a difficult horse, each step becomes a major training session in and of itself, and you may want to spread the lessons out over a period of several days.

One of the many advantages of breaking training down into small steps is you are never more than a few seconds away from a positive quitting place. When training stops on a good note with the horse feeling calm and relaxed, he'll often begin the next session already presenting the next layer in the training. You can make tremendous progress even if you can only work for five or ten minutes at a time.

Is it worth it? Let's look at all the things you will have worked on, and all you will have accomplished.

Go back over the goals.

1. We want the horse to stand quietly, without moving his feet while he is being bridled.

That means you've taught your horse to ground tie. Depending upon how you shaped this, you will have also worked on his leading. You've taught him a cue to come forward, a cue to move over, and a cue to step back. You've tuned up his brakes and his steering wheel. You've improved his transitions, worked on picking up the correct lead, and introduced lateral work, all without ever leaving his stall.

2. We want the horse to lower his head within easy reach, and to keep it down.

Head lowering is a wonderful behavior to teach your horse. With head lowering you have a cue to calm down, and a cue to stop rearing. For the behind-the-bit horse, you have a cue that says, "Stretch out and reach for the point of contact." Head lowering is your antispook cue, your "relax and take a break cue." Of all the things you can teach a horse, it's one of the most useful behaviors.

3. We want the horse to take the bit easily.

Here you've also worked on getting your horse to take a paste wormer, to have his teeth floated, and to have his whiskers trimmed.

4. We want the horse to keep his head down while we take the headstall up toward his ears.

Think of all the reasons you need to handle your horse's head, from brushing and sponging him off, to putting on fly repellent, and doctoring wounds. You're also making him safer to ride. Head-shy horses tend to be spooky horses. You want your horse to be comfortable with things around his head before you ever get on him.

5. We want the horse to leave his head down while we take the bridle over his ears.

You're preparing your horse for having his ears clipped and for putting on fly repellent.

6. We want the horse to continue to stand quietly while we fasten the throat latch, and check the bridle.

7. We want the horse to continue to stand quietly until we are ready to go.

These two steps are very similar. You're teaching consistency. You've got the horse ground tying. Will he continue to stand even when he knows he's about to go out? He'll be safer and so will you, when he does.

You can never do just one thing. If you have an easy-mannered horse, chunking bridling down into tiny steps like this may seem like overkill. Fine. Treat the steps like a checklist. "Yes, my horse stands quietly." "Yes, he keeps his head down." "Well, no, he doesn't take the bit very well." That's the step you work on.

If you're teaching someone green, either horse or human, chunking the process down will simply mean you'll have a better product at the end. You'll have a leg up on all these other skills you're going to want them to know.

REVIEWING THE STEPS

Here's a review of the process of designing a shaping program.

1. State your overall goal. I want my horse to ___.

2. Recognize that your overall goal is too general for training purposes.

3. Visualize the process. Take yourself through the behavior as it now exists, and state your goals clearly for each step in the process.

4. Remember to include, not exclude. Go through your goals. If any of them are saying what you don't want, rephrase them to state what you do want your horse to do.

5. Go through the list of the nine methods for changing behavior (see Ch. 7, Nine Easy Steps to the Perfect Horse: Retraining Behavior Problems), and develop a training program for each step in the process.

Practice makes perfect

"Okay," you're saying. "I can see how this works for bridling, but what else can I teach my horse?"

Here are some suggestion to get you started. Use these simple behaviors as exercises to develop your training skills. Go through the goal-setting sequence I've outlined for each one. Develop your training goals. Rephrase them as needed into positive statements, and develop a training program for each step.

Take the time to go through this exercise now, before you've read the rest of the book. Write down your training steps, even if you can only think of one or two for each behavior. Think about how you would teach your horse. When you've finished the book, repeat this exercise. I think you'll find your goal-setting skills will be even better than they are now, and you'll have lots of new ideas for things you can teach your horse.

SAMPLE TRAINING EXERCISES

Saddling: "I want to saddle my horse." This is too general a statement. After all, even the rider with a horse who flips over backward every time the girth is tightened is managing to get the saddle on. You need to be more specific.

1. I want my horse to _____.

2. I want my horse to _____.

3. I want my horse to _____.

4. I want my horse to _____ .
5. I want my horse to _____ .
6. I want my horse to _____ .

Clippers: "I want to be able to clip my horse without tranquilizers." A good beginning. Now get specific, and remember to state how you want him to be. Walk yourself through the process of clipping. Include all the skills your horse will need.

1. I want my horse to _____ .
2. I want my horse to _____ .
3. I want my horse to _____ .
4. I want my horse to _____ .
5. I want my horse to _____ .
6. I want my horse to _____ .

Braiding (or mane pulling): "I want my horse to stand still without fussing while I'm braiding him." Your goals are getting clearer. Now state the same thing in positive terms and go through the steps.

1. I want my horse to _____ .
2. I want my horse to _____ .
3. I want my horse to _____ .
4. I want my horse to _____ .
5. I want my horse to _____ .
6. I want my horse to _____ .

Rein backs: "I want my horse to back up under saddle." You're being too vague again. How do you want him to back? All stiff-legged, with his nose in the air, or soft and round and light on his feet? Imagine what you want and write out your goals.

1. I want my horse to _____ .
2. I want my horse to _____ .
3. I want my horse to _____ .
4. I want my horse to _____ .
5. I want my horse to _____ .
6. I want my horse to _____ .

Lunging: "I want my horse to lunge quietly without bucking and racing around." You've stated your goal well, saying what you both do and do not want. Now break it down into small steps, shifting into completely positive images. What's the first thing your horse needs to be able to do? Even if it seems like an insignificant detail, write it down. For something as complex as lunging, you may find you have ten or twenty steps, not just six.

1. I want my horse to _____ .
2. I want my horse to _____ .
3. I want my horse to _____ .
4. I want my horse to _____ .
5. I want my horse to _____ .
6. I want my horse to _____ .

Trail obstacles: "I want my horse to cross streams." How? Leaping across them like they're some mammoth water jump, or walking calmly through?

1. I want my horse to _____ .
2. I want my horse to _____ .
3. I want my horse to _____ .
4. I want my horse to _____ .
5. I want my horse to _____ .
6. I want my horse to _____ .

Need some more suggestions? Ask your horse. He's your best teacher. He'll tell you what he needs to learn, and how many steps you need to break things down into. You don't have to live with bad manners or dangerous behavior. Every training problem can be chunked down into small steps. Break things down enough, and you'll begin to understand how easy training really is.

One thing you'll notice: The more you train, the more you'll have to work with. Look at your list for bridling, clipping, and braiding. Aren't many of the steps the same? You'll even see some of the same steps repeated for backing and trail obstacles. They all share common elements. For example, in each, you probably wanted your horse to drop his head. You taught that for bridling, you reinforced it for clipping; now when you ask him to lower his head for braiding, he does it automatically.

That's what so much fun about training: watching your progress mushroom. As you build up a solid foundation, the building blocks are there to be used no matter what the situation. You can't predict all the different things you and your horse will have to face. You don't have to. Build a good foundation, and your horse will be ready for anything.

CHAPTER FIVE

All Aboard! Mounting Blocks and So Much More: The Power of Goal Setting

SOMETHING FOR EVERYONE

Some of you who are more experienced may glance at this and think: a whole chapter just on getting your horse to stand next to a mounting block! You've got to be kidding. When is she going to talk about some real training?

This book is intended for people of all experience levels. In my own teaching, I work with many highly trained riders and instructors. I've been able to learn what their needs are, but I also work with beginners and first-time horse owners. If you haven't spent much time around horses, no exercise is ever too basic to be taught. I've given lessons in how to lead a horse into a barn, turn it around, and close the door behind you. Sound simple? If you've been around horses for years, of course it does, but to a timid, first-time owner with a pushy horse it can seem like an impossible task.

You may know how to teach your horse how to stand quietly while you get on. It's no problem for you—but for someone who has never dealt with this issue, it can be extremely frustrating. You may take bridling for granted. Then you buy that green three-year-old you've been dreaming of for years, and he throws his head up in the rafters whenever you come near him with a bridle.

I don't know what issues you're struggling with, or what you already know, and what you don't. I don't want to skip over anyone, so I've chosen to talk about some very basic training issues here. That way everyone can participate. Embedded in the discussion are principles and concepts that will help you with every step of your training. If you're an experienced rider, you'll be able to generalize easily from these examples, and apply the principles to your own training situation. If you're a teacher, I think you'll find that this is a very use-ful section you'll want all your students to read. And if you're a novice rider struggling to get along with your horse, I think you'll find that this is an excellent starting place.

Foundation is everything in horse training. So even if you're working with upper level horses, I think you'll find a great deal in this chapter that will interest you.

A VERY GOOD PLACE TO START

Training is easy once you know where to begin. Getting started is the hard part. You want to ride. You've got a picture of your dream horse in your head. You can see yourself clearing every fence on the course; galloping along a winding trail; or executing the perfect canter pirouette. That's your dream, but right now you and your horse are just starting out together. What are you going to work on today to get him to all those wonderful tomorrows? What are your immediate training goals that address the issues you are working on today?

Goal setting is an important part of training. When I'm working with someone on a regular basis, I'll ask them what they want to focus on today, in this lesson. Very often they'll say they don't know. They have an overall dream of what they want to do with their horse, but they don't have a specific goal in mind for that day's training. That's fine. The horse will always tell us what he needs to learn. We'll take him out to the ring and he'll refuse to walk up to the mounting block. Great. He's just given us the lesson for the day. Yes, we could get on some-how, but we'd be missing a wonderful opportunity to train.

We might have been planning to work on canter departs, but that's not what the day's lesson is going to be about. We're going to teach him to stand next to the mounting block. In the process we'll be working on leading; on ground tying; on lateral work; on loading into a trailer; and, oh yes, on canter departs, and even on flying lead changes. How is that possible when all you're doing is getting on? The answer is, you can never teach just one thing. You'll see what I mean by that as we go through this lesson.

WHEN YOU'RE YOUNG, YOU BEGIN WITH ABC

Getting your horse to stand next to the mounting block isn't just a matter of shoving him over until he's close enough so that you can catapult onto his back. We're going to take the time to teach him a series of cues. We're going to teach him to back up and to come forward. We're going to teach him to step sideways and to listen to lateral aids. We're going to teach him to ground tie. The result will be a horse who leads better, who stands better, and who responds better to your riding aids.

I almost always use a mounting block, even if I'm riding a very small horse. They're good for the horse's back, they're good for saddles, and they're certainly good for me. Yes, I make sure the horse will let me mount from the ground, but at some point in his training I'm going to ask him to step up to a mounting block. Most riders can eventually figure out how to get most horses to do this. You've probably got your favorite way, but let's look at it together and add the clicker.

FIRST STEP: STATE YOUR GOAL

First, let's decide what you want your horse to do. We have to know what our goal is in order to develop logical steps toward it.

Stated simply our goal is to get on our horse. As we saw in Ch. 4, Everything Is Everything Else: Bridling a Head-Shy Horse, the problem is that's too general a statement. It doesn't give us any guidelines. I want to be much more specific. The more detailed I am, the easier it will be to train my horse. I'm going to visualize step by step the entire process of getting on. From that I'll design a set of goals:

1. We want the horse to walk quietly next to us while we bring him up to the mounting block.

2. We want him to line himself up parallel to the block, so that the stirrup is even with the center

of the block, and his body is no more than eight inches from the block.

3. We want him to stand still with the reins resting over his withers while we adjust the stirrups and check the saddle.

4. We want him to stand still while we pick up the reins and mount.

5. We want him to wait for us to settle into the saddle and give him a signal before walking off.

6. We want him to walk off quietly from the block.

As you can see, the more specific we are, the easier it is to break the training down into small steps. If we had stayed with our general goal, "We want the horse to stand still for mounting," it would be much harder to see all the individual pieces we have to work with.

First what, then how

Let's start with Goal 1. We want the horse to walk quietly up to the mounting block with us. If our horse doesn't, we need to review basic leading. (See Ch. 10, Baby's First Steps, and Ch. 15, Ground Manners for the Older Horse.) We need to teach him not to drag along behind us, or skitter off to the side. If leading is the problem, we'll use the clicker to teach him how to lead.

Suppose your horse leads perfectly well everywhere else. He's just afraid of the mounting block. Rather than try to force him, we'll use the clicker to work him through his fear (See Ch. 14, Overcoming Fear: Clippers, Baths, Shots, Etc.). We can treat the mounting block the same way we do a trailer phobia (See Ch. 19, Trailer Loading: Can It Really Be This Easy?) and in the process we'll be working on our horse's loading skills.

Goal 2: Lining his body up to the mounting block. This is just an extension of his leading skills. We'll develop a cue that says come forward, and another cue that says move over. We'll click and reinforce (C/R) him as he responds correctly to each cue.

As for our other goals: Teaching our horse to stand still next to the block as we adjust our stirrups and get on is simply a matter of raising our criteria. At first all we're going to ask of our horse is that he stand next to the block for an instant. Then we'll withhold the C/R for two or three seconds, then five or six.

We'll gradually stretch him out until he's standing next to the block for as long as we like, one minute, ten minutes, you choose. Next we'll relax our time standard while we add a new criterion, pulling the stirrup down (on a Western saddle, it might be adding pressure with your hand to the stirrup). If he stands still, C/R. If he moves off, bring him back to the block and begin again. Remember he wants that reward. He'll make the effort to stand there once he understands that's what gets him clicked.

THAT'S ENOUGH TALKING, LET'S GO TRAIN A HORSE

So how does this actually work with your horse? Let's assume your horse leads well, and he's only mildly afraid of the mounting block. He'll walk up to it. He just doesn't understand that he's to stand parallel to it. As soon as you step up onto it, he swings his hindquarters away and faces you. That's what most horses will do the first time they are asked to line up with a mounting block (Fig. 12a). (If you have a more severe problem, the chapters already mentioned will help you out.)

Walk your horse up to your mounting block. It should be big enough and sturdy enough that your horse won't knock both it and you over if he should happen to bump against it. Buckets, while easy to move around, are not ideal.

Step up onto your mounting block as your horse approaches. Don't worry if he's square to it or not. He'll probably swing wide so he's facing you with his head. This is perfect. Organize the reins so your left hand is on his crest, activating the right rein. This will tip his nose to the right. If your mounting block is positioned against a fence, the way it would be in an arena, bending him to the right puts him on what will be your inside rein when you get on.

With your right hand, reach back and tap him on his right hip with a long dressage-length whip (Fig. 12b). If he doesn't understand what you want, he'll probably step to the right into the whip, swinging his hips even further away from the block. This is normal. Remember, horses (and people) push into pressure (Fig. 12c). You're going to use this as yet another opportunity to teach him to move away from pressure.

Keep tapping him until he takes a step back to the left. He'll do this as soon as he gets far enough away from the block that he doesn't feel crowded by it. Click, stop tapping him, and give him a treat.

Suppose he swings all the way around to the right? That's great. It just makes it easier for him to learn to move over from the whip cue. Stay on the block.

You don't want to teach him that he can drag you away from it. If he starts to pull back, anchor your hand. Become like a post in the ground. (If he's pulling so hard you can't hold him, he's not ready for this step. Go back and work on his leading.) If he's simply swinging his hips away, switch your hand positions to make it safer and more comfortable for both of you.

Position yourself on his right side. Hold the right rein in your right hand, and use the whip in your left hand to tap him directly on his right hip. C/R him for swinging his hips back toward the block (Fig. 12d). Once he's consistently moving over from a tap on his hip, return to your original position. Hold the rein in your left hand and the whip in your right hand. Tap him by reaching over his back.

LATERAL AIDS

Your horse may understand what you mean when you're positioned on his right side and asking him to step over from a direct tap on his hip. But when you're back on his left side and reaching over his back to tap him, that's when he gets confused. Diagonalizing your aids like this is hard for a horse to understand. Your body is on his left side, but the signal to move over is on his right. Be patient with him. C/R correct responses, and he'll figure you out (Fig. 12e).

You may find that he responds beautifully to you until he gets one or two steps from the block. This is also normal. He's feeling crowded, as if there isn't any more room for him to step over. As you tap his hip, he'll revert back to swinging his hips to the right. Keep tapping until he swings back. C/R. As you persist in asking him, he'll get comfortable enough to take that extra step closer to the box. It's jackpot time. Give him his favorite treat, maybe a sugar cube, or a peppermint. When you vary the treats, you're giving him valuable information, as well as making him more willing to try harder the next time (Fig. 12f).

YOU CAN NEVER DO JUST ONE THING

Repeat this whole sequence, taking him away from the block and leading him back up to it, until he lines himself up to it automatically. Can you see all the other things you're really working on here? Isn't this just like asking a horse to step up into a trailer? If you have a sticky loader who also doesn't stand well for mounting, take advantage of this opportunity to teach him this easy exercise.

Fig. 12a: This quarter horse has never used this mounting block before. He's not afraid to walk up to it, but he's not sure he wants to stand broadside to it.

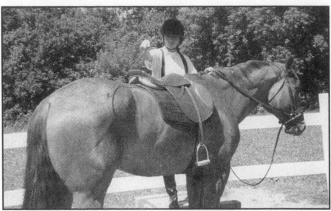

Fig. 12b: His rider is asking him to swing his hips to the left. Her left hand is on his crest, activating the right rein. This will bend him slightly to the right and make it easier for him to move his hips over. She's tapping him on the hip with a dressage-length whip. The instant he shifts his weight to the left, she'll click, stop tapping and give him a treat.

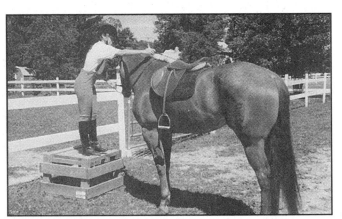

Fig.12c: Her horse responded to the whip by swinging away more to the right. This is normal. Remember, horses (and people) push into pressure.

Fig. 12d: His rider has positioned herself on his right side. She's holding the right rein in her right hand, and she's tapping him on his right hip, asking him to step to the left. With his hips this far away from the mounting block, he doesn't feel crowded. He easily swings to the left.

Fig. 12e: Now the rider is reaching across the horse's back to ask him to move his hips to the left. Horses often find this confusing. The rider is standing on the left side, but the signal to move is coming from the right. This horse kept stepping to the right, into the tap of the whip. That's normal. As soon as he shifted to the left, click, the tapping stopped AND he got a treat.

Fig. 12f: The end result: the horse is standing quietly on a loose rein while the rider mounts. The rider's right hand should be further forward on the saddle to keep the saddle from rolling sideways as it is doing here.

Can you also see how you're working on his riding? Isn't the whip like a leg aid? You're telling him to move away from pressure instead of pushing into it. You want to find as many different ways of explaining this principle to him as you can. Eventually he'll generalize the concept. It's not just a specific cue he's learning, but all cues of this type. Pressure doesn't mean "Push back." It means "Soften and move away." Everything is everything else. When you work on this one basic element in his training, you're really working on everything else you'll ever want to teach him.

These simple pieces are some of the most important things you can teach your horse. It's easy to rush through this kind of work to get to the more glamorous things like actually jumping a fence. However, if you skip too many steps, you'll usually find yourself getting stuck somewhere in your training. That's when you'll know something in the foundation is missing. Don't worry. Horses are wonderfully flexible. If you skipped a step, you can always go back and fill it in.

ADDING PIECES

So now you have your horse standing quietly next to the mounting block. You don't have to hold him there. The reins are just hanging loose over his withers. You've got the behavior consistently, and you've used a variable reinforcement schedule to get him to stand there longer and longer.

You can even step down from the block if you like, and he'll continue to stand still. Click that, because it's a new criterion. You're asking your horse to stand still and not follow you as you move around him. In other words you are asking him to ground tie at the mounting block.

Step back up onto the block and begin to go through your normal mounting routine. What would you do first? Pull down your stirrups? Organize your reins? Check your girth? Go through each step several times. Pause after each successful piece to click and treat. If he moves off, go back to the very beginning of the sequence and rebuild your steps.

VARIABLE REINFORCEMENT SCHEDULES TO THE RESCUE

At this point you may be asking yourself if you are going to have to do this every time you want to get on. Of course not. This is a teaching sequence. Until your horse understands what you want, you need to give him plenty of "right answer" cues. Imagine you are six years old again, just learning to print your letters. Your teacher is helping you. She's sitting next to you while you print the alphabet. You draw an A, and she praises and encourages you.

Remember how that made learning fun? Remember what a great sense of accomplishment you felt when you got your A's shaped just right? If someone did that to you now, you'd clobber them. Why? Because you've already learned the task. You don't need someone telling you what a great job you did. It would be annoying and even a little insulting. Once your horse has learned something well, he probably feels the same way. He'd be saying: "I can do this, stop fussing and just let me do my job." Peregrine loves learning new things, but once he's got something down, he only needs an occasional reinforcer to keep him motivated.

So once your horse is standing quietly for each individual step in the sequence, it's time to add a variable reinforcement schedule and begin to link steps together.

Up to now you've said something like this to your horse:

"Will you stand when I step up onto the mounting block? Yes." C/R.

"Will you stand when I organize my reins? Yes." C/R.

"Will you stand when I check the girth? Yes." C/R.

"Will you stand when I tighten the girth? Yes." C/R.

"Will you stand when I pull down the stirrup? Yes." C/R.

"Will you stand when I put my foot in the stirrup? Yes." C/R.

"Will you stand when I put weight in the stirrup? Yes." C/R.

"Will you stand when I stand up in the stirrup? Yes." C/R.

"Will you stand when I swing all the way over? Yes." C/R.

"Will you stand until I ask you to start off? Yes." C/R.

Congratulations! You are now on your horse and he stood absolutely still.

Walk your horse off a few steps, dismount, and begin again. (You can use the dismounting to train as well. Stop your horse. Take your foot out of the stirrup. Start to swing your leg over, then stop and sit back down into the saddle. If he stands still, C/R. Next time go a little further. Begin to swing your leg over, then reverse course, and sit back down again. It's a great way to get him used to the motion of having you mount and dismount.)

When your horse is consistent with this stage, you're going to start combining steps. You're going to say:

"Will you stand when I step onto the mounting block, and organize my reins? Yes?" C/R.

"Will you stand when I step onto the mounting block, organize my reins, and check the girth? Yes?" C/R.

"Will you stand when I step onto the mounting block, organize my reins, check and tighten the girth, plus pull down the stirrups? Yes." C/R.

Do you see how this works? You're going to continue to combine steps until you can just walk right up to the mounting block and get on. You've used the clicker and all the principles of shaping to teach your horse rock solid manners. You've also improved his leading skills, taught him to ground tie, made him easier to load in a trailer, and introduced him to leg yielding and sidepassing. Not bad for one simple lesson in basic handling.

CHAPTER SIX

The Problem with Punishment and Some Positive Alternatives

Let's begin our discussion of punishment and the alternatives to it with some definitions.

The common usage definition of *punishment* is a penalty imposed for an offense. When defined in this way, punishment becomes an unpleasant or painful stimulus applied after a behavior has occurred. It is intended to prevent that behavior from occurring again.

In contrast, *negative reinforcement* is an unpleasant event or stimulus that can be halted or avoided by changing one's behavior. It acts like a "wrong answer" cue.

In these definitions the critical difference between negative reinforcement and punishment is not the severity with which they are applied. Both can range from very mild, gentle corrections to very harsh, painful aids. The primary difference is one of timing. Punishment occurs after the unwanted behavior. Negative reinforcement occurs during the behavior and stops as soon as the horse offers a more acceptable response.

Behavioral psychologists see punishment in a different way. For them punishment is not a penalty with its moral overtones of judgment. They define punishment in terms of negative and positive reinforcement:

Positive reinforcers make the behaviors that produce them more likely. Negative reinforcers make the behaviors that end them more likely.

An animal can do something that will make us remove a positive. (A horse is pawing in his stall as we pass out dinner. We withhold his grain until the pawing stops.) It can also act in a way that produces negatives. (We go in with a whip and smack that same horse every time it paws.) Punishment occurs any time an action is followed by either the loss of a positive, or the gain of a negative.

Negative punishment is the removal of something that the animal wants. Positive punishment is the active presentation of an adversive.

These definitions can make your head swim. When most people talk about punishment, they are using the common-language definition. Yes, they want the behavior to stop, but they also want the horse to "learn its lesson." What they create instead is a problem in timing that can have very negative consequences throughout their entire training program.

The goal of punishment is to stop behavior, and it often does, in the present. When it works, it reinforces the punisher, and therefore makes punishment more likely to be used again. The problem is that the effect on future behavior is unpredictable. Punishment may or may not stop that behavior in the future. (The horse may still paw in anticipation of his dinner.) Punishment may stop other behaviors altogether, that you didn't want stopped. (The horse may stop coming to the front of his stall to greet you.) And punishment may produce other side effects that you never envisioned. (The horse may start pacing in his stall, or kicking at the walls. He might even become aggressive and lunge at you when you feed him.)

The unpredictable nature of punishment makes it a less than satisfactory training tool. Good trainers learn how to shift away from punishment as it is popularly defined. Instead they use well-timed and appropriately applied reinforcers. To understand what I mean by this, and to see how punishment works in the real world, let's begin with two very familiar stories.

THE *BLACK BEAUTY* PRINCIPLE

Imagine the following scenes. You are at a show with your horse and you are stabled next to a competitor who is having a bad day. You can see the ring from your stall so you watch him as he goes out for his class. The horse is nervous in the warm-up ring and blows up in the class. When your neighbor brings him back to his stall, he takes a crop to him and beats him.

Or consider this. You are standing at the rail watching a rider schooling over a jump. Her horse is unsure of himself, and rushes the fence. She pulls him up hard after he has jumped and hits him across his shoulders with the reins.

We've all seen or heard of people doing this or similar things to their horses, and for most of us these scenes make us uncomfortable. We've all read Black Beauty. We are good, kind people. We know this isn't the way we want horses to be treated. And yet many of us have probably done something very similar in a fit of frustration or anger. We can feel a certain sympathy toward these riders, even as we denounce their methods. But why? What is so terribly wrong about punishing a horse for misbehaving?

The first example, most of us would agree, clearly crosses the line into abuse. The second may not be so clear. Is the rider abusing her horse, or correcting an unwanted behavior with an appropriate response?

Understanding the answer to this question goes beyond simply saying I love my horse, and I don't want to hit him. Of all the ways to control behavior, punishment is perhaps the easiest to use, the most addictive, and the least effective.

OUR TRAINING TOOLBOX

All behavior is controlled by two desires: the desire to avoid pain, and the desire to gain pleasure.

Behavior in this case means anything you are trying to get your horse to do (or not do). It can range from very basic things, like standing quietly on cross ties, to work as advanced as riding a Grand Prix test. Whatever you are trying to teach, you have four tools to work with. They are:

Punishment
Negative reinforcement
Positive reinforcement
Changing the motivation

You might look at this list and say, "I'm a really gentle person. I only use positive reinforcement with my horse."

You may indeed be a very kind person, but everyone who handles horses uses all four of these elements. As long as we lead horses, as long as we ride horses, we will never get away from the "moving away from discomfort" side of the training coin. If that statement makes you uncomfortable, read on. Having a happy, well-mannered horse depends on how well you understand what this really means.

We want our horses to move away from pressure. When you put a hand against a horse's ribs to ask him to move over on the cross ties, he is moving away from pressure. When he leads next to your side at the end of a lead rope, he is yielding to pressure. Under saddle, when he moves away from your leg or softens to your hand, he is moving away from pressure. The pressure is called negative reinforcement. By giving you the behavior of moving away, he is stopping or avoiding the pressure.

These are all routine everyday responses we take for granted in a trained horse. They allow us to coexist safely with an animal that is both larger and stronger than we are. They become the signals we use to communicate with him. They are all "moving away from discomfort" responses, and they are all unnatural. They must be taught to the horse.

The horse's natural response, just like ours, is to resist pressure. If someone poked you in the ribs, or pulled on your arm, your first response would probably be to stiffen up and resist. It wouldn't be to step softly aside. So, how do we teach the horse this basic principle without confusing him, or crossing the line into abuse?

AGGRESSION COMES FROM A PLACE OF FEAR

When a horse resists, our natural response is to resist back. The horse then becomes frightened and resists harder. This in turn forces us to escalate our own response. The result is a familiar cycle in which the handler uses an ever increasing level of fear and pain to control behavior.

So how do we avoid this downward spiral? We've all heard the saying, "There's nothing new under the sun." If you look at some of the most popular trends in riding and horse training over the last few years, you will see that this certainly seems to be true.

Many of the most significant advances have come about not by inventing something totally new, but by adapting techniques from other fields. Take, for example, Sally Swift's Centered Riding. What Sally did was to draw on her own life experience and introduce the Alexander Technique and creative visualization to the horse world. Her work has helped thousands of riders improve their position and communicate better with their horses. Linda Tellington-Jones left horses to study the Feldenkreis method of Awareness Through Movement and brought that back into the horse community in the form of TTEAM.

What these examples show is the value of looking beyond traditional methods and teachings for answers to our training problems.

THE ELEPHANT CONNECTION

Several years ago I watched a video that was taken at the San Diego Zoo.* The keepers were training an aggressive bull elephant with methods they had borrowed from dolphin trainers. This particular elephant had tried to kill his keepers on a number of occasions. He was so dangerous no one had been able to go into his enclosure with him for over ten years. The keepers were worried about the lack of foot care this situation created.

Captive elephants need to have their feet trimmed just like horses do. Without proper care, the keepers were concerned that the elephant might develop painful abscesses. Because of their enormous weight, elephants can't lie down for extended periods, so any injury to the feet can be life-threatening.

The video showed the traditional methods of trimming an elephant's feet. It's a sight every blacksmith should see. The handler holds the foot much like we would a horse's. The only difference is the handler is directly under the elephant's giant belly. Any mistake on the elephant's part and the handler could be crushed. As the narrator calmly points out, handling elephants is rated by CalOSHA, the California Occupational Safety and Health Agency, as a more dangerous occupation than being a police officer in Los Angeles.

People have been training elephants for four thousand years. Traditional methods included the use of goads, beatings, food deprivation, chaining, and harsh sacking out. None of these methods were going to help the San Diego Zoo solve the problem it was having with this particular individual. What was needed instead was a new, innovative approach.

Conditioned response training

A food reward and a high-frequency whistle became the keys to the elephant's training. The video showed the elephant lifting his foot through a small window in the gate of his enclosure. He stood without restraints of any kind while the rough, pocked surface of each foot was trimmed away. It was an amazing sight. Just months before this same individual had been aggressively charging the wall when people approached. Now he was holding his foot up for a pedicure.

He also stood calmly while his ear, all one hundred pounds of it, was dragged through a narrow slot, and a blood sample was drawn.

When I saw this, I thought: We horse owners have a lot to learn.

Traditional horse handling, just like elephant handling, uses a very different approach. It relies more on the stick and less on the carrot. Pain is used as a motivator, and punishment is part of the standard training toolbox.

Think of the twitches, the chains, the tie downs, the bits, the hobbles, the whips, etc. that we as a whole so routinely use.

For hundreds of years this is how horses have been trained, so why should we change now? Is it just that we all read Black Beauty when we were little, and we want to be nice to our horses? Or are there valid training reasons why we should be moving away from punishment as a training tool? Is the traditional approach to horses really the best?

THE PROBLEM WITH PUNISHMENT

Punishment as most people use it occurs after the behavior it is meant to influence. The poor timing creates many of the problems we see as a result.

Let me give an example.

Your horse doesn't like riding in company. When other horses get too close, he pins his ears and will sometimes even kick out. Your best friend has just ridden by on her gelding, and your horse spins and tries to kick him. You respond by smacking your horse with your crop. That's punishment. The problem is, it occurred after the fact. Nothing your horse does once he has kicked the other horse will alter the fact that you are going to hit him. Nor can you say with any certainty that the horse won't try to kick again.

Supertraining: Vol. I-II. Sunshine Books, Inc., Waltham, MA 02453

Now let's look at the same example from the perspective of someone who understands how to use negative reinforcement. This person sees her friend's horse approaching and notices that her own horse is starting to pin his ears. She asks him to turn to the right and turn to the left. She gets his feet busy, and as soon as she sees him focus back on her and his work, she lets him relax by walking straight.

The unpleasant or uncomfortable stimulus in this case is the extra work of turning. But unlike the first example, the horse remains in control of his own destiny and can learn from his behavior. As soon as he stops pinning his ears at the other horse, he discovers work eases off. By changing his behavior he learns he can avoid the negative reinforcer. As defined by a behavioral psychologist, you have just used positive punishment: the active presentation of an aversive.

In this case the negative reinforcer becomes a "wrong answer" cue. It can tell the horse what not to do. Unlike the first example where the punishment happens after the fact, he can use this information directly to modify his own behavior and remove the unwanted stimulus.

If that's positive punishment, what would be an example of negative punishment? Remember the definition? Negative punishment is the removal of something that would be a positive reinforcer.

Instead of using another horse example, let's look at something that may have happened to you, or perhaps to your children. You've brought home a report card that is several grade points below what you usually get. You've been surfing the Internet instead of studying, so your parents pull the plug on your computer for a week.

Losing your computer privileges now has very little connection with the studying you didn't do a week ago. Did the loss of your computer make you study harder the next time? Maybe, but for most people the answer is no. Did you learn anything from the experience that would improve your studying skills? I doubt it.

How did the punishment make you feel? Angry? Resentful? Instead of studying, didn't you just sneak over to your friend's house to play on her computer? Punishment creates emotional side effects that for the most part we do not want, and it often gives birth to alternative behaviors that are just as undesirable as the ones you are trying to stop.

Suppose your next report card wasn't much better? What did your parents do? Ground you for two weeks? That's another problem with punishment, it tends to escalate. With physical punishment this becomes a particular problem, because pain is a distraction to learning.

Here's another example. You've had a rotten day at work. You were stuck in traffic coming home, and now your horse is being terrible. He keeps dancing around on the cross ties and won't let you groom him. Finally you just can't take it any more. You smack him as hard as you can across his shoulders.

How does it make you feel? Five minutes from now you may feel terrible. After all you are a kind person, but right now it feels good. You feel in control, powerful, and that's a problem. Punishment can be intoxicating. You can get addicted to it. It becomes self-reinforcing for the punisher, so even though your horse may still be dancing around on the cross ties after you've hit him, you find yourself using punishment as a means to "control" his behavior.

Punishment didn't get you the results you wanted. Your horse's manners aren't much better, plus he's getting sulky and resentful, but you're still hammering away at him. You're caught in a self-reinforcing trap that can be very hard to get out of. Your horse's behavior may actually be deteriorating with the use of punishment, but you find you just can't stop yourself. Your behavior is being reinforced!

ACTIVE VERSUS REACTIVE RIDERS

So how do you get out of this trap? Suppose you examine your training program, and you find yourself using punishment more than you would like. What can you do?

First, ask yourself, can your horse physically do what you are asking? Is he comfortable? Does his saddle fit, and are you giving clear and consistent signals? Does your horse understand what you are asking him to do? If not, go back to a simpler stage in his training. Remember, the fastest progress is made with the smallest steps.

Second, look at the style in which you train. Are you an active or a reactive rider? John Lyons in his clinics and seminars describes these two training styles. Let's go back to our example of the kicking horse. The first rider is a reactive rider. She is responding to her horse rather than taking charge. As Lyons points out, these riders tend to be a second or two behind their horses. You can recognize them because they are the ones who are constantly scolding their horses. You'll hear them tell you horses are stupid, and it certainly seems that way when you watch their horses struggling to learn even the most basic behaviors.

By contrast, the second rider is an active rider. She takes charge. She sees her horse pinning its ears, and before the situation can escalate, she gives him something else to do. Active riders are also easy to recognize. They're the ones riding all the smart horses. They make riding look like a dance. They tend to be very reinforcing and positive in their training. They're on relaxed, happy horses, and for them, riding is fun.

ALTERNATIVES TO PUNISHMENT

Does this mean you should never use punishment with a horse? No. There are times when a sharp reprimand is appropriate, but you will find that it is so closely linked to the behavior you are trying to change it will be hard to distinguish from negative reinforcement.

In other words, you are going to be moving away from the popular definition of punishment: a penalty imposed for an offense. Instead, you'll be coming more in line with the definitions used by behavioral psychologists. In place of punishment with all of its ethical and moral connotations, you will be thinking more about the appropriate use of reinforcers. When you do use an adversive, you're going to be aware of your timing so that your action is directly linked to the unwanted behavior. As soon as the horse changes his behavior, the correction will stop.

For the most part you will find yourself using punishment as a penalty only in extreme cases where your horse is actually biting or kicking out. For the rest of the time you will be using negative reinforcement to discourage unwanted behavior. You will also be using secondary reinforcers and positive reinforcement to promote the behavior you want.

The secondary reinforcer is the piece that has been missing from our toolbox. Its absence forced us in the past to rely more on pain than on pleasure in our training.

Add a "right answer" cue to the toolbox, and your horse can easily learn to move away from pressure. Negative reinforcers will evolve into the cues you use to communicate with him. The tap of a whip will not be seen as a source of pain or fear, but as an easily understood signal for movement. When a correct response is given, it is rewarded by the immediate removal of the signal. Punishment becomes easy to avoid when the goal of training is to teach.

WHAT THE CLICKER IS NOT

Remember, this book is designed to show you how the clicker can be incorporated into your current training program. It is not intended as a cookbook. I'm not saying, "Follow these exact steps, and you too will have the perfect horse." Training doesn't work like that. Training is a creative process in which flexibility and creativity are keys to success.

Horses tell us what they need to learn. It's up to us to notice and give them the lessons they are asking for. What do I mean by that? Suppose your horse dances around whenever you try to get on. He's telling you what he needs to work on. If you never take the time to give him a lesson in standing still, don't be surprised if the behavior persists.

Problems are just opportunities in disguise. Take the time to work on this behavior, and you'll also be working on turning, brakes, picking up a correct canter lead, half-halts, and a score of other skills, all from one elementary lesson. Good trainers take advantage of these glitches in the horse to make major improvements overall.

So how do you get a horse to stand still for mounting? There isn't just one answer. There are many, and that's the point I really want to convey. Every trainer you talk to will have a favorite way that consistently works for her (him). If you were to ask ten different trainers, you might get ten different answers, and they'd all be right.

Don't be confused or upset by all these different solutions. This is good news. It means that if you hit a stumbling block in your training, you don't have to quit and give up. There is always going to be somebody else who has encountered the same problem, and come up with a good way to solve it. There are lots of creative people riding horses, and you're probably one of them.

So how does the clicker fit in to all this? First let me state what the clicker is not. It is not a separate riding discipline. We don't have jumping and dressage and cutting, and oh yes, that weird new stuff, clicker training.

The clicker is a training tool. You use it to communicate "right" answers to your horse. Just as there are many different ways to train horses, people will find many different ways to use the clicker. That's the exciting part. We're all pioneers in this; creating, inventing, and having fun. No one person has all the right answers, or the right way to use the clicker. It's an adaptable tool that you can fit into your existing program, to be used in a way that suits your particular needs.

The case histories in the next section are intended only to get you started—to spark your own problem-solving abilities. My intent is to show you what a versatile and useful tool the clicker can be. And in case you think you have to be a professional trainer with years of experience and a talented horse to use the clicker, take a look at some of the horses and their owners I've included in this section. I have kids, amateur owners, and beginners, all using the clicker with tremendous success.

I know what your next question probably is. "If the clicker doesn't refer to a particular riding style, how do I use it? I can see from the photos in the book you're primarily interested in dressage, but I do jumpers" (or Western, or halter, or just plain trail riding.) "How do I use the clicker?"

It's a good question. The answer is we don't all have to ride alike, or train alike, to use the clicker. What I did originally was piggyback the clicker onto the training methods I was already using. This is important to understand, because I think that's the way most people are going to begin. We're all going to start with what we already know.

When I first started using the clicker in 1993, my horse was injured. I was limited to teaching him simple tricks that didn't require much movement. I shaped simple behaviors like having him touch his nose to a whip or turn his head to the side. I treated him like a dolphin in a tank. I'd wait for him to look off to the side and then click him for doing it. He caught on fast and so did I. That's a great way to start with the clicker.

When Peregrine returned to work, I was so intrigued by the clicker that I went through his entire repertoire and reshaped everything I had ever taught him. I had a lot to experiment with. I love ground work, so in addition to riding, I also had all of his liberty training, basic ground manners, leading, in-hand work, long lining, and lunging to play with and learn from. At the time that I was doing all this, I was also looking in depth at John Lyons' work. What I discovered was that the clicker adapted beautifully to his exercises. His training methods are already broken down into small steps. His system follows the rules of shaping beautifully, so it was easy to add the clicker on to his work.

Does this mean you have to use Lyons' work in order to use the clicker? Absolutely not. The examples I'm presenting are not the only way to train. The clicker is an event marker that says: "Yes! You just got the right answer." That means that you can piggyback it on to many different training methods.

The particular style of riding you enjoy isn't important. What is important is that you understand the rules of shaping. Start with small steps. Train one criterion at a time. Once your horse understands what you want, shift to a variable reinforcement schedule by asking for more. If he gets confused, and the behavior deteriorates, go back to a simple step in the training and review. It's not up to you to tell him when he's learned something. Your horse is the one who tells you when he understands the exercise, and can do it consistently.

Does this even mean you have to use a clicker? Again, absolutely not. More than anything else the clicker is about breaking training down into small steps. You can still follow the steps, even if you never intend to use a clicker or a food reward. My hope, though, is that you'll want to experiment with the clicker. Start with the simple exercises. Once you see how fast your horse learns with the clicker, I think you'll do what I did, and start using it throughout your training.

The following chapters are all designed to show you how the clicker can be used to solve real-world problems. To begin with your own horse, condition him to the clicker, then pick something that's easy to teach him. If you've got a fidgety horse, maybe you'll choose to teach him to stand quietly by the mounting block. (See Ch. 5, All Aboard!: Mounting Blocks and So Much More.) Whatever you choose, chunk the exercise down into small steps, and click and reinforce (C/R) your horse for each small success. Follow the rules of shaping, and I think you'll be delighted at how fast your horse learns.

As you become more familiar with clicker training you'll see that it doesn't change how you ride, so much as how you teach. Even if you never intend to actually use the clicker, but are reading this book out of curiosity, I think you'll find it will change the way you work with your horse. You'll become much more aware of the small steps any training exercise can be broken down to, and you'll start looking for more opportunities to reward your horse. For both of those things, your horse will thank you.

Have fun with all this. More than anything else, the clicker gives you permission to relax and really enjoy your horse

CHAPTER SEVEN

Nine Easy Steps to the Perfect Horse: Retraining Behavior Problems

It's easy to feel overwhelmed when you are dealing with behavior problems in your horse. The magazines are filled with advice about specific problems. What do I do with my horse who won't pick up the right lead? What about the horse who won't tie, or the one who won't let me bridle her, or clip her, or clean out her feet? The questions go on and on.

Some of these situations require that the owner master certain skills. Picking up a correct lead requires that the rider has control of his own body and understands the canter aids. If you're struggling just to stay in the saddle, you're not going to be able to teach your horse a consistent cue. Other situations, like teaching a horse to pick up its feet, require fewer handling skills.

Suppose you understand all that. You're a good rider. You've taken lessons for years at an excellent stable with well-trained horses. Now you've bought your very first horse, and you're having problems. He's a youngster, still very green. He doesn't pick up his feet very well. He fidgets on the cross ties. He can be hard to bridle. He doesn't always stand still when you get on. Under saddle he's a little quick, and doesn't always listen to your leg. He spooks at the far end of the arena. He's been known to buck, and out on trails he won't walk through water. Some of your friends think you were crazy buying such a green horse, but you love him. He's really very sweet, and you know with work he'll be the horse of your dreams.

But right now you're feeling a little lost. Where do you begin? What do you do? Every person you talk to about him gives you different answers. Who do you listen to for advice?

Getting rid of problems doesn't have to be complicated. All the advice, all the different techniques really come down to just a few simple solutions. Dolphin trainer Karen Pryor, in her book *Don't Shoot the Dog*, presented a list of eight ways to eliminate unwanted behavior, to which I have added a ninth.

Learning the alphabet

Think of problem solving like learning how to read. Most of us learned to read phonetically. We learned the sound the letters made and then combined them to make words. We could learn a new word simply by looking at the phonetic building blocks. Imagine how much harder it would have been if we had learned each word individually. That's really how we treat training. For each separate problem we think we have to come up with a unique solution.

Instead, what we have are nine training solutions. They make use of the desire all animals have to avoid pain or to gain pleasure. The nine training solutions are the equivalent of phonetic building blocks. Once you understand them, you'll find it's much easier to choose training methods that suit your horse and the issues you are dealing with. Whatever problems you have, the list will give you not one but several different ways to solve them.

There are no right or wrong answers here. It's more a matter of selecting an approach that suits your personality and experience level. If one approach doesn't seem to be working, be flexible. Try something different. That's the key to good training.

Creating a well-trained horse isn't just about tackling the major issues head on. Horses always tell us where we need to begin, and it usually isn't with the scream-in-your-face, attention-getting issues. That's good news for most of us. We don't have to be heroes and get on a horse that rears to solve a rearing problem. We don't have to be talented riders with years of experience to school the horse that spooks into the next county. Long before these horses ever explode into violent behavior, they've been warning us they don't have the self-control to handle what we're asking of them.

The challenge is to recognize all those fidgety, annoying, dancing-around-on-the-cross-ties behaviors as training opportunities. The best trainers focus their attention on small details. They don't struggle every day trying to bridle a head-shy horse. Instead they teach the horse to stand quietly and lower its head on cue. In the process they've given themselves a tool that says "don't rear."

Whatever approach you choose to correct a problem, you'll have the best success if you chunk your training down into small steps. Make things so simple that you both can succeed. And remember, be persistent. Many of these approaches take time. If you give up after five minutes, you aren't giving your horse a chance to change. Our goal isn't just to solve the problem. The goal of all good training should also be to keep things safe for both the handler and the horse. With time, patience, and a good lesson plan, you'll be able to do just that.

THE NINE TRAINING SOLUTIONS*

Training Solution 1: Sell the horse

Let's begin with a very straightforward solution to all our problems: Sell the horse. Get rid of the behavior by getting rid of the doer. This is an extreme, but frequently used, solution. Consider this example. You just bought a young Thoroughbred off the track, and now you discover you've gotten in over your head. This horse requires a level of knowledge and riding skills that you simply don't have. You might try to work it out, except the two of you just don't get along. Your personalities don't match. For his sake as much as yours, you've decided to sell him. It's easy to see how this will solve all the problems you're having with this individual, and in many instances it can be the best choice for both of you.

The main drawback to using this solution is you don't really learn anything and neither does the horse. The next time a horse acts up in the same way, you won't know any more about how to change the behavior than you did the first time.

Selling the horse may seem a bit extreme, and something you're not ready to do yet. Less extreme examples of this method certainly exist. Your horse

hears another horse running loose outside and starts to act up on the cross ties. You put him away in his stall. You haven't taught him anything about standing tied, but you have solved your problem, at least temporarily, by removing your horse. It can be a good choice for that moment. Your horse didn't get hurt by breaking the cross ties, and neither did you. You can work on the issues of self-control another time.

Even cross ties are really a form of Solution 1. Wouldn't it be great if your horse would just stand ground-tied? John Lyons uses a round pen to teach horses to stand quietly without any restraint while they are groomed, saddled, and bridled. You might watch the training process and say, "I'd really like my horse to do that, but I have shows to get ready for. I don't have time to teach him to ground tie. It's easier just to cross tie him." That's a clear case of Training Solution 1.

Suppose your barn has open box stalls, the kind where the horse can put his head out. You'd like to be able to hang his blanket over the edge so it can air. Your neighbor can do it with her horse. Her mare never bothers anything, but you own the one horse in the barn who just can't leave anything alone. What do you do? Solution 1 says simply take the blanket away. It's quick, it's easy, but again the horse doesn't learn anything.

Here's another example. Suppose you're a little late with the morning turn out. Your horse doesn't like to be kept waiting so he's pawed a hole in the front of his stall. You could rebuild your barn so he can go in and out to pasture on his own, or you could try:

Training Solution 2: Punishment

The common usage definition of punishment is an unpleasant or painful stimulus that is usually applied after the behavior has occurred. The intent is to make behavior stop.

You could yell at your horse for digging the hole. He probably won't understand what all the fuss is about, but you may feel better. For punishment to work, you have to catch the horse in the act. If you chase him to the back of his stall every time he paws, you might be able to stop the behavior, at least while you're around.

But suppose you say, "That's just not how I want to handle my horse. I don't want to use punishment.

---

*Derived from *Don't Shoot the Dog! The New Art of Teaching and Training,* by Karen Pryor; Bantam Books, N.Y.

I know it's not always very effective, and besides it can have some unwanted side effects."

"If I use punishment and he doesn't stop pawing, I know I may have to really get after him. I don't want to be constantly yelling at my horse, or beating on him. I've seen it happen to other people, and I don't like it. What else can I do?"

Training Solution 3: Extinction

Unreinforced behaviors tend to diminish over time. Just ignore it. Every time you yell at him, he's getting attention. For some horses any attention is better than no attention. Your making an issue of his pawing may be what is keeping the behavior alive.

Suppose your horse is tired of being left alone on the cross ties, so he starts to paw. When you walk over to correct him, you're really just reinforcing the pawing. It would be better to ignore the behavior. To cure pawing many trainers will tie a horse up for hours. They put it somewhere safe where digging doesn't matter. After a while the horse gets tired and gives up the behavior.

Many behaviors are really best dealt with by simply ignoring them. Suppose the first time your horse picked up the canter he also tossed his head. You praised him for cantering, but that's not the only message he got. He thinks the head toss is part of the package. Don't worry about it. As you reward the canter and ignore the head toss, it will diminish. Making an issue of it may just create other problems. Remember, it's always better to focus on what your horse is doing right, rather than on what he's doing wrong.

Some behaviors are self-reinforcing. If that's the case, ignoring them won't help. Cribbing is the classic example of this. Cribbing occurs when a horse clamps his front teeth down on the edge of his stall and sucks in a huge gulp of air. A confirmed cribber will wind suck for hours at a time. Anyone who has lived with a cribber knows how annoying the sound they make can be. It's like listening to a dripping faucet, only this is a faucet you truly can't turn off. Studies have shown that cribbing releases endorphins. These horse are addicted to the behavior. Simply waiting for it to go away won't work.

Training Solution 4: Negative reinforcement

Negative reinforcement is an unpleasant event or stimulus that can be halted or avoided by changing one's behavior. It acts like a "wrong answer" cue. Behavioral psychologists may argue over the definitions, but for our purposes the primary difference between punishment and negative reinforcement is one of timing. Punishment either occurs after the behavior, or is presented during the behavior but with no opportunity for avoidance. Negative reinforcement occurs during the behavior and stops as soon as the horse offers a more acceptable response.

To stop cribbing, people will often put a leather collar around the horse's neck, just behind his ears. When the horse arches his neck to suck in air, the collar tightens around his trachea. The added pressure is intended to discourage wind sucking. On confirmed cribbers a metal plate is added, sometimes with prongs that press into the neck. The collar is intended to exert pressure only when the horse is wind sucking. He can avoid the pressure by avoiding the behavior.

If putting a metal-prong collar on a horse sounds excessive, it's important to remember that cribbing is more than just an annoying habit. Horses can trigger life-threatening colics by sucking too much air into their stomachs. Does this approach work? Sometimes, but more often than not horses will wind suck through their collars. As long as these horses are confined with too little exercise, they continue the behavior.

Cribbing isn't the only bad habit horse owners have to deal with. Let's go back to our head-tosser. Ignoring it hasn't helped. You've had him checked to make sure your saddle fits. Your vet says he's not back sore, and nothing else is hurting him. You need to take a more active approach to change this pattern.

Your horse's head-tossing can be easily stopped using negative reinforcement. Horses do not like pressure on their jaws. If we will only ease off the reins and get out of their mouths, they will do amazing things for us.

You can use this idea to break your horse of his head-tossing habit. Every time he tries it, simply take all the slack out of your inside rein. You don't have to pull. Your object here is not to punish or hurt your horse. As long as he's shaking his head, you're going to hold onto the rein. The instant he stops, even if it's only for a second, you'll release the rein. He'll soon get the message. "You can shake your head all you want, but as long as you do, I'm going to be in your mouth." If you're consistent, most horses will very quickly stop their head-tossing.

That's great, you say, but before I can worry about head-tossing, I first have to get on. My horse just won't stand still. I have to have two people holding him down, and even then it's a struggle.

Training Solution 5: Change the motivation

Horses will do things that make sense to them. It's easy to teach your prancing, dancing horse to stand still. You just have to get him to want to stand still, and you do that by asking him to move his feet.

Get on as best you can, and then go to work. Ask him to turn to the right and to turn to the left. Work small circles, and figure eights. Keep his feet going actively forward through frequent changes of direction.

Your horse will soon be wishing he could just stand still. So that's what you let him do. You offer him a chance to stand, and you start practicing getting off and getting on. If he walks off again, go back to your turning. Your horse will soon learn to stand beautifully for mounting, and, as an added bonus, you'll also have tuned up his brakes and steering wheel. By changing his state of mind, you've made him easy to train.

Sometimes this is all you need to get the change you want. If your horse is sluggish and won't move, try taking him out of the little pen where you've been riding and work in a big field. If you've got the opposite problem, too much energy, trade places and spend some time in a small arena.

Suppose that still doesn't help. Your horse was ridden for years by a rider who only knew one gait—dead run. As soon as you get on that's all your horse is thinking about. It doesn't matter where you ride, he still thinks that's all you want.

Training Solution 6: Shape the absence

Shaping the absence means you're going to reward anything and everything that isn't the unwanted behavior. If he trots for two steps on his way to the canter, praise him. It won't happen overnight, but he'll gradually begin to offer more and more of the things he gets rewarded for, and less of the unwanted behavior. Couple this with changing his motivation, and you'll go a long way towards correcting the problem.

Training Solution 7: Put the behavior on cue

Putting a behavior on cue brings it under our control. If we teach a horse to paw on command and then never cue him for pawing, we can extinguish the behavior. For our horse with only one gear, fast forward, we could bring the canter completely under stimulus control. The end result would be a horse

that met the following four criteria.

1. The horse canters promptly every time we ask for it.
2. The horse doesn't canter when we haven't cued it.
3. The horse doesn't canter in response to some other cue.
4. When we ask for the canter, we get the canter, not something else.

Bringing a behavior completely under stimulus control where all four of these criteria are met may not be necessary for all behaviors. If your weekend trail horse sometimes picks up a trot instead of a canter, you may not care. Having him come in from his twenty-acre pasture whenever you call him may be far more important to you. If you're showing, your priorities could be reversed. You'll put your training time and energy into making sure the canter meets all four criteria of cue control.

Many of the problems we have with our horses come from our not being consistent about teaching cues. Go down your checklist of basic riding aids. Does your horse meet the four criteria for picking up a canter, coming to a halt, turning, etc.? If not, you need to review the steps you've taken to teach him your cues.

Putting a behavior on cue is a multi-step process. It begins with shaping the behavior. (See Ch. 2, Getting Started with the Clicker.) Suppose you are working your driving horse on a lunge line. You want to teach him voice commands. Many of us start backward. We put the cue before the behavior. We've all done it. We've stood in the middle of the lunge circle chanting, "canter," "canter," "canter," while our horse races around us at the trot. We're at one end of the line thinking we want our horse to canter. He's at the other end thinking that funny sound means trot as fast as you can.

So before you add a cue, you want to be able to get the behavior consistently. Once you can predictably tell when the horse is going to canter, you can start adding your cue. If you know he'll break into a canter every time you raise your whip, say "canter" just before you raise your arm. It will appear as though he's responding to your voice. Don't be fooled. Presenting the cue once isn't enough for your horse to learn it. You'll need to repeat the process many times, gradually fading out the original cue, before your horse will respond to just the verbal command. Now when you say "canter," even in the absence of other cues, that's what he'll do.

You're halfway home at this point. The horse understands the behavior you want, and is willing to give it to you. You've got a cue attached to it that he responds to consistently. Now you've got a new problem. He's learned cantering gets him rewards, so he might start offering you the canter even in the absence of the cue.

When that happens, don't scold him. Just quietly say "wrong," and bring him out of the canter. Again don't chant to him. Say wrong once, not over and over again. He'll soon learn "wrong" means you're not going to get reinforced now for that behavior.

Your horse may get confused at first. It won't make sense to him why sometimes you're really pleased when he canters, and other times you stop him. You need to be very consistent, and he'll begin to get the idea that if he wants to be rewarded, he has to wait for the canter cue. As his repertoire expands, you'll find it will become easier and easier to teach him to wait for a cue. Your horse will only canter when you ask, and he'll do it each and every time you ask.

Training Solution 8: Shape a conflicting behavior

Shaping a conflicting behavior is a powerful problem-solving tool. For example, a horse can't rear and put his nose to the ground both at the same time.

You'll discover lots of opportunities to shape conflicting behaviors. Suppose your horse has started to rush back to the barn after your ride. He's in a big hurry to get through the gate. You can solve this problem by asking him to halt facing away from the opening. He can't rush through the gate and stand still at the same time.

"But wait a minute," you say, "that's just the problem. He's so eager to get home, he won't stand still." Let's go back in our list to solve that problem. Work on changing his motivation. Treat him just as you did when you needed to teach him to stand still for mounting. Make him circle and turn until he's eager to stand still.

Shaping a conflicting behavior can keep you safe whether you're out on a trail ride or down at the spooky end of the arena. A horse who has learned to turn and face what's scaring him can't be running for the next county at the same instant. Teaching a conflicting behavior is a major step toward creating a safe horse, but it's more than just controlling which

way the feet are moving. You'll also be changing the way your horse thinks.

Our posture can dictate our mood. If you doubt this, try slumping down in your chair. Really let your head and shoulders droop. The chances are you're not going to feel like the life of the party. Your body posture is telling your brain to be depressed. Lift your head, perk up your face, and your brain will think it's time to be happy.

Horses are the same way. Change a horse's head elevation, and you change his mood. Most of us know we can make a calm horse out of a nervous one by simply lowering its head. We can take this a step further. Suppose your horse isn't very bold. He can't ride around your arena without spooking in all the corners. He feels all scrunched up. It's almost as though he's trying to get you to go first, and, of course, you're on top of him so that won't work. It's like the old Laurel and Hardy routine where two people are trying to fit through the same door. Horses who are afraid shorten their bodies. It's like they're saying, "No, not me. You go first."

As he tries to suck back, you're going to ask him to stretch and reach for the bit. His new body posture will say to his brain, "I'm feeling very bold and confident. Nothing scares me." Each time you feel his body changing back to its old pattern, you're going to make him stretch for the bit. He'll soon forget about being afraid.

Asking your horse to do the opposite of what he wants to do can stop an emotional meltdown, but like any other learned skill he's going to need lots of practice. The horse needs to learn how to shift his emotional states. The first time you ask him to lower his head, he's not going to leave it down for more than a split second. He won't feel safe abandoning his alert posture.

The more opportunities you give him to shift his emotional state, the easier it will become for him.

Begin with small issues. Don't wait until your horse is five miles out from home, and he's rearing on the far side of a creek, to begin his training. The time to teach your horse how to substitute one behavior for another is at home in his comfort zone where you can control the situation and keep things safe.

Training Solution 9: Learn to live with it

All this is so much work, you moan. Isn't there an easier way? Yes, go back to Solution 1, *Sell the horse*, or try Solution 9, *Learn to live with it*. Training does require a commitment of time and energy. If your horse fidgets on the cross ties, or dances about when you get on, you may decide it's just easier to live with the behavior. Trying to solve the problem is more work than it's worth to you. Habits that may annoy other people, like a horse mouthing the cross ties or pawing while he eats, may simply not bother you.

There is no one model of perfect equine behavior. Don't make yourself crazy trying to live up to someone else's standards. Training takes time and energy. Maybe you're feeling some pressure from others about the way your horse dances around when you groom him; after all, their horses all stand quietly. If it were dangerous, or truly annoying, you'd do something about it. Your horse just fidgets.

You have a choice. You can beat yourself up over something you're really not motivated to fix, or you can just relax and accept it as part of what makes him the character you love. If it starts to bother you, you'll find the time and the energy to change it, and Training Solutions 1 through 8 will give you all the tools you need.

A FINAL EXERCISE

Calm, well-mannered horses are a delight to be around. Pushy, nervous, aggressive horses soon wear out their welcome. Before we resort to Training Solution 1, getting rid of the horse, or Training Solution 9, just giving up and learning to live with rude behavior, there's a lot we can do. The best training programs use a mix of all the different problem-solving styles, and the best trainers can solve the same problem in a number of different ways.

You can easily teach yourself to be a flexible trainer. Play a game with yourself. Pick a common behavior problem and go down the list. Find a different solution to the problem from each of the nine categories. You'll quickly see some of your solutions will work better than others. Sometimes shaping a conflicting behavior will seem like the best choice. For a different situation using negative reinforcement might work better. What is the best choice for your bold, pushy gelding might not work at all on his timid, bottom-of-the-pecking-order stablemate.

Once you understand that training is made up of basic building blocks that you can mix and match, you can really have fun creating your perfect horse.

Whatever your choice, before you bring your horse out, ask yourself: "If I try this and it doesn't go as planned, can either my horse or myself get hurt?" If the answer is yes, go back to the list and find another solution. What these nine training solutions teach us is that there is always another, better, safer way to solve our problems.

PART II

PRACTICAL USES
FOR THE CLICKER

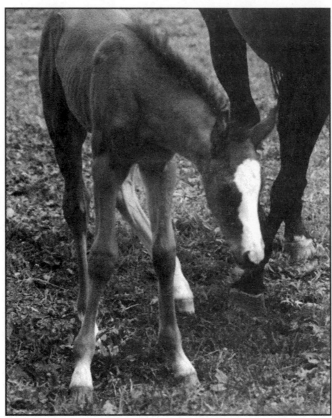

Fig. 13: Horses need teachers, not bullies. At eleven days this Thoroughbred colt is still small enough to push around, but just because you can, doesn't mean you should.

CHAPTER EIGHT

Foal Training: Early Childhood Education

WHOA THERE! JUST BECAUSE YOU CAN DOESN'T MEAN YOU SHOULD

So you don't have a foal. Your horse is twenty years old, and after your one awful experience with a green horse, you swore you'd never own a horse under fifteen. You don't need to read this section. Right?

Wrong.

When I started working on this section, I thought it was going to be a short little piece covering a few basics. I didn't realize it was going to grow into the main nuts-and-bolts section that it did. If you're having trouble with your horse, the solution can probably be found in this section. If you want to learn how to teach something new to your horse, you'll find the steps outlined here.

I admit it. I originally wrote this section so I could sneak some cute foal pictures into the book. Foals are great. I love working with them. I raised both Peregrine and his mother. During the writing of this book I added a new horse to my equine family, a wonderful yearling who you'll meet in the next section. (See Ch. 17, Lateral Work.)

Young horses are great teachers. They remind you about all the tiny steps that go into creating that beautifully trained horse we all dream of owning. Foals haven't learned to control their emotions. They show everything. It's easy to recognize when they're afraid, or when they're just being silly. They know less, so they're simpler. You can't ride a youngster, so you've got lots of time for basics. For many of us it's a lot easier to be patient with a baby having his first bath than it is an older horse "who should know better."

That's just the point of these chapters. Just because we can muscle our way through problems with an older horse, doesn't mean we should. You need to treat your hefty four-year-old the same way you would a newborn foal: with patience and care.

Horses need teachers, not bullies (Fig. 13). I'm not being sentimental when I say that. I've learned over the years that I get faster, better results when I work in small steps. Age doesn't matter. Experience doesn't matter. If I've got an older horse who has learned bad habits, I take him right back to square one and reteach the foundation. I'm not interested in patch jobs or quick fixes. If I'm living in a house with a crumbling foundation, I don't want to see the builder up in the attic plastering over ceiling cracks. I want him down in the basement fixing the problem. That's how I feel about training. Build a solid foundation, and everything else is easy.

THE CLICKER SAVES A LIFE

When Joan decided to send her five-month-old Morgan-Arab filly, Spirit, to a neighboring farm for weaning, she wasn't too worried about how she would behave. After all, Joan's friends were already calling Spirit "Miss Manners."

Joan keeps her three horses at home: Spirit, her Morgan mom, and an Arab gelding. Her barn is small. It's set up so the horses can wander in and out. When you're in the barn, you have lots of company. A foal raised in this kind of a setting could be an awful pest, pushy and out of control.

Not so, Spirit. She never demanded attention: she asked for it politely. The first time I met her I was truly impressed. This foal was a delight. She was easy to be around, safe, friendly, and perfectly at ease with people. Spirit is the kind of foal people dream about when they think about raising their own.

So Joan wasn't expecting any trouble when she sent Spirit off to be weaned. Spirit left in November just before an early snowfall officially ended the riding season. Joan checked in on Spirit throughout the winter, but mainly she let her just be a horse in a herd.

In March the vacation was over. It was time to come back home, but first Spirit needed some tidying up. She was starting to look like a wild mustang. Spirit was used to coming into the barn. She was in a stall every night, and turned out with the other horses during the day. So she'd been handled every day; she just hadn't had regular grooming.

Joan brought her brush box out and set to work. Spirit was her usual self, Miss Manners. She let Joan shed out her shaggy coat, and pick out her feet. She was fine until Joan started on her mane. Her fuzzy foal mane had grown out. She had a long mane now, full of tangles, and she didn't want it touched. When Joan tried to brush it, Spirit shook her head. Joan persisted, and Spirit responded by dancing to the end of the lead.

Joan's friend, the owner of the farm, was watching. She's an experienced breeder who has raised foals for years. Fussy weanlings were nothing new for her.

We've all heard the next piece in this story. It may have even happened to us. Joan's friend stepped in to help. She took a firm stance with Spirit. "This is silly. We're not hurting you. You can just stand there and let us do this," was her attitude.

With each stroke of the brush the tension mounted. Spirit just couldn't stand it. She started rearing up. The barn owner became even more insistent. Spirit saw no other choice. She threw herself straight up in the air. She went up high, pulled the lead away from them and flipped over backward.

That's when Joan put a stop to things. Horses that flip can damage their vertebrae. They can even kill themselves. It wasn't worth permanently injuring her filly over this issue.

FINDING SAFE SOLUTIONS

At home, Spirit was just as bad. When Joan tried to brush her mane, she started rearing up. She had learned fast from her one experience that this was a great way to keep people from bothering her. Joan had to try a different approach. Force was only going to get one of them hurt. Her thoughts were, "Now that I'm home, I have to find a safe way to stop the rearing."

Joan had clicker trained Spirit as a young foal. She had taught her a few simple tricks like touching her nose to a cone, but she hadn't yet taken it beyond that into any serious training issues. Joan was new

to the whole concept of clicker training. She was just beginning to experiment with it with her older horses. Now it was time to put this approach to a test, to see what clicker training really could do.

She knew she had to chunk the procedure down into tiny steps. She began by trying to touch Spirit's mane with her hand. Even that limited contact was enough to send her filly skittering away. Joan changed tactics. She flicked her hand over Spirit's mane as though she were whisking away a fly. Moving fast like that meant her hand was gone before Spirit had a chance to react. The result was Spirit knew exactly what Joan was going to do. She could say, "That's not so bad. I can let her touch me like that."

When Joan could put her hand on Spirit's mane for a full second, she clicked and gave her a treat. She repeated this several times until Spirit was letting her rest her hand on her mane.

The next step was the hardest: getting Spirit to accept having Joan's hands up around her ears. After that, Joan began to stroke the mane. Spirit caught on fast. She learned that if she stood still and allowed this, she would get a click and a treat.

Joan didn't want her just tolerating the contact. She wanted Spirit to be relaxed. She also wanted to eliminate the rearing, so the next step was to teach her a head-lowering cue.

Joan kept her hand on Spirit's mane. She didn't push down. She just let her hand rest up near Spirit's poll. The instant Spirit dropped her head, Joan clicked. Spirit very quickly learned that standing still wasn't enough. She also had to lower her head to get clicked.

Joan wasn't using any particular cue to drop the head. She wasn't pushing on Spirit, or chanting the word "down." She was just resting her hand on Spirit's mane. When Spirit dropped her head just by chance, Joan clicked her and gave her a treat. Spirit caught on fast. Down was good. Now that Joan had the behavior, she could introduce a cue. Raising her hand above Spirit's head became the signal to drop it.

The next step was to introduce the brush. Joan started to run the bristles through Spirit's mane. That was too much. Spirit couldn't control herself. She started to shake her neck and to wiggle about. Her head went up and she started to hop up off the ground.

Joan turned the brush over and stroked her with the smooth backside. Spirit was tense, waiting for the bristles to pull her mane. She relaxed when she realized it was an easy stroke with no pull.

Joan repeated the steps she had gone through to get Spirit to accept her hand. She put the brush very quickly on her mane, and then pulled it away. She repeated this until Spirit could relax, put her head down, and accept the brush.

Next she alternated between brushing with the back of the brush and sometimes with the bristles. She could see Spirit was really trying to control herself. It was very clear to Joan that Spirit was thinking about what she had to do. That's an exciting stage in clicker training. You can see the horse change. They aren't simply reacting. They are making decisions.

Spirit very clearly wanted her treat. As Joan phrased it, she had her heart set on getting the goody. She knew what she had to do to get it. It was her choice. She could continue to fuss and not let Joan brush her mane, or she could hold still. She had the game figured out. Accept the hairbrush, get a treat. She started to make rapid progress. Minutes after this breakthrough Joan could brush out the entire mane.

Fig. 14: Spirit is now calm and confident. The end result of training should be a bright-eyed, happy horse.

This process sounds as if it took a tedious length of time, spread out over many days. In reality, it took one twenty-minute session to get to the point where Joan could brush out her mane. Spirit wasn't totally relaxed yet, but she was really trying to control herself.

The second day she was much better. She would only occasionally shake her head. By the third day she was perfect. She gave one little head shake at the start of the session, but as soon as she had her first click she settled right down. It was as if she was saying, "Oh yes, it's the goody game. I know what I'm supposed to do." She was absolutely rock solid. She lowered her head every time Joan asked, and stood perfectly still while her mane was brushed out.

Joan didn't end the training there. She taught Spirit to touch the brush. She was perfectly happy to target on this object that only a short time before had sent her rearing into the rafters. She learned to touch it anywhere Joan put it. It didn't take her long to learn to walk over to the shelf where the brush was kept, touch it, and ask for the mane-combing game.

Joan told me this story when Spirit was about ten months old. We went out to the barn for a visit. Spirit showed off her lovely manners, including how well she stood for grooming. You'd never guess that she had ever had a problem with anything. She was totally relaxed and at ease (Fig. 14). What could have become a dangerous habit had been stopped in its tracks.

CHAPTER NINE

You're Never Too Young to Learn: Introducing Your Foal to the Clicker

Joan's experiences with Spirit show us that you don't have to wait for a horse to grow up to begin clicker training. Older foals and weanlings can be introduced to the clicker the same way you taught your adult horse. Start with the same trick. Ask your foal to touch his nose to a cone. Foals love to explore new objects. You'll probably be amazed at how fast he'll learn this new game.

EARLY SOCIALIZATION

Even if your foal is too young to be interested in treats, you can still use the clicker. Remember, it's click and reinforce, not necessarily click and treat. Very young foals love to be scratched and rubbed. You can use this to condition them to the clicker. Put your foal in a large stall with his mother. If the foal is still afraid of people, he will probably skitter away to hide behind mom. That's okay. Just reach under your mare's neck and rub the foal's neck and withers with your fingers.

Remember Spirit's lesson. Don't try to hold onto him. Pretend you're just flicking a fly off his shoulder. Click, and take your hand away before he has a chance to react.

It's not very flattering, but at this point every time you take your hand away you're giving your foal something he wants: the removal of your presence. So click him when he lets you touch him, and reinforce him by leaving. That way your foal will know exactly what your intentions are. He won't feel trapped because you're not trying to grab hold of him. All you're doing is rubbing his neck, just like his mom does. Your foal will love the feel. It won't be long before he'll be coming over to you to get more attention. The rubbing will become a primary reinforcer, which you can pair with the clicker. You'll use it to teach your foal to accept more and more contact.

Let a person touch you, *click*, get rubbed and scratched.

Let a person stand next to you, *click*, get rubbed.

It's an easy, no-fuss way to socialize your newborn.

MAKING MOM COMFORTABLE

One word of caution before you begin. Make sure your mare is comfortable having you in the stall with her foal. Many mares love sharing and enjoy having a "baby sitter." But some new moms are very protective of their foals and will go after you if you get too close. A vet I used for many years forgot this simple warning. He got between a mare and her foal. She went after him, and he spent many months having plastic surgery to reconstruct his face. If your mare isn't totally comfortable sharing her foal, you need to work on that before you go any further.

Put your mare on a lead so you have control of her head. Position her so her foal is on her far side. Reach under her neck to scratch him. When he lets you rub him, click, and give mom a treat. You're rewarding her for letting you touch her baby. As you progress you will gradually be asking the foal to let you stand next to him. At each step in the process C/R mom for allowing you to have more access to her foal. Continue to work in this way until she is totally at ease with you handling her foal. Essentially, you'll be training two for the price of one.

Even before your foal is born, it's a good idea to spend some time clicker-training your mare. Use it to get her comfortable being handled all over her body, and especially up around her udder. Many mares are ticklish about having anything touching them in this area. It's easy to get her over this with the clicker. Think about how Joan got Spirit used to having her mane touched. Start in your mare's comfort zone. If she's ticklish around her girth, start up on her side. Brush your hand quickly under her belly, and click her if she stands still. You want to move your hand so fast she doesn't have time to react.

Once she's accepting that, slow your hand down, then gradually begin to move your hand back along her belly. C/R her each time she accepts more contact. If at any point she gets anxious and begins to react, either go back to where she's more comfortable, or speed up your hand. Within one or two sessions you will probably find she is very comfortable having you handle her anywhere you need to. (This is the same thing you would do to get stallions and geldings used to sheath cleaning.)

You also want her to be totally comfortable having you in her stall. Groom her in her stall. Hang a plastic cider jug up and teach her to touch a target. (See Ch. 4, Everything Is Everything Else: Bridling a Head-Shy Horse.) Work on her leading skills. (See Ch. 10, Baby's First Steps: Early Leading Lessons, and Ch. 15, Ground Manners for the Older Horse.) You want her to be a good role model. The time to be working with her is before your foal is born. When you're trying to lead a newborn, you don't want to be fussing with mom.

HALTER TRAINING

So now you've done your homework. Your foal is here and mom is totally at ease having you in the stall fussing over him. He likes people. He loves having his neck rubbed and his back scratched. You've played with his ears and run your hands down his legs. Now it's time to put his halter on (Fig. 15).

Haltering can be broken down into a series of easy steps. Use a soft cotton rope to introduce the foal to the feel of things on his head:

Bring the rope up toward his nose. C/R.

Rest the rope briefly on his nose. C/R.

Leave the rope there longer. C/R.

Let the rope slide up and down on his face. C/R.

Leave the rope over his nose and move your free hand up toward his poll. C/R.

When he's accepting your hand on his poll, add the rope. Let him feel it against the side of his neck. C/R.

With one end of the rope looped free over his nose, bring the other end up over his poll to create a "halter." C/R.

Introduce the real halter. Repeat all the previous steps as needed.

Once he's comfortable with this, you can put it all the way on. C/R.

Remember, your treat is lots of scratching of your foal's neck and back, something most foals love. If at any point your foal shows concern, go back to a previous step in the shaping.

These steps are suggestions only. Your foal may be totally comfortable having a halter put on, and

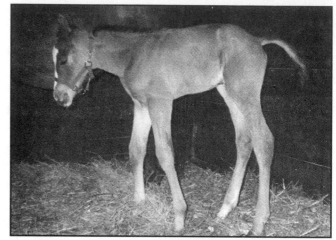

Fig. 15: Eight hours old, and this little fellow is peacefully taking a nap in his new halter.

you'll breeze through this sequence wondering what all the fuss is about. Another foal may be quite concerned having anything near his face. You'll need to take extra time with each of these steps and you may even need to chunk them down even further. Before you approach him with the rope, you may need to go through all these steps using just your hand (Figs. 15, 16).

FOOD AS A REWARD

Once the foal has started to show an interest in grain and other treats, you can use food as a reward. If you use grain, monitor how much of his daily ration you use. Overfeeding can lead to degenerative joint disease. Measure out his total daily grain ration and take a portion out for clicker training. (Don't worry if it's the major share; even a foal can work for his living.) You can add some surprise treats for extra good responses. Chopped up pieces of apples and carrots are great favorites. If you want something easier, animal crackers work great. You can buy big bags of them at the discount stores. Peregrine loves peppermints. I buy a big bag at Christmas time, and it lasts all year.

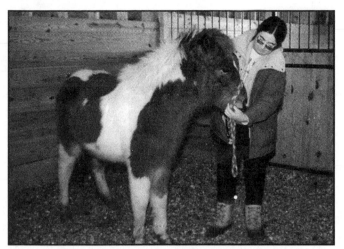

Fig. 16: I can introduce this Icelandic filly to halters by first getting her used to the feel of a rope over her nose. The promise of a click and treat keeps her interested in the lesson.

Food isn't the only treat you can use. As with very young foals, a good scratch around the withers and neck can continue to be a powerful reinforcer. Making that part of every reward will help to socialize your foal, and will associate grooming with good things.

When you first introduce the clicker and treats, your foal will mug you. He'll nuzzle your hands looking for treats or try to put his nose in your pockets. Don't worry. You are not teaching him to bite. In fact, quite the opposite. He'll very quickly learn that bumping your hands or your pocket is not the behavior that gets the "vending machine" to work. Just like an older horse, he'll soon learn he has to wait for the click.

EARLY LESSON PLANS

What can you teach your foal? All the basic skills he's going to need to be a successful riding horse. Obviously, you aren't going to put a saddle on your weanling and ride off into the sunset, but you can certainly lay a great foundation for doing just that.

Many people worry about the attention span of young horses. They think five or ten minutes is all a foal can handle. I think you'll find that your foal is capable of doing much more than that. After all, this is a prey animal who must remain attentive to the herd in order to survive. In the wild he would be learning new things all through the day.

The clicker is a fun game your foal will want to play with you. You can start with simple things like teaching him to lower his head, or to pick up his feet. You do this the same way you would an older horse. Let's take picking up the feet as an example.

TEACHING THE BASICS: FOOT CARE

Your foal is now comfortable having you next to him. He loves having you scratch him around his withers. He arches his little neck out, and keeps asking for more. You get tired of it long before he does. This is a good time to introduce the idea of allowing you to handle his legs and feet.

Your foal lets you:
Stroke your hand down his foreleg. C/R.
Run your hand down his cannon bone. C/R.
Put your hand for an instant on his ankle. C/R.
Begin to leave your hand there longer. C/R.

As he becomes comfortable with that, ask him to shift his weight off his foot. Do not push him over. Wait for him to shift his own body. C/R.

Ask him to lift the foot. All you want him to do is lift it off the ground. Do not take hold of it yet. Let him lift it. C/R.

Repeat this step several times until he is lifting the foot consistently off the ground. C/R each time.

Now take a hold of the foot. Support it briefly. C/R.

Extend the amount of time he's holding it up. C/R.

Repeat these steps for each of the other legs. Your foal may find it easier to balance on one foot than the other. Just because he can pick up his left foot easily doesn't necessarily mean his right will be the same. Put as many steps into your sequence as you need to keep him comfortable with the process.

For the hind feet you may want to start by stroking him with a long whip, or letting a rope brush against his legs. If he kicks at a whip, he'll probably kick at your hand. A foal may be small, but those hind feet can still hurt. To prevent an accident, simply extend your reach by using the whip or rope. Stand by his shoulder well out of striking range and stroke down his legs with a long dressage whip. C/R him when he stands still. Wait until he's totally comfortable having things bumping against his legs before you start running your hand down below his hocks.

Once you understand the basic principles of shaping, you'll find all kinds of ways to use them. Let your foal tell you what he needs to learn. And remember, everything is new to him. Everything is a surprise. Take your time to chunk down these early lessons, so your horse really has a chance to learn how to learn.

Here is a summary of Karen Pryor's list of things to remember about shaping.

1. Train one criterion at a time.

2. Get a response, get it consistently, then improve on it.

3. Raise your standards in small enough steps that the horse continues to be successful and can be reinforced.

4. Once the behavior is established, shift from a fixed to a variable reinforcement schedule.

5. When adding a new criterion, temporarily relax the standards of the old.

6. If behavior deteriorates, go back to a previous step in the shaping process.

7. If one shaping procedure is not creating progress, find another. There are always many different ways to build the steps to the desired behavior.

CHAPTER TEN

Baby's First Steps:
Early Leading Lessons

Early socialization and good grooming manners are only the beginning. You can use the clicker to teach your foal how to lead. With very young foals most people simply put their arms around them and direct them as they follow Mom (Fig. 17). As the foals get a little bigger, people add a butt rope.

Fig. 17: It's day three in this foal's life, and he's going out for only the second time. He's already comfortable with people, so it's easy to guide him out to his paddock. The problem is he's going to outgrow this method fast. The time to teach him to lead is before he gets too big to handle.

All this works great for a few days until the foal decides to add some side trips on his way out to his paddock. That's when most of us decide it's time to teach him about halters and lead ropes.

The time to start this is not when he's leaping around, full of energy after a night in his stall. Turn him out in his paddock. Let him play. Later, when you've brought him back into his stall for his afternoon rest, spend some time teaching him how to lead.

What you are going to be working on are two fundamentally important concepts. First, you are going to be telling your foal, "When you feel pressure, yield to it." And second, "When you're afraid, listen to your handler. Don't just bolt off or spook." Neither one of these responses is natural. They both have to be taught.

DOING WHAT COMES NATURALLY

Horses (and people) naturally respond to pressure by resisting back. Put pressure on the end of a horse's halter, and he'll throw his head up and back away. That's why horses pull back on cross ties, or rear up under saddle.

Yielding to pressure is a learned response, something you have to teach. You can certainly muscle your way through this lesson with a young foal. I've seen this done in a variety of ways, from hanging on tight while the foal leaps and plunges, to tying the foal to his mother's halter and letting him try to drag her. The foal resists against his halter until he finally gives up and walks quietly forward. The message the handler wants him to learn is there's no point in pulling back. The person (or horse) at the other end of the rope is bigger than you are. The goal is to have the horse think people are stronger than he is. If you can hold onto a foal when he's little, he'll grow up believing there's no point in even trying to pull away.

The problem with this approach is it's easy for one of you to get hurt. This is especially true if you've put off handling him, and he's no longer a tiny newborn, but a 500-pound stud colt ready for weaning. Holding on then may not be easy. The clicker gives you an alternative approach. You're going to engage the foal's mind, not his muscle. You're going to use it to teach the horse to yield to pressure, and in the process you're going to make him a much safer horse to be around.

I'm going to take you through a step-by-step sequence. Before you get involved in the details, I want you to visualize the overall picture. Pick any spot on your foal's body. It can be anything from the tip of his nose to a tiny dimple on his rear. There are six different directions that spot can move. It can move forward or back, left or right, up or down. Whatever spot you pick, you can ask it to move in each of these six directions. If you can get the dimple on his left hip to move forward, you can move the whole horse forward.

The general principle you want to teach any horse, no matter what its age, is to yield to pressure. You want to teach your foal to follow a feel. It's a very simple concept. You aren't trying to drag the entire horse around. Instead you are going to teach him to move any part of his body you select in any direction you indicate. You'll be able to ask your foal to step forward or back, left or right, all from just a light signal.

This is not a new concept. What I am describing is an approach shared by many good trainers. This is what Pat Parelli teaches in his programs on Natural Horsemanship. John Lyons presents similar concepts in his College Level Leading and round-pen training. I am building on their general approach, but I've added the clicker for clearer communication.

STEP ONE: BACKING

You can begin to teach your foal to yield to pressure right from day one, during his first grooming session. You'll start by asking him to take a step back out of your space. You're probably already doing this without even thinking it's part of his formal training. Simply press your thumb against his chest. Right in the crease where his front leg joins the shoulder is the best place (Fig. 18).

The object here is not to push him backward, but to have him feel the pressure and to respond to it by stepping back. When you feel even a subtle shift of weight back, click and reinforce him by rubbing his neck and face. Make lots of physical contact with him. Rub him, and hug him, and tell him he's wonderful. You're going to be teaching him that verbal praise and scratches are good things he wants to get more of.

Ask him to back up several more times until he is shifting his weight easily and quickly. Now withhold

Fig. 18: This Icelandic filly is learning how to back. I'm working her in a large stall. She can see mom and the rest of her friends, so she's relaxed and willing to work with me. I can get her to back by placing my hand on her chest and applying gentle pressure. I am NOT pushing her back. As she shifts her weight in response to the pressure, I'll click her and take my hand away. Her treat will be a scratch on the neck.

your click until he has taken a full step back. Again repeat this, gradually drawing out the number of steps he must give you before you click. Your foal isn't even going to be aware he's having a serious training session. You're just grooming him and scratching him the way you always do, but he's also backing up whenever you ask. If he starts to crowd into you asking for more attention, you now have an easy way of telling him to be more polite about your space.

SIGNALS: STARTER BUTTONS OR A CONSTANT "ON" SIGNAL

You can use your thumb in one of two ways, as a constant "on" signal, or as a starter button, In the first, you will leave your thumb pressing in against his chest until you click him. What you are saying is, "Whenever you feel pressure here, keep backing up until it stops." If you want three steps, you'll leave the signal on for three steps; five steps, the signal stays on for five.

We often use this kind of constant "on" signal with horses, and we may not even realize that's what we're doing. Think of the riding lessons you've watched where the horse drops out of the canter, and the instructor scolds the student for not maintaining the canter with his seat. The rider didn't keep his signal going.

The other way you could use your thumb is as a cue. It initiates the behavior and then disappears.

It's like turning a key to start up an engine. Your signal gets things in motion. In this case it means "start backing up, and keep backing up until I click you or ask you to do something else."

We also use this kind of "starter button" signal in riding. In that same canter lesson where the rider was scolded for not maintaining her seat, she may have also been corrected for leaving her leg on. "Don't keep kicking him once he's going," is probably something we've all heard from an instructor.

Somehow our horses learn to figure out what we mean even when we don't always know ourselves. They know which are the "full-duration" signals and which are the "starter buttons." They understand that we can have both operating at once. Somehow they manage to make sense out of it all and give us the behavior we want.

So how should we think of our signal to back? Is it a constant "on," or a starter button? Both work, but I like to think of the thumb signal as being like the rider's leg. If I have to leave my thumb on the whole time the horse is backing, by analogy I'm also saying I have to leave my leg on through an entire movement.

Quite apart from any other training considerations, my leg is going to get awfully tired riding like that. So I want my foal to understand that the signal from my thumb is like a starter button. It's an "on" switch that says "Start backing up and keep backing up until I tell you to do something else." If he stops, I'll press my thumb against his chest to get the engine started again.

You can never do just one thing. That's certainly true in horse training. When you press your thumb against your foal's chest, you're going to be turning in to face him. As he backs up you'll be stepping with him into his space. Your body becomes like the rider's seat saying, "Keep moving with me until I click you or ask for something else." You are still teaching your foal to move away from pressure, just a different kind of pressure. He's learning to listen to a complex array of body signals.

VERBAL COMMANDS

Even a very young foal can begin to learn voice commands. Once your foal is consistently backing up, if you want, you can add a verbal command.

You've already got the first steps of putting the behavior under stimulus control.

We began by first getting the behavior. We did this by using negative reinforcement, pressing our hand into his chest to get him to shift his weight back, and removing it the instant he did. With the clicker we were able to shape this response very easily and quickly. The combination of the pressure from our hand and our shift in body position became a signal that the foal responded to by stepping back.

Now we want to transfer that very natural cue to an artificial cue, the spoken word. We have the behavior. We know that every time we turn into him in a particular way, he'll back. So now, just before you move, say the word "back," and click him when he responds correctly. Repeat this consistently over a number of trials, and your foal will begin to associate this particular sound with the action. He'll know that if he backs up when he hears this word, he'll get a treat.

You're now part way through the process of having the behavior under stimulus control. Here are the criteria:*

1. The horse backs up promptly every time we ask for it.

2. The horse doesn't back up when we haven't cued it.

3. The horse doesn't back up in response to some other cue.

4. When we ask for backing, we get backing, not some other behavior.

Your foal may be backing even when you haven't asked for it. Don't click him. This can be a really hard step for the handler. The horse will get frustrated when he doesn't get reinforced. He's not sure why the vending machine isn't working. It was working just a few seconds ago. Very often what he'll do is back up even more. You'll see some of the strongest responses of the session. It's as if he's doing the equine version of kicking the Coke machine. "If a little backing doesn't get the human to click, maybe a lot will."

It's really hard not to reinforce this extra effort, but if you're going after stimulus control, keep your finger off the clicker. Wait for the behavior to stop, and then ask him to back. C/R when he does. Repeat this, sometimes presenting the cue and reinforcing

---

*Based on *Don't Shoot the Dog*, by Karen Pryor, Bantam Books.

him when he backs, sometimes withholding the cue and the reinforcement. Backing in the absence of a cue will gradually extinguish. Eventually, he will only back if he is given the signal to do so.

The last step in this is fading your original cue. Suppose you want him to back from a verbal command only. He understands back as a complex signal made up of body language and sound. To find out what he is listening to, present only the verbal cue. Does he back? If not, add in your body cues until the behavior comes back up to full strength. Now you know all the elements he's reading. Begin to fade out the gestures until only the word "back" is needed to get the response.

This may seem like a lot of effort to be putting into a foal, but it's well worth it. By the time your horse is ready for riding, he'll know something far more important than a series of individual cues. He'll know how to learn, and he'll be able to generalize concepts. He'll be an active participant in his own education—trying to find out what you want, and trying to do it right.

BASIC LEADING STEP TWO: GOING FORWARD

Once you have your foal backing up from a signal, you can use the same basic approach to teach him to step forward. Stand by his shoulder. If you're on the left side, you can support him a little by holding your left arm across his chest. Reach back with your right arm and press your fingers against the point of his hip. When he shifts forward, click him and give him a scratch (Fig.19).

You'll build this sequence in the same way you did the backing up, gradually adding more steps as he understands what you're asking him to do. Don't worry about trying to stop him at this point. Remember, we can't ask him to do something we haven't taught him. The halt will come later. For now let the clicker do it for you. He'll stop as you do to get his scratch. This way you never have to pull on your foal. The clicker ends behavior. When you use it, you're putting your foal in a learning situation where his head is never jerked on.

If he starts to surge forward too fast, you can steady him with your left arm. Your goal isn't to hold him. If he's comfortable having you next to him, he won't be trying to break away. Your left arm is just there for guidance, not restraint. Turn this into a game. Find lots of different ways you can ask

Fig. 19: I am asking the foal to step forward. I use my left arm across her chest to steady her. At the same time I am reaching back with my right hand and pressing my fingers against the point of her hip. As she takes a step forward, I'll click her, take my hand away, and give her a treat.

him to move. Loop a soft cotton rope over neck. Don't tie it around his neck. He isn't ready for that yet. Simply hold the two ends together. That way if he panics, you can just release the rope. Teach him to move forward and back from the feel of the rope.

Be creative and have fun. What you are doing is teaching him to follow a feel. If you touch him on his shoulder, you want his shoulder to soften to the pressure and move over. The same is true for his hip, his ribs, his neck. In fact, you want every inch of his body to come alive and respond to you. Pair correct responses with lots of rubbing and praise. He won't even know he's having a training session, but he'll be learning to be a light, responsive horse who never pulls on his handler. Later, if you want to put a figure-eight body rope on him to help with the leading or to teach him to ground drive, he'll already know how to respond to pressure across his chest.

If at this point you're feeling left out because the only horse you own is all grown up and over 16 hands high, don't worry. All these exercises apply just as much to your horse as they do to a foal. Whatever the age, these are valuable lessons for every horse.

Once your foal understands how to move away from pressure, it's easy to take him for a little walk around his stall. Stand by his side with your left arm across his chest, and your right hand reaching back toward the point of his hip. Ask him to take a step or two forward. You'll be angled slightly forward to do this.

As soon as he takes those first couple of steps, get ready to back him up. The more steps forward he takes, the more likely he is to want to keep going. You're going to ask him to back up just as soon as he's in motion. Simply rotate your body so your left side angles toward his left shoulder and reach down with your left hand to ask him to back. As he takes a step or two back, C/R.

Continue this, gradually lengthening out the number of steps you ask him to go forward, and always having him take those one or two steps back out of your space to stop. Start with just a few steps at a time, and build slowly. If you let him take too many steps at first, it will be hard for him to stop. "Make haste slowly" should be your motto here.

You have now taught your foal the two basic responses that are the building blocks for everything else you will ever ask him to do. You have taught him to step forward and to step back. Your foal may only be a couple of days old, but you've already introduced him to the two elements you'll need to solve every training problem you'll encounter, and to build a top performance horse.

CHAPTER ELEVEN

Circles and Turns: Putting an End to the Pushy Horse

You've taught your foal to step back out of your space, and to come forward when you ask. He's responding beautifully, but now you have a new problem. When he walks forward, he crowds into you with his shoulder. It's time to teach him to move out of your space.

Even very young foals can learn to displace their hips and shoulders and step laterally out of your way. Press your thumb against your foal's ribs, and click him when he shifts over. It's tempting here just to shove him over. That's not what you are trying to do. You want your horse to respond to a signal, not a push. You don't have to press hard to have an effect. It's your foal's job to move his body, not yours. If you push your foal over, he'll never learn what you really want. Pushing will mean to him, "Brace yourself. Get ready to stagger sideways."

Pressure that isn't a push teaches your foal to think and listen to you. He has to figure out what you want, and come up with the right answer.

TURNING TO THE RIGHT OUT OF YOUR SPACE

To solve the crowding problem you're going to teach your foal to turn away from you. You'll begin by getting him to move his head and neck out of your space.

Your foal's first response will be to walk straight ahead and crowd into you. Before you can ask for a turn, you'll have to get him to step back out of your space. In effect you'll be teaching your foal to redistribute his weight forward and back. The shifts in weight will create a balanced turn. Another way of saying this is you will be teaching your foal to respond to half halts. Pretty fancy for a horse that isn't even weaned yet, and barely knows how to lead.

ASSEMBLING THE PIECES

You've taught your foal to back up, go forward, move his haunches over, and turn his head away. From this beginning you can teach your foal to lead. You just need to add one other piece, lowering the head (Fig. 20).

To teach this you can use the same basic principle Joan used with her foal to solve Spirit's rearing problem. (See p. 55, The Clicker Saves a Life.) Joan began by putting her hand on Spirit's poll. She didn't push down. She simply rested it there. She was relying on the principle that behavior is variable. Spirit wasn't going to hold her head rigidly in one position any more than we would. She shifted it about.

When Spirit dropped her head even slightly, Joan clicked her and gave her a treat. As she repeated this, Spirit began to drop her head right down to her knees. Spirit was learning that when she felt pressure

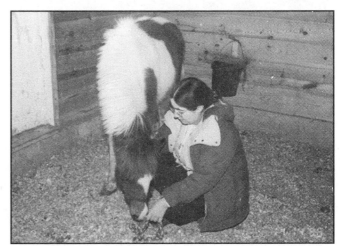

Fig. 20: This filly is learning to follow a feel. When I put gentle pressure on her halter by taking the slack out of the lead, she lowers her head in response. My goal is to have her nose on the ground. By kneeling down, I make it easier for her to lower her head and share a peaceful moment with me.

on her poll, dropping her head earned her a treat. It also made the pressure go away. Pushing up against Joan's hand never earned her a treat, and simply made the pressure worse.

Joan could now transfer the cue (pressure on the poll) from her hand to the lead rope. She did this by taking the slack out of the lead. She didn't pull down on the lead, any more than she had pushed with her hand. That would have provoked a fight. Instead she simply put enough pressure on the rope so Spirit could feel the halter pressing against her poll. At the slightest tendency to drop her head, Joan released the pressure, and clicked her.

Now we've developed signals to step back, to step forward, to step over sideways, and to lower the head, all of which the foal understands and responds to consistently. He's totally comfortable having you stroke him anywhere and everywhere on his body, but he also understands how to move away from pressure. If you ask him to shift over, you don't feel rigid muscles braced against you. You feel a relaxed foal who understands what you want and is happy to give it to you in exchange for praise and a good rub.

The next step is to combine these pieces to teach the foal to lead next to you on a cotton rope. Let's start by teaching your foal to walk with you from the left. Use your left hand to ask him to lower his head. It's easy and natural for him to take a step forward as he does so, especially since you'll also be reaching back with your right hand to give him a go forward signal on his hip. As soon as he takes a step, C/R. Since the clicker ends behavior, you won't have to worry about brakes yet.

Repeat this several times until you can gradually fade out the go-forward signal from your right hand. Your foal will be following your body and the feel of the rope. He'll not only be walking next to you, he'll be softening and lowering his head in response to the lead.

As he walks forward, you'll want to switch the lead from your left to your right hand, so you can walk with both shoulders facing forward. If you have trouble making the switch, practice it without a horse until it becomes automatic.

When he's moving off consistently, have him walk forward two or three steps, then ask him to back. Prepare for this step by switching the lead back to your left hand as you turn to face him. Then use your right hand to signal him to back up. If you're not sure how to do this, borrow a friend's horse, or better yet, borrow the friend. Pretend the person is a horse and practice with him.

Have your friend hold the lead with both hands out in front of his body. His hands represent the horse's head. Begin by leading him around the way most of us do. Don't signal him, just drag him. See how long it takes for your human "horse" to become an unwilling participant. Now change and use the signals you've taught your foal. You'll be delighted at how easy everything becomes. When you've got the coordination worked out, and you're using your signals instead of pulling on his hands, you can move on to the real thing.

Once your horse is going forward and back smoothly, you'll very easily be able to teach him to halt. Walk him forward a few steps, then ask him to back using the signal you taught him earlier. As he begins to shift his weight back, C/R him. You will see that he'll very quickly learn to read a subtle shift in your body position as a signal to halt.

The key here is that you aren't relying on the lead to do all the work. You aren't pulling on his head to drag him around the stall, or to haul him into a halt. You're teaching your foal to pay attention to the position of your body, and to respond to cues.

The lead tells him how far away he can be from you. If he should skitter off and hit the end of it, he's not going to rear up or pull away. Why? Because you've changed his response to pressure on his head. You've taught him through the head-lowering exercise to soften and yield. Originally it meant "Brace yourself, you're about to be dragged." Now it means "Relax, you're being asked to give."

What these exercises will create isn't simply a foal who knows how to lead. In just a few short sessions, you have developed cues that you're going to use for everything. As he grows up, you'll be able to ask him to move over on cross ties, to step out of your space in his stall, to load onto a trailer, to drop his head on command, to follow you over trail obstacles, and to stand tied quietly even in the most distracting of environments.

As you teach him these cues from the left, you should also switch sides and teach him the same thing from the right. It may feel awkward to you at first, but spending time working both sides of your horse will pay huge dividends once you start to ride him.

START WITH WHAT YOU KNOW

This is just one way you can teach leading, whether it's to a foal or a full-grown horse. There are lots of other approaches. For example, I've seen leading taught much the way some people teach dogs. The handler anchors the hand that holds the lead firmly at his hip, and marches forward. He walks a set number of steps. Halts, pauses, and then marches off again. If the foal surges ahead, or lags behind, he'll get pulled on by the force of the handler's steady walking. The handler never gets in a tug of war with the foal. He just keeps his hand firmly anchored by his side, and doesn't deviate from his path. What the foal learns is, "If you don't want your head pulled, you better follow this person." It's easy to see how you could add the clicker to this approach.

You may have your own favorite way of teaching leading that works well for you. Don't feel as though you have to use the steps I've outlined in order to use the clicker. Begin with what you know. Chunk your training down into simple steps following the rules of shaping, and reward your foal for each small success. The clicker will make it easier for him to understand these early lessons very quickly (Figs. 21a, b).

Fig. 21a: Taking the show on the road: This filly has never been invited out the front door before, and she's not sure she wants to go all by herself.

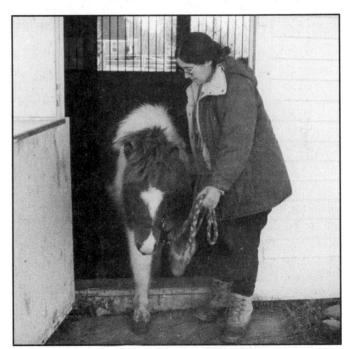

Fig. 21b: Instead of trying to drag her out i'm going to use the cues I taught her. I'll reach back with my right hand and use the "go forward" cue. The result: she's now willing to step up out of the stall.

CHAPTER TWELVE

A Clicker Training Session:
Taking the Bounce out of Your Baby

So far we've only worked the foal in his stall. When you want to lead your foal outside, you're still basically just embracing him and guiding him behind mom. He's young enough that he still wants to follow her, and small enough that you can still hold onto him.

You've taken a few minutes during each of his grooming sessions to teach him the basic leading cues. Your foal hasn't even known that he's having a formal lesson. He thinks it's all just a wonderful game. He moves his feet, and these wonderful two leggeds scratch his withers.

In less time than it's taken to write this section, you've got a foal who leads beautifully—in the stall. That doesn't mean he's going to lead beautifully outside, on his way to the paddock, when he's feeling fresh, and the wind is blowing, and his best buddy is already out there, and the neighbor's dogs are barking at his heels, and . . . Well, you've got the picture.

THE IMPORTANCE OF CONSISTENCY

The lessons you taught your foal in his stall with mom right there for security have given you the tools you'll need to deal with ever-increasing distractions. How well he learns to lead in the real world depends on how consistent you are in using them. John Lyons has a wonderful phrase that's worth remembering here: "The horse doesn't know when it doesn't count."

Get him in the habit of walking quietly and listening to you, and he'll grow up to be a quiet and responsive horse. Let him play on the end of the lead or pull on you, and he'll grow up rude and pushy. Just because you're in a hurry to get your chores done doesn't give you permission to slack off on your end of the bargain. If you let him pull on you today, don't be surprised if he pulls even harder tomorrow.

If you want good manners in your foal, you have to be consistent. Why? Because variable reinforcement schedules are at work even when we're not thinking about them. Think of the small child in the grocery store who is begging for candy. If mom gives up and buys him the gum he's whining for, she has just guaranteed that he will whine even longer the next time. Let your foal pull today, and tomorrow he will pull harder.

Build the habit of consistency for both of you by beginning with simple, easy steps. Have a helper lead mom. At first just ask your foal to follow her. Have your helper stop mom once or twice on your way out to the paddock. C/R your foal when he stops next to her. Once you get him into his paddock, click him before you turn him loose. For your foal, play time is a huge jackpot of a reward. Pairing the clicker with it is too good an opportunity to miss.

Once your foal has had time to play, you can give him a mini leading lesson out in his field. With mom along for security, lead him a few steps away from her, C/R. At first stay close to mom. You don't want either of them feeling panicked if he gets too far away. You're teaching your foal to listen to you instead of simply following along beside mom.

A CLICKER TRAINING SESSION

I am going to show you how all this works in the real world by taking you step by step through a clicker training session (Figs. 22a-m). This foal's owner is holding mom off to the side. If you have a helper, this is the safest way to work. Mom isn't fretting about her foal, and he isn't distracted by her.

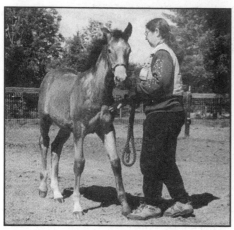

Fig. 22, The Leading Lesson:
a. I'm teaching this four-month-old foal to lead. I am asking him to back by keeping a light feel on his halter and using my right hand on his chest. My body is turned in to face his shoulder. He is responding by taking a step back. I click and give him a scratch on the withers.

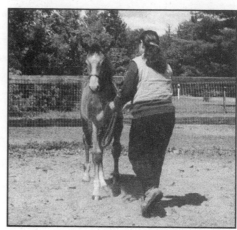

b. Several minutes later he is backing easily. I no longer need to touch him. As soon as I face his near shoulder and gesture with my hand, he backs. Now I'll change position so we're both backing together.

c. Now I'm ready to teach this foal a "go forward" cue. I've placed my right hand on his hip, and am steadying his head with my left hand. I'm careful to keep my hand forward, so I don't restrict his movement.

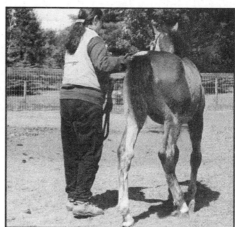

d. I'm cueing with my hand on his hip. As soon as he walks forward, I'll take my hand away. I want this to be a "starter button," not a constant "On" cue.

e. I am teaching the foal to move his head and neck out of my space. I want him to turn inside the circle I am walking. I begin by pressing my fingers against his face as I walk towards him.

f. The foal is getting the idea. He's turning away from just my hand. I have a light feel of the lead, but I'm not restricting his head. If he were to rush off, however, I could easily close my hand around the lead.

g. Horses (and people, too) have ups and downs. Now he's stuck. Note the ears pinned back in annoyance, the elevated head, the inverted, ewed neck, and the hollow back. This is not the look I want. It's time to change the lesson to help him through this phase.

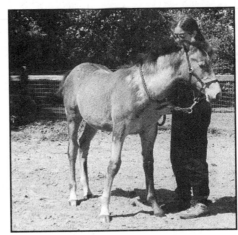

h. Introducing a neck rope. I want him to back up from the feel of the rope. He doesn't understand, so I've added an already familiar cue, my hand on his chest.

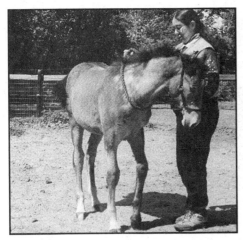

i. He's starting to under-stand. I've taken my hand away, and now he's backing from just the pres-sure of the rope. Note the dramatic difference in head carriage between this picture and that of Fig. 22g, above.

j. I am asking him to walk forward from the neck rope. Again he doesn't understand. He's telling me that he doesn't like the feel, by throwing his head up and pressing his outside shoulder into the rope.

k: I respond by using the neck rope and the lead to encourage him to bring his outside shoulder back toward me. I am NOT pulling on his head, but I've stabilized my hand so he feels steady pressure on his halter. I'll soften my hand and release the pressure as soon as I feel him move toward me.

l. He's starting to relax and walk with me. I'm leaning forward and down to encourage him to stretch and lengthen his topline. Now he undertands. Click!

Fig. 22m: The end result is a foal who leads quietly beside me on a slack lead. Note the relaxed head position, attentive ear, and lengthened neck. This would be a good place to end the training session for the day.

CHAPTER THIRTEEN

Taking the Show on the Road: Trail Obstacles

AFTER BASICS—PLAY

Once your foal is leading well, you can really have fun with him. You can teach him to walk over and around ground poles. You can create trail class obstacles and get him to walk over bridges and sheets of plastic.

When you first lead your horse over a sheet of plastic, or up to a trailer, his natural response may be to pull back. As you train him to step forward instead, he'll be learning to override his flight instinct. He'll learn to trust you to guide him through frightening new situations. You'll gradually develop a rock-solid horse who simply never spooks. He'll know how to listen to you instead of his fears.

Pulling back or running over the top of you is one problem you want to eliminate. Spooking is another. You want to teach your horse that when he's afraid, he's to listen to you and not simply to leave town. Teaching the basic leading exercises gives you a way to control where your foal moves his feet. You can ask him to step forward and back, right and left. You can also say "drop your head and relax."

These cues and the clicker are all you need to teach your foal to accept clippers, to walk through mud puddles, to load on a trailer, to stand quietly in a ring with other horses, to walk past cars, to take a bath, and to accept all the other scary things that are going to be part of his life.

COOKBOOKS AND MOUNTAINS: DIFFERENT SHAPING RECIPES

There is no one correct way to shape any of these things. Training isn't a cookbook, and it isn't a linear progression from one step to another. Think of it this way. Imagine you have five people standing at the base of a steep hill. They all want to get to the top. Not one of those five people is going to take the same route up.

One person may enjoy a challenge. He'll pick the hardest, rockiest climb up. Another may pick a nice leisurely route with lots of scenic overlooks. Someone else may look for a well-worn path that goes straight to the top, while the fourth person explores all the little side trails along the way. Someone else may not bother walking up at all. He may get in a jeep and go blasting past everyone else.

These are all different ways to train. (I'm the person taking the side trails. Which one are you?) If we had ten people, or twenty, or a hundred and twenty, we would find there are just as many different ways to the top of the hill as there are people. Conventional training gets us to think that there is only one way that's correct. In shaping, there are many ways.

Let's look at just one exercise we can teach our foal. We want our youngster to walk over a sheet of plastic. Our foal is curious, but afraid. He's slammed on the brakes about five feet away and is refusing to go forward.

Our goal is to get him over the plastic, but our rules of training say that neither the handler nor the horse can get hurt. That means that tying him to the back of a car and dragging him over the plastic, while it might indeed get the job done, isn't an acceptable answer. Nor is whipping him acceptable, or dragging him forward, or putting a chain around his tongue, or blindfolding him, or tying a rope around his hindquarters and dragging him over it. All of these may work, but they stand a good chance of violating our rules. (If you think I'm a bit too dramatic with my examples here, think about all the different ways people try to load horses into trailers.)

We don't need to do any of these things because we have a foal who understands some basic cues and loves to play the clicker game. We also know that there are lots of different ways to shape any behavior. There isn't just one way I can get my foal over the plastic. There are lots of ways. I'm going to review three different approaches just to show you what I mean. You'll probably be able to think of three or four other ways yourself.

SHAPING METHOD 1: TARGETING ON A STATIONARY OBJECT

You may have taught your foal to touch a cone, as his very first clicker game. Now you can put the cone on the ground and ask him to touch it. If your foal is worrying about the plastic, he won't be able to focus on the cone.

You may know how he feels. Remember when you were little and you had to perform in the school play? Your teacher helped you learn your lines until you were letter-perfect, but when you got out on that stage with all those parents watching you, you couldn't even remember your own name, let alone your part.

That's how your foal feels now. He's so distracted by the plastic, he doesn't even notice the cone. Help him out. Take him away from the plastic until he's back in his comfort zone. That's where you're going to begin this game. Whether he balks five feet from the plastic, or five inches, put the cone down within his comfort zone, and ask him to touch it. When he does, click him and give him a treat. A lack of enthusiasm is a good indicator of the level of his fear. A horse who is very afraid will be sluggish in his responses. As he relaxes and gets comfortable, the behavior will come back up to its previous level.

Once he's energetically touching the cone, inch it closer to the plastic. How far and how fast you move it will depend on your foal. Obviously, you'll be able to take much bigger steps with a bold foal who is only a little bit concerned about the plastic. A timid foal who is truly frightened will need more steps. Remember, if behavior deteriorates, go back to a previous step in your shaping. If you go too fast, your foal will tell you. He'll stop touching the cone.

Inching the cone forward like this will give your foal plenty of time to get comfortable with the plastic. He'll hear it crinkle when you walk on it. He'll put a front foot on the edge and jump back, and when

nothing horrible happens to him, he'll step forward again to touch the cone. It won't take long before your foal will be walking right over the plastic to get to his favorite target sitting on the other side (Fig. 23).

Fig. 23: I can get this Icelandic filly to cross the plastic by asking her to touch her nose to a cone. Each time she touches it, I'll click her and give her a treat. I'll gradually inch the cone forward so she has to cross the plastic to get to it.

Should your foal be loose or on a lead for this? The answer to that is there are lots of different ways to climb up the hill. You can teach him either way, and in fact, if you teach him both ways, you're really getting your foal to think and respond to two separate behaviors.

SHAPING METHOD 2: FOLLOWING A MOVING TARGET

Get two long strips of plastic instead of one. Lay them down in a V formation, but leave a gap to walk between (Figs. 24a-f). Before you ask your foal to go between the plastic, teach him to follow a target stick. You already began this process when you taught him to touch his nose to a cone. It's easy to transfer this over to other objects. If you've already taught him the word "touch," simply place the cone next to the whip and say, "touch." Do this several times and then take the cone away, but continue to offer him the whip. When he bumps into the whip, click him.

The next step is to move the whip and get him to follow it. As always, start with just a step or two and gradually build it into a longer sequence. Targeting is something horses understand. Watch your horses wander in for supper at the end of the day. You'll often see them walking in single file, targeting on the tail of the horse in front.

Fig. 24a: Same filly, different method. We've spread out two sheets of plastic into an open V. This filly isn't too worried about the plastic. She's more interested in touching the whip handle, her moving target stick.

Fig. 24b: An instant before this shot was taken, the plastic blew up in the air. Her body language shows us how concerned she is. Her left ear is pivoted towards the plastic and her body is arched away from it. We need to pay attention to the subtle signals she's sending us.

Fig. 24c: She's afraid, and yet she's still willing to follow the target through the plastic. But just because she's walked through the plastic once, our job is not over. Her left ear is telling us that she's still concerned about the plastic.

Fig. 24d: I've closed off the end of the V. Now she'll have to walk directly over the plastic. She's feeling more confident. She's even throwing in some variable behavior—"If touching the target is good, how about biting it?"

Fig. 24e: She's starting to relax enough to check out the plastic, but her ear is still telling us our job is far from over. It's important to be aware of these signs of discomfort. We can spread this lesson out over as many sessions as we need, but our job isn't done until she's completely at ease.

Fig. 24f: We've overlapped the plastic even more. She's following the whip over it without any hesitation. Her top line looks relaxed. She's not rushing, or crowding into her owner, but that tell-tale ear is still telling me that we need more work.

That's all you're asking your horse to do, just follow the target stick over the plastic. As he steps forward, click him and give him a treat. When he gets comfortable walking between the strips of plastic, gradually narrow the gap, until the ends forming the tip of the V are touching. He'll be able to step over the plastic without actually touching it, but the next time through you'll overlap the ends even more. As you close in the V, your foal will be following you over a wide section of plastic.

SHAPING METHOD 3: USING YOUR STEP FORWARD CUE

In your basic leading lessons you taught your foal to move away from pressure. You taught him cues to back up and go forward. If he tries to knock you down like a bowling pin, you have cues to tell him to step out of your space. This time, we're going to use these tools to get him across the plastic.

Set out your plastic and put a cone in the middle of it. Your initial goal is going to be to keep him looking at the cone. You could treat him like a dolphin and turn him loose. Every time he looks at the cone, or walks toward it, you could click him. Eventually you can shape him to walk right onto the plastic to touch the cone, and you won't have ever touched him. Or you could put a lead on him and use your leading cues.

Ask him to step forward by tapping him on his hip. If he balks and backs up instead, keep tapping him, until you feel him shift his weight. As soon as he's even so much as thinking forward, you'll release your go forward cue and C/R.

Even if he backs up twenty feet, that's okay. He'll eventually be far enough away from the plastic that he'll feel comfortable enough to listen to your cue. That's where you begin. Your goal isn't to get into a fight with him. Remember that frightened little first grader standing up on the stage? Do you think he'd remember his lines any better if his teacher started yelling at him? Of course not. So, if you wouldn't yell at the first grader, you don't need to yell at your horse either. All you have to do is be persistent. Keep asking him to go forward by continuing to tap his hip. Stop the tapping as soon as he responds to you, and C/R.

The next time you ask him to step forward he'll be far enough away from the plastic that he'll be able to listen to you. You'll go through the same series of steps you did when you first taught him the

Fig. 25a: The beauty of training with the clicker is it allows you to be so flexible. I'm using a moving target, in this case a cone, to get this Icelandic filly to walk over a tarp. I've laid it out in a big square instead of just giving her a V to walk through.

Fig. 25b: She just needed a few seconds to think about it before she was willing to follow the target to get her click and treat.

go-forward cue back in his stall, only now it's a different exercise. You're asking him to step forward even when there's something scary in front of him (Figs. 25a, b).

You may find that as he gets close to the plastic he'll start to back up again. Don't try to hold onto him and force him to stay. Back up with him. Just keep tapping his hip until he stops, then C/R. What you will find is that your foal will back up fewer and fewer steps each time, and he'll be going closer to the plastic before he hesitates.

No matter how far he backs up, just keep his head oriented toward the cone, and keep asking him to go forward. It's easy to relate to how he feels. We've all been in frightening situations where we freeze up so much we can't hear the instructions someone is trying to give us. It doesn't matter if they shout them at us, we simply can't respond. That's perfectly normal, but imagine what would happen if the airline pilot froze like that during an emergency. He'd crash the plane.

So how can pilots keep doing their job, even when a plane is going down? Are they so much braver than the rest of us? Not really. I'd say anyone who works around horses is pretty brave, so that's not the answer. The pilots are simply better trained than the rest of us. They've gone through all kinds of exercises, including flight simulations, to change their natural response to fear. They've learned how to stay calm and think their way through situations that would panic most people.

That's what we want our horses to learn. Training exercises like walking over plastic are just "life" simulations. The world is full of scary distractions. The lesson you want your horse to learn is: "It's okay to be afraid, just stay calm and keep listening to me."

Your foal is learning that the cue to go forward doesn't go away until he steps toward the plastic. When he does, he gets clicked for it. Going away from the plastic intensifies the pressure he feels from your cue. Going toward the plastic gets the vending machine to work. It won't take long before your foal is eagerly walking over the plastic. He's made a conscious choice to set aside his fear to get something he wants.

The first time you take your foal through this kind of exercise, it may take quite a while to get him up to the plastic. Then maybe you'll ask him to walk over a sheet of plywood or between two strips of plastic your friends are holding up. Or maybe you'll ask him to walk over a teeter totter, or past a mailbox, or through a mud puddle. You'll find that with each new scary obstacle, it will become easier and easier for him to walk forward.

He is learning how to stay focused and continue to listen to you even when he's afraid. Every time he overcomes his fear, he's getting a boost to his confidence. He's literally getting braver and harder to scare. Through these exercises he's discovering that trolls don't bite. In fact, quite the opposite; he's learning that good things happen to him when he walks up to them (Figs. 26a, b).

Fig. 26a: "Whoa! Slam on the brakes. There's that plastic again!" I've spread the plastic out in a square. We aren't using a target anymore. Instead her owner is asking her to come forward from a cue from behind. This filly isn't sure crossing plastic is the smartest idea in the world.

Fig. 26b: Her owner is tapping her on her hip, a clicker-trained cue. The filly understands the cue and responds by stepping forward. Note the slack in the lead rope. Her owner is doing a great job keeping her left hand inviting and soft. If she had a tighter grip on the lead, her filly might feel trapped and pull back or barge forward over the top of her.

TRAILER LOADING MADE EASY

So now you've taken one simple goal, getting your foal to step over plastic, and you've taught it at least three different ways. You've taught him to touch a target that's sitting on the plastic (Method 1); to follow a target over the plastic (Method 2); and to orient toward a target and step forward from a body cue (Method 3). What you've done is given yourself all the tools you need to get your horse safely on a trailer.

Imagine your horse doesn't want to walk anywhere near the trailer. Use shaping method 3 to get him to step up to the bottom of the ramp. You could continue to use this to load him all the way on, or you could switch to shaping method 2, and ask him to follow a target into the trailer. Once he's on the trailer, ask him to stand touching the target until you ask him to back off. Stretch the time out, and you will solve the problem of the horse who backs up fast off the trailer.

You can think up your own combinations and variations on the theme to teach your horse how to load. Remember, we're all going to find our own way up the hill. We can watch other people to see how they've done it. Let's continue the metaphor of our hill. If we haven't done much climbing before, it's probably a good idea to follow someone else's path the first time. If they slip and fall, we'll know their way isn't safe, and we should look for a different path. After we get the hang of climbing, we won't need to depend so much on following someone else's lead. We'll be able to branch out on our own.

That's the same way with training. We need to begin by learning the established methods. As we gain experience, we can branch out and use our imagination to come up with unique solutions tailored to fit our personality and horse. That's what all good trainers do, and that's the challenge for each of us. With the clicker, we can take training beyond basics. Remember, if you can dream it, you can do it. Each small step you take with your horse just gets you closer to your goals (Fig. 27).

Fig. 27: You can never do just one thing. It's obvious this filly is getting an early lesson in saddling, but how many other things is she learning as well?

CHAPTER FOURTEEN

Overcoming Fear:
Clippers, Baths, Shots, Etc.

Using the clicker with your foal gives you a head start whenever you have something frightening to deal with. Whether it's loading into a trailer, walking into a wash stall, crossing bridges, going under a sheet of plastic, or walking over hoses, you'll have the tools to help your horse stay calm.

And speaking of hoses, you can use the clicker to introduce baths, clippers, paste wormers, sheath cleaning, shots, and all those other must-do tasks.

To get your horse comfortable with all of these things is just a matter of chunking them down into small steps and applying the basic rules of shaping. To show you how this works, let's use a hose bath as the behavior we're going to shape.

BATH TIME

If your foal is afraid of baths, it's easy to chunk that down. Think of all the elements your foal has to accept in order to be totally comfortable with baths. It's not just the water coming out of the hose that may worry him. Maybe your foal tripped over a bucket once, and now he's afraid of things around his feet. If that's the case, you could get him comfortable around hoses and still have trouble giving him a bath. You have to include all the elements that go into the behavior, not just some of them.

I first met Peregrine's mother when she was just a yearling, and baths were one of the things she definitely did not do. If you tried to take her anywhere near a hose, she would either plant her feet and refuse to move, or she would go up in the air. She wasn't just playing, either. She'd aim for the handler's head as her front feet went up.

How had she gotten like this? Her original handler had forgotten she was a baby and the world was full of things she hadn't yet seen and didn't understand.

She needed to learn in small steps, and he was treating her like an experienced, adult horse.

In his mind she was a Thoroughbred racehorse. His reasoning went like this: Thoroughbreds are racehorses and racehorses take baths. This horse is a Thoroughbred, therefore she is also a racehorse. Since racehorses take baths, she takes baths. He left out the step that this horse was a baby and needed to be taught things. The result was a frightened, overfaced yearling with a growing reputation for dangerous behavior.

Long before I ever heard of clickers or shaping, I learned to chunk training down for her. I knew she wasn't the witch everyone was calling her, but a frightened youngster who needed to have things explained. Today I would probably follow very much the same procedure I did then, only I'd add in the clicker.

HOW SIMPLE CAN YOU GET?

So where do you begin? At least one step back from where your foal tells you she's starting to feel uncomfortable. That may mean you go all the way back to getting her used to being handled.

Start your bath training with your foal loose in her stall, or standing with you on a halter and lead rope. Do not tie your foal. If you were to proceed too fast, and your foal became frightened, she might pull back and hurt herself. Begin with just your hand. Until she'll let you rub her anywhere and everywhere on her body, she's not ready for the next step. Be aware of the signals she's sending you. A swish of the tail, a tightened muscle, a flattened ear, are all signs of discomfort.

Once she's accepting your hand, repeat the same procedure using a dry bath sponge. If your foal is afraid to let you touch her with a dry sponge, she's sure not going to like it any better when it's wet. So go through a sequence of steps very much like the one you used for getting her used to the halter. Use Joan's approach with Spirit and the hair brush. (See Ch. 8, Foal Training.) Touch her only for the briefest of seconds. Remove the sponge before she has a chance to react. When she is standing still letting you rub her neck with it, C/R. Gradually extend both the time you can leave it on her, and the parts of her body you can touch. With some foals this whole sequence may take only a few seconds. With others it could take the better part of a session (Fig. 28).

Fig. 28: I'm bundled up and so is this shaggy Icelandic filly. It's too cold to be giving her a bath, but I can still get her ready for the experience. I want to be able to touch her all over her body with the sponge. If she's uncertain about a dry sponge, she's not going to like it any better when it's wet.

You never know what exactly is going to bother any horse until you take the horse through the steps. The time to find out that your horse is ticklish, and will kick at anything that touches her hind legs, is not when you're leaning over her with a wet sponge. Taking the time to go through these steps can help keep things safe for both you and your foal.

ADDING WATER

Once your foal accepts the dry sponge, dampen it. Some horses just don't like getting wet. Before you make them stand under a hose, you need to get them comfortable with the idea of a sponge bath. Follow the same series of steps you went through to get her comfortable with the dry sponge.

Look for signs of tension in your foal. You want to train yourself to see the muscles that are tight; the look of concern in the face; the swish of the tail. That's the way your foal says, "I'm not yet comfortable with what you're asking me to do."

Don't just gloss over this. Acknowledge her fear, and chunk down the piece you're working on into smaller steps. Maybe the water bucket really is bothering her. Turn standing near buckets into a training session. C/R her for standing still while you set a bucket down three feet away, then two feet away, then inches away.

Ask her to touch it, and to stand still while you pick it up. You could even chunk buckets down. Start with a small plastic pail, and gradually progress to clanging metal buckets. Use the bucket like a giant sponge. Get her used to having it touch her anywhere on her body. When you can bump it over her back and against her legs without her moving, she's ready for the next step.

WALKING OVER SNAKES

Hoses are something else you may need to chunk down. Suppose your foal (or older horse) is really afraid of things on the ground. What would be scarier: walking over a hose or walking over a lunge line? Start with the lunge line. Put it out on the ground, and walk figure eights over it. C/R your horse for walking calmly over it.

Next introduce the hose. Where you begin will depend on your foal. She may walk right up to it without any concern. Walk her over it a few times, and then go on to the next step. If your foal is anything like Peregrine's mother, going anywhere near a hose may cause a panic. Back then I didn't have the toolbox I have now to solve behavior problems. I just had patience.

I began by grooming her about fifteen feet down the aisle from the hose. Each night we moved the grooming station a little closer, until we were standing right next to the hose. The hose became associated with things she liked: attention, grooming, scratching, praise. She was giving me an early lesson in the power of shaping and positive reinforcement. One night I took her out for grooming and instead of stopping in front of the hose, we just kept on walking. She stepped right over it, and never again showed any fear of hoses.

A PRETEND BATH

Once your foal is comfortable walking over and around hoses, C/R her for standing still while you pick the hose up. With the water turned off, pretend you are giving her a bath. C/R her for letting you raise the hose above her neck and back. This is the time to get her comfortable with having things moving above her. You definitely want to introduce this step before there's water gushing out of the hose.

Run the hose down the back of her legs. Let her feel it bumping up against her hocks. C/R her for standing still. If she skitters sideways, don't punish her for moving. Simply ask her to step back in the opposite direction.

Remember: It's move, countermove. Use your leading skills to get her to stand still again (see Ch. 10, Baby's First Steps: Early Leading Lessons). Go back a step in your sequence. Clicker-trained horses want to succeed. Your foal is going to be trying really hard to control her fear. Keep things simple now, and she'll grow up thinking learning is fun. Your early successes here are building a strong foundation and a confident, willing horse (Fig. 29).

Fig. 29: This is a "pretend" bath, with a friend nearby for reassurance. I'm holding the hose just as I would if I were giving a real bath. I'm deliberately letting the hose bump against the filly. I'll click and give her a treat for standing still. If she moves off, I won't punish her. I'll just use the leading skills I've already taught her to bring her back to a standstill. Clicker-trained horses want to succeed. This filly will grow up thinking learning new things is fun.

FINALLY, THE REAL THING

Once you can give your foal a pretend hose bath, turn the water on to a gentle trickle. Begin with her front feet and lower legs, and gradually work your way up. C/R her for each small success.

Taking the time to chunk things down into small steps like this will give your foal tremendous confidence. She'll grow up knowing how to learn, and how to trust people. She'll know how to stay calm and focused in new situations. She'll know how to handle her body. She'll know how to wait for signals, and how to respond to them promptly. She'll be a joy to be around. You'll have a fun, super horse with a real head start on life.

A QUICK REVIEW

We began by socializing our newborn foal using the clicker. And we taught our older weanlings and yearlings a simple trick—touching a cone. That in turn opened up dozens of opportunities to teach them how to overcome their fear, and to yield to pressure. We taught them to lead, and to walk up to scary objects. Using the clicker has kept the training safe and fun.

By the time these horses are physically mature enough to ride, they will already understand the basic riding aids. They'll be soft in your hands, and they'll know how to listen to you. Whether your horse is going to be a thirteen-hand pony or a seventeen-hand giant, that's what they all need to learn in order to be fun and safe to be around.

CHAPTER FIFTEEN

Ground Manners for the Older Horse

STEP ONE TO RIDING SUCCESS: GROUND WORK

"Prepare, prepare, and let it happen." That's an expression I heard my teacher, Bettina Drummond, say many times. She was quoting from the late dressage master Nuno Oliviero.

When I was scanning through an online dressage e-mail list, I saw a wonderful statement. "Horsemasters are master beginners. Upper level teaching is only teaching basics very well." I absolutely agree, and that's why I place so much emphasis on ground work. Preparation is everything (Fig. 30). My horses have taught me that good ground preparation is a major key to success under saddle (Fig. 31).

In the foal section I showed you how to socialize a horse, how to get it used to being handled. That's important no matter what the age of your horse may be. I don't want to get on a horse that doesn't want to be touched. A head-shy horse that flinches at whips, shies from saddle pads, and dances away from grooming is telling you he's not ready for a rider. Maybe you've been getting on his back every day for the last ten years, but in my opinion that horse is just an accident waiting to happen.

You can go right on riding him if you want to, but I've never learned how to be a good rodeo rider, and I don't care to start now. If we were working together, I know what we'd be doing, and that's tons of ground work. I wouldn't get on that horse until he was comfortable with people, and telling me he was ready to be ridden.

My goal is always to ride, but I'm not in any hurry to get there. Beyond simply getting on a horse's back, I have other things in mind. I want more than a mediocre performance on a stiff, unhappy horse. I

Fig 30: Prepare, prepare and let it happen. This three-year-old Icelandic is having the first ride of his life—on a single rein, to start.

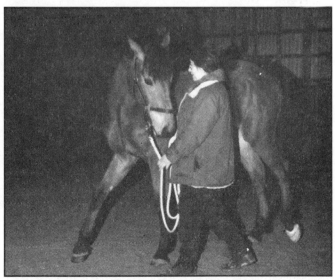

Fig. 31: Preparation is the key to riding success, and that means doing your homework on the ground.

have ridden well-trained horses. I have experienced excellence, and that's what I want. I get there by doing my homework on the ground.

LEARNING TO RIDE ON THE GROUND

Through ground work I establish my relationship with the horse: one of respect, trust, and understanding. It's also where I learn to speak with my body. It's where I learn to turn and flow in rhythm with my horse's movement. In a very real sense it's where I learn to ride.

If you're having trouble getting your horse to canter, or to stop, or to turn when you ask, spend some time on the ground. If your horse jigs out on the trail, or spooks in the show ring, you need to spend time with the basics. It isn't just a matter of making your horse more responsive. As you learn to move in rhythm with your horse, you'll become a better rider. The body language of good in-hand work is the body language of an organized rider (Fig. 32).

When I lead a horse, whether it's on a short lead beside me, or out at a distance on a lunge, I'm teaching the horse to soften to me; to yield to my hand and my body; to follow suggestions; to go against natural instincts; and to give to pressure instead of resisting it.

I'm setting the horse up to be light under saddle. I'm teaching him how to flex; how to respond to half halts. I'm learning, myself, what a half halt means. I'm learning that turns are nothing more than a rebalancing of weight forward and back. I'm learning how to ask a horse to yield sideways, and how to get him to stop, all without pulling or pushing him, or relying on leverage. I'm learning how to be clear in my signals, and how to chunk down my lesson plan. In other words, when I lead my horse, I'm learning how to ride.

Ground work is a major key to riding success. When riders start focusing on ground work, I always see a major improvement in their riding. If you have a problem under saddle, very often the best solution is to get off and address it from the ground. The trainers who understand this are the trainers with successful horses.

GETTING READY FOR GROUND WORK

If your horse happens to be the grown-up variety, he can still benefit from the basic handling skills I described in the foal section. Even if he leads well, going back to basics is a great way to polish skills.

Fig. 32: You don't have to be in the saddle to improve your riding. It may not look like it, but this handler is having a riding lesson. She's learning how to use her body to communicate with her horse. The positioning she uses to balance him here will carry over directly to her work under saddle.

And if he should happen to be one of those horses who grew up never really having learned good ground manners, these are great exercises for teaching him to respect your space. Unlike the foal, you'll probably have your older horse in a halter and lead rope, and you'll be working out in your ring where you both have plenty of room to move.

Old habits can be hard to break, yours as well as your horse's. Most people drag their horses around both on the ground and under saddle. Ask a rider to back up a horse, and chances are he'll haul on the lead. The object of this lesson is to teach the horse to respond to cues. We want the horse to move his own feet. When you drag him back, he's learning a different lesson.

To help you keep your hands out of it, fold the excess lead into tidy loops so it won't be dangling in your way. Give yourself twelve to fifteen inches of lead between your hand and the horse. You want him to be able to stand next to you at a halt with no tension on the line, but not to have so much slack that he can pull very far away from you should he rush forward.

I like to think that the lead acts just like the walls of a round pen. It sets limits. Suppose I've got a horse who is turned out in a five-acre pasture. I want him to walk next to me back to the barn, but he has other ideas. He charges off to join his friends. When he leaves my immediate space, I've got five acres to go chase after him in.

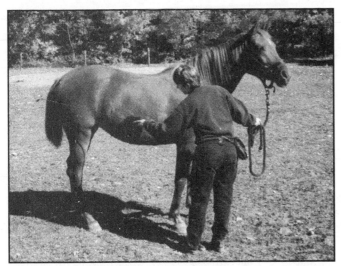

Fig. 33: This horse is learning to relax while her handler strokes her with a whip. When the whip is used as an extension of your arm most horses can readily accept it.

If I put him in a sixty-foot round pen, he can't get quite so far away. If I put him on a six-foot lead rope, he has even less space to run off in. He can circle around me on the end of the lead, but he'll always be within six feet of me. In a sense I've put him in a twelve-foot round pen.

The problem here is, if he runs all the way out to the end of the lead, I'm going to be looking at his hindquarters. That may not be the safest position to find myself in, so I need to decide how big a round pen I really want to be in. If my horse takes off, how far do I want him to be able to go before he hits the end of the lead? The answer may be only eight or nine inches, and so that's how much slack I'll give the rope.

STEP ONE: TEACH HIM TO BACK

Begin just as we did with the foal by first teaching your horse to back up. If you're working on his left side, hold your lead in your right hand. Stabilize your hand against your side. This will keep you from pulling back. Pretend you're in a dog obedience class, and you can't give signals down the line. Now turn in toward your horse's shoulder and ask him to back.

There are lots of different ways you can ask him. You can use your thumb in his chest just as we did with the foal. You can press your hand against the bridge of his nose. Or you could shake the lead at him as if it were a wiggly snake.

I want my horse to understand all of these cues, but I generally start by teaching him to move away from a whip. If he's afraid of whips, I'll begin by

stroking the front of his legs. Treat his fear just like we did everything else. Click if he stands still. Stop stroking before he has a chance to react. Show him the whip is just an extension of your arm (Fig. 33). Once he's accepting it, tap him just below his knees to ask him to move back. If he shifts his weight even a little, C/R (Fig. 34).

Some horses do better if you use the whip out in front of them, or if you tap the ground instead of their legs. Experiment, and find out what works best for your horse. And remember to ask yourself: Do you want this to be a starter button or a constant "on" cue? Are you going to signal once, or keep tapping with the whip as he backs? Decide which it is, and then be consistent in how you use it.

LEARNING RESPECT

Why start with backing? Several reasons. The first thing you teach a horse to do is often the hardest because he's not really paying attention to you yet. That means you want to start with a step that gives you the most control.

From the handler's point of view, backing is an easy behavior to prompt. To ask a horse to step forward, you have to reach back toward his hip. That puts you in an awkward position. To ask him to step back, you're going to turn in to his shoulder and use the whip directly in front of you. If he pulls,

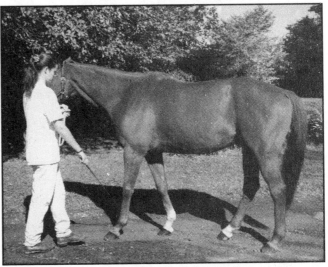

Fig. 34: Teaching an older horse to back: The handler is asking for the rein back by tapping her horse with the whip just below his knees. Note that she is NOT pulling on his head to get him to back. The whip and body cues tell the horse to back. Her Thoroughbred responds by giving her a lovely rein back. Note the relaxed line of his back and neck and the engagement of his hindquarters.

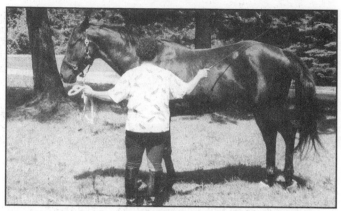

Fig. 35a: Teaching a "go forward" cue. Step one: The handler holds the whip in her right hand, and the lead in her left. The tap of the whip on his hip is the "go forward" cue. Her left hand is held slightly forward so there's no pressure on the lead. She'll wait for him to move in response to the whip before she moves.

Fig. 35b, Step two: As the horse begins to walk off, the handler steps forward with him. She's bringing the whip towards his shoulder so she can transfer it to her left hand. The horse's topline continues to be relaxed and lengthened as he walks forward from behind.

Fig. 35c, Step three: Here's the end result we're looking for. The handler has switched her whip to her left hand and the lead to her right. Both she and the horse are walking off together. She's established a connection with him which she's maintaining by looking at him. Many of us were taught not to look at our horses when we lead them, but this horse is comfortable with people and is not threatened by eye contact.

you're in a very strong, grounded position, and you can see where you're using the whip. That makes it a much easier cue to control.

Horses do not like to back. They can certainly do it, but you're not going to see too many horses out in the pasture backing up. That makes backing a very powerful tool. When a horse is comfortable backing, that's a signal that he's also comfortable with you. You want your horse to glide back smoothly. If he feels as if he's pulling his feet out of deep mud, you need to work some more on this exercise.

Anytime the backup cue becomes sticky, you'll want to review this basic step. You're going to need a good rein-back to create balanced turns, half halts, smooth transitions, and a soft mouth. Horses that are pushing into your space need to learn a backup cue. What you are saying is very simple: "I don't care how big the emergency is, running me over is never an option." When you teach your horse to back, you are really teaching him to respect your space and to listen to you.

STEP TWO: GOING FORWARD

To get him to go forward, stand at his shoulder. Again, we'll assume you're working from the left. You can cue him in one of two ways. One, hold your lead in your left hand and the whip in your right. It's similar to the position you'd be in if you were going to lunge him. Reach back with the whip to tap his hip. As he comes forward, C/R. As you start to ask for multiple steps, switch your whip to your left hand, the lead to your right, and walk forward with him. You may have to practice this maneuver a few times before you are fluid doing it (Figs. 35a, b, c).

The other way to signal him to step forward is to hold the lead in your right hand, the whip in your left. Stand next to him, facing forward. Reach back behind you with the whip. You don't need to be able to see how far back you are touching him. Your horse will know where the whip is and will be able to respond to it.

You can lean forward slightly in your upper body as though you were about to walk off. Just be careful. It's easy to walk off without your horse. You want him to move forward from a signal from behind. You don't want to end up dragging him forward. Your feet should not move until his do (Figs. 36a, b). If you feel him respond even a little, C/R. Again you don't have to worry about getting him to halt. The clicker ends behavior.

CROWDING

If your horse is crowding into you with his shoulders, you'll solve the problem the same way you did for the foal. You'll teach him to circle out of your space. Decide how large a "round pen" you want him to be in. Eight or nine inches is probably all you want to give him.

Hold the lead in your right hand. Press it against your side so you're not pulling on him, and reach up with your left hand to ask him to turn. To get him to move, flick your finger tips against his face. If the horse surges ahead of you, you'll feel him pulling on the lead. Immediately stop your feet. Make yourself like a post. Anchor your hand against your side, and use your whip to ask him to back up. When he's repositioned, begin again.

Once he's turning away from your hand signal, switch to your whip cues. Swing the whip behind you to get his feet to move. If he surges ahead instead of turning, bring the whip around in front of him and ask him to back. The balance of the two requests coupled with your body position will create a turn.

OVERCOMING FEAR OF WHIPS

If your horse is afraid of whips, you can still use this exercise. The best way to help a horse work through his fear is to use whips as cue sticks. I have yet to meet a whip-shy horse that could not accept whips within a very few minutes. With horses that are very afraid I often begin by stroking their legs. I'll C/R the horse just for standing still and letting me touch it with the whip.

If I have a second person helping me, I'll hold the horse while my helper strokes him with two whips. When you stroke a horse with a whip, you are using a very different body posture from someone who is about to strike a horse. Horses read our intent from our bodies, and very quickly learn to relax. When the cues are paired with a C/R, even a very whip-shy horse will relax.

Why should you bother using a whip around a frightened horse? You don't want your horse teaching you what you can and can't do with him. If your horse shies away from something, you want to get in the habit of dealing with it.

Don't let your horse tell you you can't touch his ears, put him on cross ties, pick up his feet, or any of the other things he's nervous about. Work with him instead. Help him through his fear. He'll be a much happier, healthier horse.

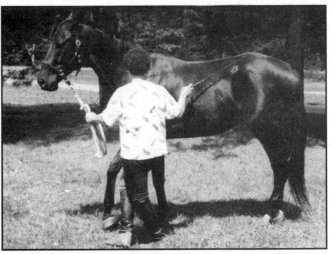

Fig. 36a: Problems. Here the handler is compressing her horse by pulling back on him with her left hand. The horse's feet are in motion, but he's got nowhere to go. Note the compression in the horse's topline. His back is hollow and his head is elevated. His neck doesn't have the lovely forward stretch that you see in Fig. 35a.

Fig 36b: Problems. Here the handler didn't wait for her horse. She walked off without him. He's got his feet planted in the ground. If she had waited for him to respond to the "go forward" cue of the whip, they'd be walking off together. Compare to Fig. 35c.

Imagine the stress you would feel if every day when you went to work, you felt afraid. That's how many horses spend their entire lives. Think of the riding horses you've seen who even into their late teens are still anxious about grooming, hate being tied, and are nervous wrecks under saddle. You owe it to your horse to be a good teacher, and not let him go through his life worrying about what goblin is going to jump out and get him next.

Remember, all resistance is is just your horse's way of telling you that he's afraid or he doesn't understand something. If that were you, you'd want a teacher who was patient and kind. Once we understand something, it's a lot easier to be brave. Your horse is the same way.

CHAPTER SIXTEEN

Lunging and Liberty Training

GETTING TO KNOW YOU

While I was writing this book, I bought a Cleveland Bay/Thoroughbred cross. When I first saw Robin in December, he was twenty months old, and he'd just been pulled out of a herd up in Canada. He trusted people. He confused me at first because he was so willing. He'd follow you on the end of a lead. He'd even stand in cross ties, so I assumed he'd had a fair amount of handling. But that didn't match some of his other responses; in fact, he knew almost nothing.

We discovered the hard way that Robin had never had his feet picked up, never mind trimmed. On the day the blacksmith came to do his feet, Robin shook like a leaf. When Robin started kicking, the blacksmith backed right off. The blacksmith struggled through the front feet, but had to leave the hind feet for another day. Robin had clearly never had his feet worked on. The blacksmith described him best. He said Robin was like a four-day foal, only, of course, this foal was twenty months old and almost sixteen hands high!

I visited Robin several times before I brought him home. What became increasingly clear was just how little he knew. Robin is the kind of horse who sails through the early stages of training simply because he is so trusting and so steady in his nature and then gets in trouble later because he really doesn't understand what's been taught to him.

Robin would follow behind a person, but he really knew nothing about leading. If you swished the lead rope behind him to ask him to come forward, he'd freeze up trembling. He just didn't know what you wanted. He was wary about grooming. He didn't want his legs or his belly touched, and his feet were very much off limits. He wasn't mean or dangerous. He would just flinch and try to tuck himself away from you. My first job was simply to get him comfortable with basic handling.

An unbroken horse will move away from a driving aid out of fear. I have seen trainers use this fear in their training. Their horses may be responsive, but they never look as beautiful as the horses who have learned through understanding and respect rather than fear and intimidation.

I do not want my horse afraid of anything I do around him. If I tap him with a whip, I want him to move over because he understands the signal, not because he's afraid of the pain. Fear is a bad deal. It interferes with learning, and it's dangerous. If my horse is afraid of anything that I'm doing, I need to change my lesson right away to work directly on removing his concern.

Fear is different from respect. I want my horses to respect me. I am an authority figure. If I ask my horse to step aside, I expect him to move over without an argument. If I carry a bucket of grain out to his paddock, I expect him to wait to eat until I tell him he can have it. I do not need my horse to be afraid of me to teach him this lesson. My horse is going to be my partner. I want my partner to trust me, not fear me. I build that trust by setting my horse up for success, and never for failure. That means I am always looking for positive things I can reinforce, not negative things I can punish.

I introduced Robin to the clicker while he was still at the seller's, but I waited until I got him home to begin really working with him. Phase one was all the early socialization and handling I described in the foal section.

I began by sacking Robin out with my hands. (See Ch. 8, Foal Training; Ch. 20, Biting: Learning to Read the Language of Horses; and Ch. 21, Crossing the Line into Aggression.) I approached Robin gently with my hand. Just before the contact became uncomfortable for him, I took my hand away. If I thought he was going to move away from me in three seconds, I took my hand away in two. If he moved before I could take my hand away, he would be left with a question mark. He wouldn't know what I was going to do. By moving away first, I was telling him exactly what my intentions were.

GETTING TO LIKE YOU

The clicker is a great way to introduce yourself to a new horse. Through it I learned what Robin understood, and what he didn't. Robin didn't mind if I touched his neck, so that's where I began. If Robin stood still while I stroked him, I clicked and reinforced him with a little grain. My goal was to click him before he got uncomfortable and shifted his feet away.

Robin wanted the grain and the social attention. He caught on fast to the criterion: "If I stand here and let her touch me, I get clicked." The clicker gave me an easy, low-key way for us to get to know each other. I could teach him to move away from pressure, to back up and step sideways, to lower his head, and to pick up his feet, all without ever getting aggressive with him.

This is truly resistance-free training. I left the barn every night thinking how lucky I was to have found such a phenomenal horse. He was so quick. He was so easy. But then that's how I describe most of the clicker-trained horses I work with.

I took my time with these early lessons. This wasn't a weekend clinic situation where I had to pack a lot of training into a short time frame. I was in no hurry. We were going to have a lot of years together. Some nights all I did was groom him. I focused on being consistent. If Robin started pulling on his lead, or running over the top of me, it would be because I let him.

That's a really important message with any horse, and especially a young one. Now is the time to build consistency. My job was to pay attention to small details. It's all too easy to let a horse slip into bad habits. If I asked for something, and then didn't follow through to make sure I got a response, I was just setting myself up for bad manners down the road.

LIBERTY TRAINING

One of my first priorities with Robin was to teach him liberty training. In liberty training the horse is completely free. You have no bridle, no leads of any kind attached to him. The horse learns to circle around you at a walk, trot, and canter. You can ask him to change direction through inside and outside turns, to halt, to come when called, and to lead, without ever putting a halter on him.

Liberty training for me is the foundation of everything else I do with a horse. I had just one small problem. The ideal place to teach liberty training is in a sixty-foot round pen. All I had was an arena twice that size, with footing that was frozen and slippery. My only option was to teach Robin "liberty training" on the end of a lead rope. To do this I used Pat Parelli's Seven Games of Natural Horsemanship.

This is a perfect example of the way I like to train. There is nothing I enjoy more than looking at someone else's work and seeing how they do things. That to me is the fun of training. There are only so many ways a horse can move its body. We can put different kinds of tack on. You can ride Western, and I can ride English. When we go sideways, you can call it a sidepass, and I'll call it leg yielding, but it's all the same movement. We can ask for different degrees of engagement, or different head positions, but the basic steps will still be pretty much the same.

So the difference isn't in what you teach, but how you teach it. Every time your horse learns something in a new way, he becomes more flexible. The more different ways you teach something, the better he's going to understand what you want and be able to respond to you. He'll be able to offer you the behavior under any and all circumstances. You're literally making him more intelligent.

If your horse gets confused and resistant when you add something new, he needs to learn this mental flexibility. If you can't think of new things to train, don't worry. You don't have to. Just keep finding new ways to teach old behaviors. Pat Parelli's Games gave me one more way to teach the same old thing. When I started Robin, I simply piggybacked the clicker onto his methods.

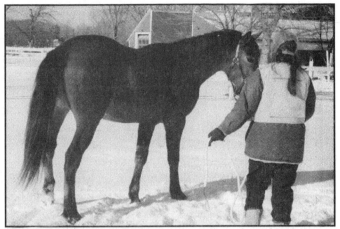

Fig. 37a: Robin at twenty-two months is learning the beginning stages of lunging. I've got him on a twelve-foot lead. I am asking Robin to change direction in front of me. My right arm shows the new direction I want him to head off in. I'm swinging the rope at his right shoulder to get him to move off.

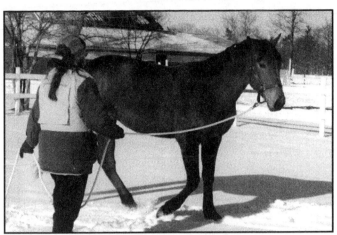

Fig. 37b: He's beginning to move off around me, but . . .

Fig. 37c: . . . now he's pulling on the line. I'm swinging the end of the lead at his hindquarters, asking him to move on.

Fig. 37d: Adding more energy helped. Now he's circling around me on a soft lead, so . . .

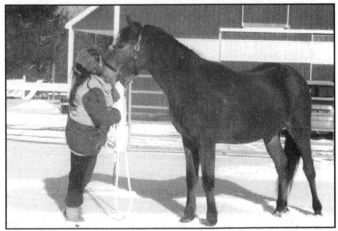

Fig. 37e: . . . Click! He's going to get a treat: some grain, and a rub on the forehead.

PAT PARELLI'S SEVEN GAMES OF NATURAL HORSEMANSHIP

Parelli's first game, the Friendly Game, is essentially just another version of sacking out. Rubbing and stroking become Parelli's way of reinforcing and reassuring the horse. When I played the Friendly Game, I simply added a C/R each time Robin accepted my hand in a new place.

When Robin was comfortable being handled all over his body, I added the next game in the sequence—the Porcupine Game. This is a very basic exercise to teach the horse to move away from physical pressure. You press against the side of the horse's face, or on his neck and shoulder, to get him to take a step over. Anywhere and everywhere you touch him, you want him to learn to follow your suggestion and move away from a light touch. I played porcupine games all over Robin's body, but I added the clicker. When he gave me correct responses, click! He got a treat.

LUNGING

From Porcupine Games I continued with Parelli's Games to teach Robin to move away from me and to change directions. If I wanted Robin to move off to the left, I would hold the lead in my left hand and extend my arm out to the side. Stretching my arm out put pressure on Robin's halter, but I didn't try to pull him to the left. Instead the lead simply offered a suggestion. I asked for movement by swinging the free end of the rope at his shoulder. As soon as he moved off to the left, click! He got a treat.

I very quickly added a variable reinforcement schedule to this exercise. I would wait for him to move a little further each time before I clicked him. I did the same thing to the right. In less than ten minutes I had him lunging around me on perfect circles in both directions (Figs. 37a, b, c, d, e).

Liberty work evolved easily out of this simple exercise. When I finally turned Robin loose, he seemed to know exactly what I wanted. I didn't have to worry about him blasting around the arena and getting himself hurt. He stayed on a perfect circle around me. Not everyone is after the same thing when they lunge a horse. With the clicker that doesn't matter. The results you get depend entirely upon what you choose to reinforce. I wanted to teach Robin to flex to the inside and give to the pressure of the lunge line (Figs. 38a, b, c, d, e, f). This sequence of photos taken over a five-minute time period shows a dramatic transformation in his balance.

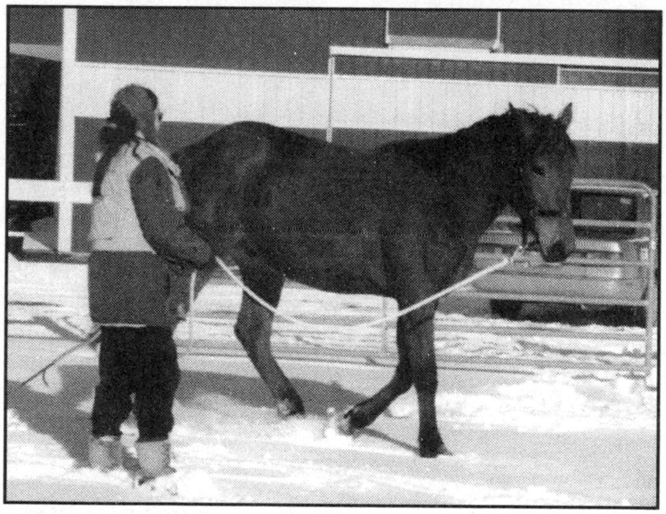

Fig. 38a: Robin is starting off well. There's slack in the line. His ear is riveted back on me, and he looks relaxed. However, he's leaning down onto his shoulders.

Fig. 38b: I'm behind his hindquarters sending him forward, but my positioning keeps him circling around me. He's responding by offering me the beginnings of a lateral flexion. His hips are engaging more underneath his body, and his neck has more of a bend to it.

Fig. 38c: Robin is bending even more. His outside shoulder is beginning to lift, and he's showing even more engagement through the hind end.

Fig. 38d: This is a beautiful flexion. Note how much more bend there is in his hocks than in the previous pictures. As he engages his hindquarters, he can lift his shoulders. His head and neck are yielding softly to the side. What I feel in my hand is a totally light, responsive horse. Compare this with Fig.38a, and see how much higher his front end is now than it was just a few turns before.

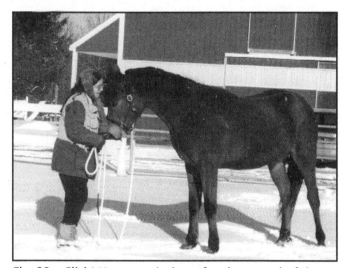

Fig. 38e: Click! He gets a jackpot for that wonderful flexion. And, because that movement was clicker-shaped, he'll remember it and show it to me on purpose in our next training session.

Fig. 38f: The result: a youngster who can trot in beautiful balance even on a small circle. I'd like him to release his neck forward a bit more than he is, but overall I like the balance and the energy he's showing me.

CHAPTER SEVENTEEN

Lateral Work

WHY SIDEWAYS?

If you've never worked a horse laterally, you're missing an important element in your horse's training. The sideways movements we train in dressage are not only very beautiful to watch, but they can also dramatically improve your horse's gaits and overall balance. If you want to make a huge difference in your horse, teach it to go sideways.

Lateral work isn't just for show. Horses that crowd into you with their shoulders need to learn lateral work. Horses that jig, or run over the top of you, or are stiff as two-by-fours, need lateral work. If you want to improve your horse's brakes, or eliminate a bad spooking problem, you need lateral work. In other words, lateral work is good for just about every aspect of a horse's training.

One of the easiest ways to teach your horse lateral work is to begin it from the ground. Long before a horse is ready to be ridden, you can ask him to displace his shoulders and hips and step over sideways.

SHOULDER-IN AND HAUNCHES-IN

When a horse is traveling straight down the rail of an arena, it is traveling on two tracks. You can picture it like a train track. The outside front and hind feet land in the outer track, and the inside front and hind feet land in the inner track (Fig. 39).

When a horse steps laterally, it can travel in three or four tracks depending upon how steeply angled its body is off the wall. When it's traveling in three tracks, the outside hind foot steps in the outer track. The inside hind and the outside front foot step on the same track, and the inside front foot steps in the inner track. When a horse is walking on four tracks, its body is steeply angled, and each foot lands in a separate track.

There are two basic bends a horse can travel in: the dressage movements of shoulder-in and haunches-in. In shoulder-in, the horse is bent away from the direction of movement. In other words, the horse would be bent to the right but traveling to the left (or vice versa). In haunches-in, the horse is bent in the same direction it is traveling. If it's bent to the right, it is traveling to the right.

LATERAL WORK

I used Parelli's Friendly Game and Porcupine Game to introduce Robin to lateral work . The first time I ask a horse to step over sideways, I don't try to get the entire horse to move over all at once. That would be too hard. I just ask parts of the horse to respond to me. Think of it as if you were moving a heavy couch by yourself. You don't try to pick the whole thing up. Instead you shift first one end of it, then the other, until by degrees you've moved it across the room. I'm going to treat the horse in the same way, except instead of my pushing him over, he's going to move his own body (Figs. 40a, b, c).

I began with Robin by asking him to bend his head to the inside while I pressed on his shoulder. I clicked him for the neck bend, and soon he offered it freely. Now my finger tips told him what part I wanted to move, and the bend in his neck made it easier for him to step over sideways. As soon as he shifted his shoulders away from my hand, click, he got a treat for his first effort.

I taught him to move his hips over in the same way. I asked for a bend in the neck, and as he looked back at me, I pressed on his hips. Note, I was not pushing against him. That would only stiffen him. When you push against someone, what is their natural reaction? Isn't it to brace back against you?

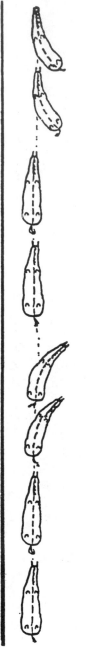

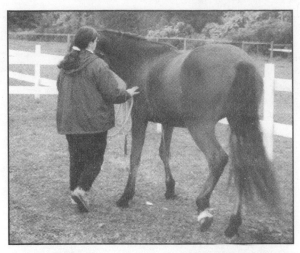

Fig. 40a: Here's an easy way to introduce lateral work. Robin has his head deeply flexed to the side, and I'm stepping in towards his shoulder asking him to step over sideways. He's made a good effort, and I'll click him and give him a treat for this first attempt.

Fig. 40b: I'm helping him to get more organized by asking his hindquarters to move over. My right hand is pressing gently on his hip. Note: I am not pushing him over. I apply light pressure and wait for him to respond. Again, the deeply flexed neck makes it easier for him to move his hips. When he gives me a correct response, I'll click him and give him a reward.

Fig. 39: A horse can travel straight on two tracks, or laterally on three or four tracks. In Shoulder-in, the horse is bent in the opposite direction from which it is traveling. In Haunches-in, the horse is bent in the same direction.

If Robin were to become stiff in his joints, stepping over would be something hard and unpleasant to do. He'd start to resent his work, instead of enjoying it. If he resisted me, he'd also be more likely to injure himself. I needed to be especially mindful of that, given his very young joints.

I wanted him to step over with ease. I got him to do that through shaping. When I put my hand on his hip, I was offering a suggestion only. By asking for the bend in his neck, I was setting him up so that stepping over was easy, I clicked and reinforced any tendency he had to shift his hips to the outside. I was looking for the inside hind leg to step

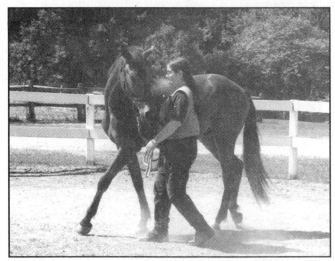

Fig. 40c: A lovely moment: Compare this with Fig. 40a, and you'll see how far we've come from that first awkward step. Robin is beautifully balanced. He's wrapped around me and we're moving together like dance partners. Note the lift of the shoulders, the engagement of the hind end, and the lightness of the lead. I am not pulling Robin's head to the side. He's maintaining this position on his own.

more deeply under the line of his body. I could feel the shift happening under my fingers, which made it easy to click him the instant I got even the tiniest response.

Robin stepped over right away from the left side, but he got stuck on the right. Horses, like people, usually have differences between their left and right sides. The most common pattern is for the left to be the overflexed side, and the right to be the stiff side. A trainer once told me that was because foals tend to lie in utero curled to the left, so they are born with the left side naturally overflexing. I have no idea if that is indeed the case, but it makes a good story; and it certainly matches the patterns you normally see.

Robin ran true to form. He could bend well to the left, but when I switched over to the right, he had trouble balancing on his left leg. He didn't want to shift his weight onto that leg. I could have just ignored the problem and only worked him from the left. This is a bad deal for any horse, especially a young one. The time you spend working your youngster from both sides will pay huge dividends when you start riding.

Rather than ignore the problem, I needed to spend some extra time working on it. I could have simply pushed Robin over and forced him to step sideways; or chased him over with a whip; but those options would have created resistance. Remember, I was dealing with a very soft, inexperienced horse here. I might be able to force him over physically, but I'd be creating mental and emotional resistance that would get in my way later. Being kind wasn't just a matter of sentiment: it was good training.

I spent more time on the right side. I asked for a deeper bend of the neck. Then I asked Robin to move his shoulders over. Once I had his shoulders moving where I wanted them, I slipped my hand back and asked for the hips. From this new position it was easy for him to move his hips over. *Click!* We had our first step of engagement.

By the end of the session, Robin was moving easily into lateral flexions on both the right and left side. I had a horse who understood how to organize his balance and move fluidly sideways. I had the beginnings of shoulder-in, haunches-in, collection, and engagement. And I had it all on video, too.

YOU CAN TEACH AN OLD HORSE NEW TRICKS

Shaping lateral movement in this manner is an easy, no-force way to trigger the reactions in a horse who has never gone sideways before. Your horse doesn't have to be young to benefit from this learning. Oliver is an eighteen-year-old Anglo-Arab who lives in the same barn as Peregrine. He had been ridden for years in a martingale. When I first met him, he was a stiff, arthritic, nose-in-the-air, skittish horse. At some point in his life he'd had laminitis, a potentially crippling inflammation of the feet. He was sound now, but his left front was permanently deformed.

In the winter of 1996, Oliver was turned out as usual with another horse. None of us saw what happened, whether he got kicked or just slammed his head against the arena wall playing, but he came in with a shattered jaw. His lower jaw was so badly broken the vets couldn't set it. They got him stabilized on antibiotics and then sent him home. With luck, they hoped the jaw would heal on its own.

The vets wanted him fed only wet mashes. Oliver wanted his hay. He went on a hunger strike. Within days he had his world back the way he wanted it. He had his hay, and his grain. When he ate, it sounded as if he were rolling marbles around in his mouth. We all tried to be somewhere else in the barn at mealtimes. It was the most grotesque sound, but Oliver seemed oblivious to it. If you didn't know he had a broken jaw, you would never have guessed from his attitude that there was anything wrong.

By midsummer Oliver's jaw was healed enough for him to be ridden again. I started working with his owner, and one of the things we introduced him to was lateral work. I used the same approach I had used with Robin. Oliver wasn't just stiff in his body, he was stiff in his mind. In eighteen years, he'd never been asked to bend, and now all of a sudden I wanted his feet to move in directions he had never in all his years known they could go. Getting Oliver to step over laterally did more than just free up his joints. It freed up his mind as well.

TRAINING WHEELS FOR THE HORSE AND HANDLER: NECK ROPES

A natural extension of the preceding exercise is to use a neck rope to move the horse around. This approach isn't just good for horses. It's also an easy way to improve your skills if you have never worked a horse laterally before (Figs. 41a, b, c).

HOOKING INTO THE CIRCUIT BOARD

You'll use the lead end of the rope attached to the halter if you need to ask the horse to soften his neck and bend laterally. You'll also use it for security, to give you a little extra control if he starts to walk off; but mainly you are going to be controlling the horse from the neck rope. You want him to get used to responding to the light pressure he feels on his neck. This is a great exercise for teaching your horse to be soft in your hands under saddle, to neck-rein, and even to ride bridleless! When you get done with this exercise, you'll be able to stop, turn, rein back, and move laterally, all from a little string looped around your horse's neck.

Think of it like hooking into a giant circuit board. The horse was born with certain natural abilities. He doesn't need you to teach him how to do anything. He could pick up a canter and do flying lead changes within hours of his birth. Training doesn't teach him new motor patterns, it just hooks those patterns into cues that say "do this now." What you are programming is a giant circuit board that says "rein back," or "canter now."

Most of us hook into that circuit board in a just a very few ways. We connect to the horse's head via a halter or a bridle, and we connect to a couple of spots on his sides.

That system is very much like the cable that hooks into your computer. There's just one slot the cable will fit. You have a machine with incredible capabilities, but only one way to connect into the system. That's too limiting for me. I want my horse to have connections all over his body through which we can put information in and get a response back.

I've worked with horses that felt as if they were made of wood. You touch their sides and nothing happens. Those horses have learned to tune out their riders. They can still feel a fly landing on their side; they are every bit as sensitive as they were on the day they were born. These exercises teach the entire horse to tune into your signals. Touch him anywhere, and you'll feel his focus shift onto you.

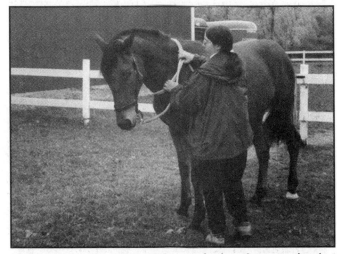

Fig. 41a: Introduce the neck rope by looping your lead around your horse's neck. I am asking Robin to back by lifting the rope so it puts pressure on the base of his neck. I'll click if he moves or even shifts his weight.

Fig. 41b: As Robin catches on to the neck rope, I'll just throw the rope over his neck. The rope becomes like two reins. I can ask him to step in any direction I want just by changing the pressure he feels against his neck. In this case I am asking him to step forward by adding pressure to the top of the rope.

Fig. 41c: I can introduce Robin to lateral work by adjusting the pressure he feels from the rope. Working in a neck rope is great not only for the horse, but for the handler as well. The rope lets you feel where the horse is leaning his weight, so it's easy to learn what adjustments need to be made.

BABE: OVERCOMING RESISTANCE IN THE OLDER HORSE

If your horse has become resistant to leading, working in a neck rope can go a long way toward breaking up the log jam. I was reminded of this recently when I was asked to work with Babe, a middle-aged quarter horse mare belonging to a very patient teenager.

The first time I saw Babe, her young owner was struggling to get her into the indoor arena. Babe had planted her feet and was refusing to move. She had her ears pinned flat, and she was threatening anyone who came near her. The standard response to horses like her is, "Oh, she's just being a mare." Attitudes like that are worse than no help. I suspected Babe was being a grump because she hurt. The only question was, where?

It's hard to do a lameness exam on a horse who refuses to move. When that same horse tries to kick you anytime you get near, it's even harder. I've met horses like Babe before. They've become so defensive you have only to look at them and they'll strike out. It's hard to tell what, if anything, is really bothering them because you get a reaction no matter what you do.

Babe's entire body couldn't hurt. She had to let us in under her defenses so we could find out what specifically was wrong. Before we called in a vet, we needed to review some basic leading and handling lessons to make her safe to be around. We did it with the clicker.

Babe was an interesting horse to clicker-train. First, we taught her, in her stall, to touch a cone. Between touches she pinned her ears flat and threatened her neighbor in the adjacent stall. We were giving her grain, and she wanted to be certain he stayed away. There might be a solid wall separating the two of them, but she still had to warn him off. We kept back a safe distance ourselves. Her ugly faces weren't reserved just for her neighbor. Babe had absolutely no tolerance for frustration. If she couldn't figure something out right away, she shut down or became aggressive.

In all her years of riding and being around people, she had never learned how to learn. Anything new simply stopped her in her tracks. She wanted the grain, but she didn't know how to get it. She went into a sulk. She tried threatening us, then ignoring us, and, finally, she came forward and bumped the cone. *Click!* She got a treat.

We made it as easy as possible for her to be successful. Without actually pushing the cone at her nose, we got her to keep trying. By the end of the session she was consistently touching the cone. The first tiny flicker of light had turned on.

Our next job was simply to get Babe out of her stall and down the aisle. If Babe thought she was going out to work, she would plant her feet and refuse to move. Force wasn't going to work. That's how she'd been handled all her life. If you got tough with her, she just shut down even more.

We began by teaching her to lower her head, and then asking her to target on a cone. We inched her out of the barn by asking her to follow the cone. After each touch I would move it slightly ahead of her. Once she was out of the barn, her attitude shifted. She walked along without any further balkiness over to the arena.

Our system worked well until a winter storm iced in the driveway. Babe didn't like walking on ice. She'd balk at the doorway and refuse to move. We broke her pattern by adding the neck rope. She was used to resisting against her halter, but this was something new. The rope gave her confidence. We could use it to help steady her balance for the short walk over to the indoor arena. That simple addition put an end to her planting her feet as if they were buried in cement.

The next phase of her training involved sacking out (see Ch. 8). Reinforcing her with the clicker during these lessons taught her that we were people she could trust. With just those few new behaviors, Babe's entire attitude toward people shifted. She became a much safer and easier horse to be around.

Babe's story has a happy ending. Once she stopped threatening us, we could look for the underlying causes for her behavior. Babe was indeed lame. Xrays showed major arthritic changes in her right ankle. She'd probably been hurting for a long time, but her general grumpiness and overall resistance had made her a hard horse to diagnose. With patience and training, she'd reached a point where her owner could see the problem and get her the medical attention she needed.

SHOULDER-IN

Adding lateral movement

Once you have a horse coming forward and backing up from the neck rope, you're ready for sideways. You create lateral movement by simply walking where you want to go. The suggestion from your body tells the horse you want to go sideways. Lyons has a phrase that's useful to remember here: "Get the feet to move. Get them to move consistently, then take them in the direction you want them to go."

To help you understand how this works, imagine that you and your horse are standing at the center of a large clock. If you want him to walk straight ahead, you're going to step toward twelve o'clock. If you're on his left side and you want him to step sideways off to the right, you'll angle your body toward two o'clock instead. As you step forward along that track, the neck rope will automatically press against the inside of his neck.

If he ignores your suggestion and walks forward, he'll be in your way, dragging you off your intended track. Immediately stop your own feet, and ask him to rein back using your neck loop to signal him. Remember to use your body. You may have to turn so you're facing his inside shoulder to get him to shift back.

Once he's stepped back out of your way, ask him to come forward again and to follow you over toward two o'clock. If he walks through you, simply ask him to rein back again. Repeat this pattern until you get that first step sideways, then click him. Most horses catch on very fast to this exercise, especially if you've prepared them with the earlier leading lessons.

This is a great way to learn lateral work. With the neck rope it is very easy to feel when the horse is pulling against you. If you feel pressure, you simply ask the horse to shift his balance so he's no longer leaning against the rope. If you feel him leaning into the front of the rope, ask him to shift back. If he's pulling into his outside shoulder, you'll rein him back and over to you.

The horse as a drill team

As you get your horse moving laterally through longer sequences of steps, you'll become comfortable with the flow of the movement. You'll learn how to take him through corners without loosing the bend. One of the challenges of lateral work is keeping the hips and shoulders lined up within the arc of the movement. It's easy to push the shoulders outside the line of the body.

What does all this mean? Think of the horse as a drill team. The team is made up of four members, inside and outside shoulders, inside and outside hips. When a horse goes through a corner, even when he's just walking on two tracks, the outside of his body has a greater distance to travel than the inside of his body. That's why horses become unbalanced through their turns. They don't know how to keep the drill team lined up.

When a horse walks sideways through a corner, his hindquarters have a much greater distance to travel than his front end. It's easy for his hips to get left behind. When this happens, you need to swing his hips over to get them to catch up with his shoulders. Look back at his hips and put a little extra pressure on the top loop, as you steady the bottom loop. That will slow his shoulders and allow him to swing his hips over.

Swinging his hips over will help him to engage more so he can lift his shoulders up into the lateral movement. The lifting is what we're after. We want the horse to learn to pick himself up through the movement, and not simply lean into his outside shoulder. If you feel him pushing against the neck rope, rock him back and ask him to begin again.

As you become coordinated with the system, and your horse tunes in to the signals, you'll find you'll be able to hold the top and bottom of the loop like you're holding two reins. The top of the loop says come forward. The bottom of the loop says shift back, and your body indicates the direction of travel. By regulating the top and bottom "rein" you'll be able to walk your horse sideways in a beautiful shoulder-in position, all without ever putting a bit in his mouth.

You will be learning that all lateral movements evolve out of adjusting the horse's balance forward and back. As you and your horse get good at this you won't need anything on his head. You'll be able to work him with just a short lead thrown over his neck. You'll ask him to rebalance as needed with very subtle adjustments on the top and bottom "rein."

Working a horse in a neck rope is a great way to learn the basics of lateral work. Once your horse understands how to move his feet sideways, you can easily switch to a bridle.

LATERAL WORK UNDER SADDLE

If you're working an older horse, it's easy to transfer the ground work to riding. One simple way to begin is to put a friend up on your horse. At first the rider sits quietly and lets the ground person cue the horse. As the horse engages into shoulder-in, the rider can learn the feel, and gradually begin to add seat and leg aids.

As the horse tunes in more and more to the rider, the ground person can hand the reins over to the rider and slip back by the horse's hip. Positioning yourself here helps back up the rider's seat and leg, and is a less abrupt transition than if you were to simply walk away from the horse (Fig. 42).

Working a horse laterally makes the difference between riding a horse who is forever stiff and green in his balance and one who flows. Soften a horse through lateral flexions, and you gain control of more than just his feet. You open the door to his mind.

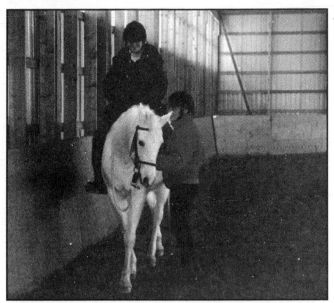

Fig. 42: Once the horse understands lateral work in-hand, the ground person can assist in transferring the cues to riding. This helps both the horse and the rider. This is Magnat, an Arabian, and his owner giving a novice rider her first experience with lateral work.

Part III

DON'T SHOOT THE HORSE: CLICKER-TRAINING FOR BIGGER CHALLENGES

CHAPTER EIGHTEEN

Clicking, Clucking, and Other Assorted Sounds: A Few Words about Clickers

Have you gone to a tack shop recently, or thumbed through the mail-order catalogs? You can buy all kinds of fancy bits for twenty, thirty, forty dollars. Martingales, chambons, draw reins, they're all there waiting to drain your checkbook. I always think of that when I pull out my clicker. I chuckle when I say to someone, "You can set up a two-thousand-dollar round pen, or you can spend a couple of dollars on a clicker." They usually opt for the clicker (which isn't to say the round pen isn't a fun tool to have, too).

My little plastic clicker is the cheapest piece of training equipment I have ever purchased, and it is also the most powerful. So, if you're one of the people who asks, "Do I have to have a clicker?" the answer is no. You can get by without one, but why would you want to?

CLICKERS VERSUS VERBAL COMMANDS

I know I've talked about this many times before, but it's worth repeating here. The function of the clicker is as an event marker. The horse drops his head. You click. The horse shifts his weight exactly where you want it, you click. What the clicker gives you is speed and precision. The result is that the horse knows clearly what it is you want.

Speed

Think about the very first thing I have you teach your horse: touching the cone. The first time you present the cone, your horse is going to be curious about it. He wants to sniff it and feel it with his nose. You'll have plenty of time, that very first time, for a "that's right" signal.

Your horse may bump into the cone a couple more times before his curiosity is satisfied. After that he'll be focused on his treats. Now when he brushes against the cone, you want to be ready with a fast event marker. It takes a lot longer to say the word

"good" than it does to click. By the time that final "d" rolls off your tongue, your horse may have left the cone and be mugging your hand trying to get his treat.

So what does your horse think he's being rewarded for? Chomping on your fingers. This happens all the time in training. We think we're saying "yes" to one thing, but from the horse's point of view, he thinks he's being reinforced for something entirely different. The clicker is fast enough to capture the precise event you're really trying to reinforce.

Unique sound

The clicker also offers another wonderful feature: unique sound. Most of us already cluck to our horses. Why do we do this instead of just saying "hurry up?" We've learned that horses respond well to this kind of signal. They can hear it amid all the verbal chatter we present. When I make a clucking sound, my horse knows that I'm talking to him, so he should pay attention. I do use words with him. He understands and appreciates the different tones I use; but he listens to my chirps, squeaks, and clicks because he knows those contain messages that are important to horses.

So does that mean that you should never use words in training? Absolutely not. Words are an important part of a good trainer's toolbox. To understand how to use them, let's distinguish between five primary functions words can serve. If you understand clearly what they are supposed to be doing, you'll be able to choose the best place for them in your own training situation.

THE FIVE FUNCTIONS OF WORDS
I. Attention

The first is for attention. We all use verbals in this way. How do I know this? Simple. I'm sure your horse has a name, and that's all a name really is: a signal for attention.

II: Cues

Verbals also function as cues. They become the green light that says "You may now perform a given behavior." (See Ch. 6, Nine Easy Steps to the Perfect Horse, and Ch. 10, You're Never Too Young to Learn.) Verbals are often used for cues. We tell our horse to trot, or to canter. We shout "Whoa!" when we want him to stop. We have other signals and body cues that do the same thing, but verbals are definitely part of the toolbox. Used as commands they are a very useful and appropriate tool.

The key to teaching a verbal command is to get the behavior first, and then to present the cue just before you know the behavior is going to occur. (Remember how this works? You've got the horse touching the cone consistently. You've got the behavior, so now you say "Touch" just before he moves his nose. Repeat this over a series of trials, and the word "touch" will become paired with the behavior. Once this link is firmly established, you can say "Touch," and the horse will look around for the plastic cone.)

Do I use verbals as cues? Yes, but sparingly. The reason is more one of convenience rather than philosophy. I'm usually teaching a human while I train. If I'm carrying on a conversation with a person, it's hard to use verbals consistently with the horse. I have to interrupt one conversation to initiate the other. For me, body language works better when I need to be able to present a consistent signal to the horse. Once I have a behavior firmly established on visual cues, I can transfer it to a verbal. Peregrine knows a few verbal commands, a larger assortment of chirps, squeaks, and clucks, and a huge array of touch and gesture cues.

III and IV: Encouragers and bridging signals

Words also function as encouragers, and as a bridging signal or conditioned reinforcer. These two need to be talked about together because people often confuse them, and let their encouragers act as bridging signals.

The bridging signal is your event marker, and it needs to be fast. "Good" is fast, but a click is even faster. And there is one other feature that is important to remember. Your conditioned reinforcer ends behavior. Do you really want your horse stopping every time you say "Good?" I certainly don't. I want "Good" to mean "You're on the right track, keep going." Think of it like the children's game "Hot and Cold." Someone picks out an object in the room, and you have to tell them what it is. As you move around the room, they tell you if you're getting hot or cold. Move away from the object, and you're getting colder. Move closer, you're getting warmer.

For me, that's how "Good" functions. It's an encourager. It means: "You're doing great. I like this. Keep doing more of the same and you may get clicked." It does not mean stop and look around for a treat. That's what the bridging signal means. When a clicker-trained horse hears a click, he's going to stop.

V: Rewards

The fifth function for verbals is the actual reward the horse is working for. Understanding praise is a learned reaction. Tell an untamed horse he's wonderful, and I doubt you'll get much of a reaction. Say the same thing six months later, after you've been working with him, and you'll see him blossom. Why the change? You will have linked praise with things he wants, like food, physical comfort, and security. He's learned that pleasing you creates opportunities to get these other things. When you tell him he's wonderful, you often follow that with a good scratch on his neck. He likes the social grooming, so he's started to link verbal praise with the good things in life. Over time, as your relationship develops, praise may even become the most powerful motivator he works for.

There's a reason for this and it isn't just that he loves you. Praise alone will begin to create conditioned pleasurable responses. Suppose, when you scratch him, he begins to feel relaxed and calm. Your horse likes this and looks forward to being scratched. Now you start pairing verbal praise with the scratching. Do this consistently over a series of trials, and the praise alone will cause him to feel those same pleasurable sensations.

It's just like Pavlov's ringing bell. Most of us have heard about his experiment with dogs. Pavlov knew dogs salivated in the presence of food, so he rang a bell just before he fed his dogs. After a time he could ring the bell, and that stimulus alone would cause the dogs to salivate. The same process is at work with our horses. Horses are not contact animals. They do not naturally enjoy being hugged, but we can teach them to enjoy affection. That's an important part of the relationship most of us have with our horses. If your horse is standoffish and grumpy, you may not be as patient with him as you would be with a sweeter horse. Getting horses to act as though they like people is more than just a matter of sentiment. It's good training. Even cowboys hug horses.

BEAR HUGS

If you're having trouble connecting with a horse, this is an important point to remember. I want my horses to love praise and affection, and I know this is something I have to teach them to appreciate. I want to be able to do more than just stroke the horses I work with. I want to be able to wrap my arms around the base of their neck in a huge bear hug.

If a horse won't let me do this, I teach him. I begin wherever I have to. If he's not used to people, I treat him like a young foal and work on socializing him. (See Ch. 8, Foal Training, and Ch. 9, You're Never Too Young to Learn.) I sack him out with my hands. I stroke him. If he's fidgety I take my hand away fast, so he knows exactly what my intentions are. Then I leave my hand on him a little longer. I stroke down his neck, and then I turn and walk away.

Once he's accepting my hand, I change tactics. I ask him to move away from pressure. I teach him to shift away from a gentle suggestion. With these pieces in place I can teach him to accept a bear hug. I throw my arms around his neck, and if he tries to squirm away, I can ask him to move back to me with a little touch of my finger tips.

This is a great thing to do with a grumpy horse. Over this past year Peregrine has been on extended stall rest because of a foot injury. He's gone weeks at a time without seeing the sun. I can't blame him for being a grouch, but I also can't let him make ugly faces at me. So I hug him. If he grumps at me as I walk past his stall, I rush in and throw my arms around him. If he squirms and tries to move away, my finger tips tell him to shift back. When he's holding himself still, I rub up and down his neck. When his ears go forward, I click and give him a little treat. I've found for both of us it's a better response than getting mad at him when he grumps. And anyway it's hard to give someone a hug and be angry at the same time. It just doesn't work.

I do this with other horses as well, and it's not for sentimental reasons. I want the horses I ride to be comfortable with me hanging all over their bodies. I've been on horses that are still afraid of people, and it's never a safe feeling. I want a horse to be totally accepting of me before I climb aboard, and hugging is one test of his attitude. Think of it from his point of view. What I'm asking the horse to accept is something that's really very frightening and intrusive. Isn't that exactly how a predator would grab him? A horse who has learned to enjoy this kind of contact is a horse who is telling me he trusts people.

I can establish the same pleasurable associations for verbal praise. I find out where the horse's itchy spots are. While I'm scratching him, I'm telling him he's wonderful. I want him to have a solid link between praise and pleasure. With very little effort on my part I can turn a simple word into a very powerful tool. Put "good" in front of a bridging signal and it functions as an encourager. Put it after, and it becomes a reward. The key is not to let it become the bridge itself. For that you want the high-speed clicker.

TONGUE CLICKS

So we're all agreed clickers are good things. The problem is, they aren't always very convenient. When you're working with horses, you need your hands free for other things. You can't be holding a clicker at the same time you're trying to organize the reins, and you don't need to. Mechanical clickers are great for starting horses, but eventually you're going to want to switch over to a tongue click.

Chirps, squeaks, kisses, and all the other assorted sounds we horse people make to encourage movement are not clicks. We make these sounds out of the corner of the mouth, or with our lips. They are signals that ask the horse to move, and they should be kept solely for this purpose.

A click is a single clear sound made with the tongue on the roof of the mouth. And no, it won't confuse your horse to use both. (Can you tell I've been asked these questions before?) Your horse can distinguish between "go" and "whoa," so he can certainly distinguish between a cluck and a click.

If you're one of the many people who has trouble producing a good clear click, check out Appendix Two for step-by-step instructions.

CHAPTER NINETEEN

Trailer Loading:
Can It Really Be This Easy?

WELCOME TO LIFELONG LEARNING

I always groan a little inside when someone calls me about a trailer loading problem. By the time someone is desperate enough to call around for help, it's never a simple situation. The refusal to load is just a reflection of deeper problems that have been allowed to fester. I should know. I have a bad loader.

I don't pretend to know all the answers when it comes to trailer loading. If nothing else, Peregrine has taught me that. I'm always looking for better, safer ways to get horses onto trailers. Who knows, by the time this book comes out I may have learned some new technique I like even better than the methods I'm describing here.

Having said that, let me tell you there are three important lessons here that I know won't change. First: I agree with John Lyons. Trailer loading problems are just leading problems in disguise. Second: Whatever method you use, the clicker can help. Third: any time you think you have all the answers, some horse will come along to tell you you don't. You can never stop learning and evolving. The key to good training is to always be looking for new ideas to add into the mix. My search for a consistent, safe way to load horses keeps reminding me of that point (Fig. 43).

If you have a hard loader, you probably already know this. You've already learned that more force only makes for a bigger wreck. The solution lies in taking the horse away from the trailer and reviewing basics. At this point in the book that should sound familiar. Trailer loading isn't any different from any other training problem. It's just that a frightened horse trapped inside an unyielding metal box can be a lot more dangerous.

My first goal, as with everything else, is to keep things safe. I've mentioned trailer loading in the

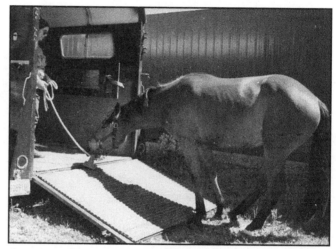

Fig. 43: Robin is doing the "elephant-on-a-drum" trick trying to touch his target. As soon as he realized he could step on the ramp, he walked right into the trailer.

previous sections. Maybe you've already worked through the basics, and your trailer loading problems are a thing of the past. But, just in case your horse still digs in his heels whenever you bring out the trailer, here are three success stories that may help you.

And remember, everything is everything else. Even if your horse loads like a dream, if he shies past trail obstacles, or hates the far end of the arena, I think you'll find something useful here.

LEARNING FROM CONTRAST

I introduce most horses to the clicker by teaching them to touch a cone with their nose. When I first started doing this, I wasn't thinking this simple trick had any practical value. I was just using it to learn about clickers. Well, I was wrong. This so called "simple trick" is one of the best tools I've discovered for getting a horse on a trailer.

There is no sweeter sight than a horse who loads

calmly, comfortably, and easily onto a trailer. Until you've had to load a difficult horse, you just can't appreciate what a delight a good loader is. By contrast, there are few things more frustrating and dangerous than a horse who won't load.

Anyone who has been around horses for any length of time has seen a variety of trailer loading methods used. We've all been there. We've seen it at shows and clinics. Someone has a horse who is refusing to go on. Maybe it's just standing frozen to the ground, or maybe it's rearing back and trying to bolt away.

That's when the "helpers" come out. Everyone has a suggestion, a sure-fire way to get that horse on the trailer. I've seen horses chased onto trailers with brooms, pulled on with butt ropes, pushed on with ground poles, lured on with food, and dragged on with war bridles. I've also known the horses who wouldn't load no matter what anybody did. I've seen the horses who could simply plant their feet and outlast the people. I've seen the horses who flipped over backward or who had their tongues severed before they would let someone force them inside a trailer.

I've watched all sorts of things and I've even tried some of the more humane methods. They all work— some of the time. The problem is, many of them can get you or the horse hurt, and they may end up making the horse harder to load the next time.

EARLY LESSONS

Several years ago, just as I was starting to experiment with the clicker, a two-year-old Appaloosa was brought to a clinic I was giving. Her owner borrowed a big, very inviting stock trailer, and had a friend load the horse for her. It was the filly's first experience with a trailer, and she wasn't so sure she wanted any part of it.

The friend knew how to load difficult horses. He'd learned the style of horse training that says if you give a horse enough pain, you can get it to do anything you want. To his credit, he was trying to learn alternatives to his old ways, but in this situation he felt under pressure for time. He did indeed get the filly on the trailer. He told me later I didn't want to know the details. It involved a war bridle and pulleys. He was right. I didn't want to know.

We spent a pleasant morning working with the filly, and then it was time for her to go home. We backed the trailer up to the barn and led her up to it. If she thought she didn't like trailers before, she was sure of it now. She was not going to load, and she was not going to let anyone hurt her. We had terrible conditions to work in. The safest place to put the trailer was halfway up a steep driveway. We had rocks to trip over, a cramped work space, and a frightened, determined horse.

LEADING: THE TRUE PROBLEM

The man who had loaded her in the first place wanted to learn John Lyons's trailer loading methods. My assignment was to talk him through the sequence. At least that was our plan. The horse had other ideas. She was not going to let this person, or any one else for that matter, take her anywhere near the trailer. She started rearing and spooking into him. She was so afraid, she didn't even know he was there. I had to put a stop to things before one of them got hurt. That meant I got the job of convincing this horse that trailers were not really the evil things she knew them to be.

My working premise was that a horse who doesn't follow you onto the trailer really doesn't know how to lead. Framing the problem in this way takes you right to the solution. Instead of trying to stuff the horse onto the trailer, you work on the leading. You go back to basics and teach the horse cues to back up, step forward, turn right and left. (See Ch. 11, Baby's First Steps: Early Leading Lessons, and Ch. 16, Ground Manners for the Older Horse.)

All the pushiness that we'd seen earlier when I worked the filly during the clinic was magnified by her fear of the trailer. Twenty feet from the trailer she tried to bolt out of my hand. When that didn't work, she tried to knock me down. At one point I caught my foot on the edge of a rock and couldn't dodge her shoulder in time. She bolted right over the top of me. Luckily she didn't step on me, but the rock I fell on left me limping. We regrouped and went on. The alternative was to bring out the war bridle, and I wanted to spare her that.

We had a long two hours. We started a good thirty feet back from the trailer. At first, if I got any closer than that, she'd panic. I kept reviewing her basic leading skills as I slowly expanded her comfort zone. In the end she was loading herself onto the trailer. Part of me was elated. The other half of me was saying, "I don't ever want to go through anything like that again."

ENTER THE CLICKER—AND CALVIN

What I knew then about trailering was that if I could hold onto a horse, I could load it. I also knew I could do it without getting the horse hurt, and with the horse ending up relaxed and comfortable. Loading was not the issue. Working with traumatized, frightened horses was. I had to find a way to make the initial stages of handling easier and safer for both of us. I was sure the clicker was the tool I was looking for.

I had a chance to test my theory on Calvin, a six-year-old Halflinger gelding.

The first time I worked with Calvin he tried to bite me. And when he wasn't trying to bite me, he was trying to kick me. And when he wasn't trying to kick me, he was trying to knock me down, and when none of those things worked, he tried to bolt off. He was ever so charming.

Calvin was originally going to be a breeding stallion, but a low sperm count spoiled those plans. He was gelded as a three-year-old and sold into the pleasure horse market, but it seems that nobody told Calvin he'd had a change of careers. He still thought of himself as a stallion. People were something you controlled and bossed around, and if somebody tried to hit you, you flattened them before they could do it a second time. When I first met Calvin, he was a powerful, strong-willed, and very frustrated animal.

Among the many things Calvin didn't do was load onto a trailer. That is what first prompted his owner, Lindsey, to contact me. She had trailered Calvin the previous summer to ride with friends. On the return trip he refused to load. Lindsey lived through the all too familiar story of all the "trainers" coming over to help her. When simple urging failed, they went on to strong-arm tactics.

Calvin was not going to let himself be hurt. He turned into a bulldozer. He plowed into anyone who got in his way. When one particularly determined man persisted in holding on, Calvin reared up and flipped over backward. At that point Lindsey sent everyone away. She took her horse and her trailer to a quiet corner of the fairgrounds, and after several hours of patient cajoling managed to convince Calvin to walk onto her trailer.

When Lindsey first called me, it was the middle of winter. Her riding ring was under two feet of snow, and her driveway, the only other workspace available to us, was glare ice. Obviously, we weren't going to be doing much with Calvin before spring. Still Lindsey wanted to get started, so I suggested she come visit me in the indoor arena where Peregrine lives, and I'd introduce her to clicker-trained horses

Lindsey is a quick study. She got the idea of the clicker right away, and went home to try it on Calvin. A few weeks later I heard through a mutual friend that she didn't like it. Calvin got really pushy around food. Haflingers aren't very tall. Calvin is only fourteen-and-a-half hands, but he's a massive horse. When he starts pushing, you feel as if you're being run over by a Sherman tank.

Calvin figured out the food part of the clicker really fast. He just wasn't connecting it to behavior. Most horses go through this. They discover your pockets have food in them, and they start trying to mug you. You have to let this stage work itself out. The horse needs to learn it never gets food directly. It has to do something to unlock the vending machine. As you keep linking the clicker to behavior, the horse will settle down and leave you alone. Lindsey hadn't seen this stage in the training. She just knew her horse seemed even more out of control than before.

I heard all this second-hand from our mutual acquaintance, so I was surprised when Lindsey called me again and asked me to come work on Calvin. Lindsey told me more about him over the phone. She was truly puzzled by him. Some things he did extraordinarily well. He could be wonderful to ride, especially out on trails. He had lovely manners in the cross ties. He ground-drove beautifully, but he'd attack you on the lunge line. If he didn't feel like going into his stall, he'd balk and refuse to move. And, oh yes, he did kick and bite.

CALVIN'S STORY

I got a taste of Calvin's power the first day I saw him. I started in the barn aisle by checking out basic leading skills. I discovered Calvin went where Calvin wanted to go. His center of gravity was so low he was actually harder to control than a much larger horse. When he tanked off, there was no stopping him.

One thing was clear. We had a lot of work to do. Never mind loading. Calvin had to learn an even more basic principle—you don't run people over. Calvin used his body like a Sherman tank, and his head like a battering ram. When he got frustrated, which he did easily, he kicked. In many ways it was more like handling an unruly foal than a fully grown horse, except this foal was built like the middle linebacker on a football team.

Calvin had to go back to nursery school and learn to lead. I didn't think I could hold onto him with just a cotton lead rope, so I put a bridle on him and took him out to Lindsey's sand arena. It was mid-April and we were having an unusually wet spring. To get to the ring we had to slog through deep mud with Calvin protesting every step. For the next hour, Calvin tried every tactic he knew to get rid of me. I stuck to him like a limpet. I tried briefly to use the clicker. Lindsey was right. He just got excited and started demanding food. At this stage the clicker was too much of a distraction to be useful.

I still needed some positive way to tell him he'd done something right, and for that I used the bridle. I tightened the inside rein to say this isn't what I want. I let go of it to say that was wonderful, do it again. I was carrying a whip, but I didn't use it. Calvin's body language was telling me that if I hit him, I'd regret it. Getting into a physical fight with him would have gotten me hurt. I had to rely on persistence and patience. Pain and punishment were tools to avoid.

By the end of the session he was starting to see things my way. He was giving softly to the bridle and beginning to lead quietly.

Back in the barn he balked and refused to go into his stall. Lindsey's barn is a converted sugarhouse. Its original purpose was to make maple syrup, but now it houses her two horses. Calvin's stall is about twenty feet long, with an open half wall separating it from the rest of the barn. It's a bright, inviting, wonderfully airy box, only Calvin didn't feel like going into it just yet. Lindsey often had trouble getting him into his stall. The design of the barn didn't help. To get to his stall, Calvin had to step up through a narrow passageway. It's an awkward arrangement, not unlike going onto a trailer.

Perfect. Calvin was presenting us with a wonderful opportunity to work on the skills he'd need to actually load onto a trailer.

I stood at the foot of the step and tapped Calvin on his hip. He understood the go forward cue from our session out in the ring. As Calvin stepped up, I threw the lead over his back and let him "load" all the way into his stall by himself. Once he was in his stall Lindsey asked him to touch his nose to a whip. Click. He got a treat. With the wall separating them, Calvin didn't have the opportunity to mug her. We could work on trailer loading and condition him to the clicker, both at the same time.

Calvin was a long way from being ready to trailer, but we'd made a good start. Lindsey asked me to come back the following week to work with him. We figured by the time the ground dried up enough to bring the trailer out, he'd be ready to load.

Fig. 44: A reformed Calvin, without halter, bridle, or lead line, quietly participates in an "off-leash" leading lesson.

It turned out that that spring was one of the wettest in years. We kept waiting for the mud to dry up, and it never did. As far as I was concerned, that was a good thing. Calvin needed the time.

I started introducing the clicker into Calvin's leading sessions. It meant tolerating a burst of overwhelming enthusiasm. His attitude was: "You clicked me!! Click me again! Hurry up! What are you waiting for? Ask me for something else. Hurry! Hurry! Hurry!"

Again it was a matter of patience. As I was consistent, he settled down. By the third session the clicker was a useful tool, and Calvin was a different horse. He wasn't menacing me. He was beginning to understand what I wanted him to do. He loved getting the right answer. He loved being asked to work. I think part of his problem originally was that he was just so eager. He was overwhelming to his handlers. He got frustrated because he was trying so hard. His exuberance got him punished, and that made him even more frustrated. Now he was thriving. The clicker, instead of causing more problems, was solving them (Fig. 44).

In June Calvin's only stablemate went to summer camp with Lindsey's young son. Calvin was left all alone in the barn. He was lonely, and it showed up in his work sessions. He was grumpy and depressed. He started to get pushy again. Lindsey asked if I'd take him for a month or two of training so he could have some company. To get to my barn meant that Calvin had to load onto a trailer. We'd had a total of five sessions together. I hoped it was going to be enough.

We stacked the deck in our favor by borrowing an extra large stock trailer that was built for draft horses. So many trailers have cramped, dark interiors; it's no wonder horses are afraid of them. I generally prefer stock trailers for difficult loaders. The step up is easier for most horses than the ramp of a two-horse trailer, and the interiors are much less claustrophobic.

The owner of the trailer was a friend and experienced handler. I wanted her to lead Calvin on. She hadn't had to deal with Calvin's pushiness, so she wasn't expecting any problems. Her expectations were that horses love her trailer, and that they always walk right on. She led him toward the back of the trailer. Calvin walked right up to it and slammed on the brakes.

He wasn't particularly afraid. He just wasn't going to go on. By now I knew that look. We had to change Calvin's mind. My friend was carrying a whip. I told her to ask Calvin to touch it. The instructions confused her. She wasn't used to using the whip as a target.

While she was hesitating, Calvin started backing up. I took him from her and offered him the whip to touch. He stretched his nose out. Click. He got a carrot. You could almost feel Calvin's surprise through the line. He never got a whole carrot as a treat! He forgot all about being afraid of the trailer, and concentrated on getting more carrots. It was as if he was saying: "This is a great game! Let me play it some more."

Two more clicks and Calvin's front feet were up on the back of the trailer. Another stretch of the nose, and he was in the trailer. Click. Click. Click. We were all the way in. We loaded him on and off a couple of more times, and then shut him in and sent him on his way. It had almost been too easy.

REINFORCERS VERSUS BRIBES: A MAJOR DIFFERENCE

I have to say something here about food and trailer loading. Years ago I remember helping a friend teach her two-year-old Hanoverian to load. He was as balky and determined to have his own way as Calvin was. Nothing was working, so finally we resorted to food. We didn't know about the clicker then. We used the food as a bribe. "If you'll only come on the trailer, we'll give you this nice handful of grain," was our approach. The horse learned to stretch and stretch his neck out as far as he could reach, but he never really loaded. He'd grab the food out of our hand and fly back off the trailer.

His owner tried feeding him in the trailer. I've seen that suggested many times in articles and books. The horse would go right up into the trailer to eat, but he was always in control. As soon as he'd wolfed down the last mouthful of grain, he'd fly back off the trailer. If anything, we had made the situation worse by using the food. Yes, he was on the trailer, but the horse was clearly in control.

Over the years I've watched many other people use food as a bribe, but I've only seen it work in a couple of cases. I know of one Arab mare who came close to having her tongue severed by an overzealous professional hauler. While her tongue healed, her owner put the trailer in her paddock and left her hay and grain in it. After a few days she was loading onto it comfortably, and a few weeks later went for her first trailer ride without any further fuss. I've also known horses for whom this approach didn't work. It didn't matter how long the trailer sat in their field, or how many meals they ate in it, when you wanted to take them somewhere, they still wouldn't load.

Does it sound like I'm contradicting myself? After all, first I'm telling you I used food to load Calvin, and now I'm telling you food doesn't work. The key here is the difference the clicker makes. It puts us both in control: horse and handler. The food is no longer a bribe, something you're using to entice the horse on. The horse only gets reinforced when he offers correct responses. He has to keep offering us more of what we want to unlock the vending machine. Everything is regulated through a variable reinforcement schedule. The horse has to go a little further into the trailer, or to stand in it a little longer before he is clicked. He is learning another kind of control. He can't just grab the food and run. He has to hold himself on the trailer, and when he does, he gets a treat.

Breaking the ice

Horses breathe when they eat, and that helps them to relax. You'll often see horses who are simply too afraid to eat. They get behind a trailer, and their brains shut down. They can't think, they can't eat. They can't even move. I don't want to close a horse up in a trailer until I see him eating normally. That tells me he's comfortable with the situation and has accepted being on the trailer. Giving the horse an easy and very familiar task to do, like touching its nose to a target, helps to break the ice and get the feet moving in the right direction.

For Calvin that wasn't a problem. He wasn't afraid of trailers. He was willing to load once he knew what was wanted. His problems in the past had developed because someone had skipped over his early leading lessons. When they tried to force him to do things, he rebelled. Now that he understood what was wanted, he was delighted to oblige.

MOZART

Mozart was another nonloader. Mozart was a bright, energetic young Morgan who needed to be given interesting things to do, or he'd invent his own games. One of his favorite games was spooking. At times it seemed as though he spooked just because it was fun. If he were a person, he'd be the type who goes on all the scariest rides at the county fair, and he'd be laughing the whole time he was being whirled around upside down. Mozart liked the thrill of a good spook. That was originally why his teenaged owner, Amy, asked me to help her with him. She was getting tired of bouncing off the arena walls with him.

Shavings bags

One of the first things Amy used the clicker for was to get Mozart over his fear of shavings bags. Normally she used bulk shavings, but over the winter she occasionally had to supplement the supply with baled shavings. The paper bags they come in sent Mozart to the farthest corner of his stall. He'd plaster himself up against the wall while the shavings were spread around.

Amy used the clicker to get Mozart first to look at the bag, then to touch it. It didn't take more than a session or two before he was playing with it, grabbing it out of her hand and stepping on it. Amy developed her own shaping sequence for this.

First she stood outside the stall holding the shavings bag. When Mozart looked in her direction, she'd click him.

Next, he had to turn toward the stall door. C/R.

Take a step toward her. C/R.

Walk up to the stall door. C/R.

Touch the shavings bag. C/R.

Play with the shavings bag. C/R.

From there she stepped just inside the door and repeated the sequence until he was grabbing it from her, shaking it up and down, and stomping on it. Mozart loved the game. Playing with the bag was much more fun than spooking at it. It appealed to his sense of humor.

Amy shaped this in just one session. She was so delighted, she could hardly wait to show me what Mozart had learned. He put on a brilliant display for me, stomping on the bag with both front feet. Amy was convinced. The clicker was a great way to train Mozart.

Trailer loading: Can it really be this easy?

So did the clicker help with his trailer loading? I'll let Amy tell you:

"My horse Mozart had a huge problem with trailers: He wouldn't go near them. He would stand behind the trailer and plant his hooves on the ground and not even touch the ramp, or he would take one step onto the ramp and rear up over the back of the trailer and get even more scared. But, that was before we built a clicker into his toolbox. With a pocket of grain and a few simple clicks Mo can now walk onto the trailer without a hassle, and he'll stand there quietly.

"I started by just asking him to get as close to the trailer as he would go without me pulling on him and then, *Click!* Then I asked him to come that far again plus another step then, *Click!* I kept asking for another step and rewarding each extra step he would offer, *Click! Click! Click!*

"If he got scared or backed out, then we walked a small circle and started again, asking him to go as far as he could and then *Click!* I kept changing my goal for him to ask him to step further and further into the trailer. At first, the goal was stepping onto the ramp, and then stepping his front feet into the trailer, and then stepping his back feet inside, too. Eventually he was all the way in the trailer standing quietly and not wanting to back out anymore. I gave him clicks and rewards of grain and petting for standing inside.

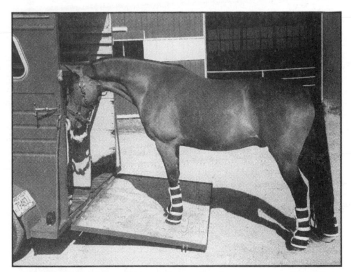

Fig. 45a: All dressed up with somewhere to go. Note the stretch of the neck, the forward ears, and the attentive expression in this Morgan's eyes. In just a few short sessions he's gone from being a difficult loader to an eager traveler.

Fig. 45b: Mozart walks onto the trailer easily without any hesitation. The trailer we're using is bright and inviting, which helps. For safety reasons I'd like to see mats on the ramp, and a leather halter instead of nylon.

"Getting him in the first time took the longest, and that was only a few minutes. The key was just to be patient and wait for him to move forward and reward him when he did. After he stood on the trailer for a while, I asked him to back out slowly one step at a time, and I made sure not to let him back out too quickly. Then I asked Mo to come out onto the trailer with me again, rewarding each step. After loading him a few times like this, all I had to do was walk him right up inside the trailer. He didn't need to be rewarded for each step, he could just walk on without having to stop part-way anymore. On this good point, with Mo having just loaded quickly, smoothly, and most importantly, safely, I let him be done with his lesson."

The key to both Calvin and Mozart was introducing the clicker well in advance of our needing it. Preparation and patience were the keys to our success (Figs. 45a, b).

TRY IT, YOU'LL LIKE IT

I can hear some of you saying, "this might work with those horses, but my horse is a really difficult loader. All my horse has to do is see a trailer and he's in the next county." I can sympathize.

The first time I trailered Peregrine he loaded perfectly. The next time he wanted no part of it. He was like a little kid who's had a plate of broccoli shoved under his nose. He's tried it, he knows he hates it, and he's not going to eat any more of it.

The first few times I trailered Peregrine his stifles were still rigidly locking. I'm sure the movement of the trailer must have made the trips horribly uncomfortable. I could sympathize with his difficulty, but there are times when you have to transport a horse.

I don't own a trailer, so I don't get many opportunities to practice loading. Over the years I've tried different approaches. All the different techniques worked—once. I'd get Peregrine loading easily, and he'd give me a coupon. It would say: "Good for one trip." When I used up my coupon, we'd be right back where we started. Just like that little kid with his plate full of broccoli, Peregrine was saying, "I tried it, and I don't like it."

Today, thanks to the clicker, Peregrine will load onto a trailer. With Peregrine I set up two very clear zones. One is outside the trailer well beyond the ramp, and the other is the ramp and the trailer itself. In the first zone he's working hard. Trailering brings out some old, dormant patterns, the worst being his tendency to try to bolt out of my hand. I have to tell him that's not an option. He can't solve his problem by leaving.

MOVING THE FEET

I load most horses in a halter and a cotton rope (no chains). I use a whip to cue them. Out away from the trailer you tap the horse on its hip, establishing a cue to go forward. If the horse responds by blasting forward and trying to run out over the top of you, you tap his chest or front legs until he backs up. With both aids you are saying, "Move away from pressure: Come forward, step back." With just these two simple cues you can place a horse's body anywhere you want. (See Ch. 10, Baby's First Steps: Early Leading Lessons; Ch. 13, Taking the Show on the Road: Trail Obstacles; and Ch. 15, Ground Manners for the Older Horse.)

What you are saying to the horse is, "I am going to ask you to move your feet. We are going to practice going forward and back, turning right and turning left. As long as you are thinking about running backward or bolting off, this is what we are going to be doing. If you start to get tired and want to stand still, I will let you do that, provided your nose is facing the trailer. If you walk forward quietly when I tap your hip, I'll let you stand still again. If you try to run over the top of me, or back up, we'll go back to work practicing our leading skills."

The horse loads on the trailer because it's the one place where he gets to stand still. The primary motivator in this case is fatigue. Initially the horse sees the trailer as a terrifying trap you are trying to force him into. Now it's a quiet place of sanctuary where he gets to rest.

You don't need the clicker to get a horse on a trailer using this method, but it sure does help. It takes the fight out of the exercise. Now when the horse first comes forward from a tap on its hindquarters, click, and give him a treat. The entire time you are practicing your leading skills, you can be clicking and rewarding.

As the horse starts to relax and work with you, you wait until he is facing the trailer to click. Next he has to walk toward the trailer, C/R. Suppose he sticks at the bottom of the ramp. No problem. Tap his hip. If he shifts his foot even a little, click and give him a treat.

With the clicker your horse now has a choice, and it's the classic one of the carrot and the stick. He can stand there with you tapping on his hip, or he can come forward and get a treat. Every time he shifts forward, you immediately stop tapping (remove the negative reinforcer), and you click him for the effort.

Even with a really sticky horse, the hind end will eventually load the front end onto the trailer. He'll be bringing his hind feet further and further under his belly. Eventually the horse will have no choice but to move his front feet. He'll do one of two things. He'll back up. No problem, you just go back to working on your leading skills until he's ready to approach the trailer again. Or he'll step up into the trailer to take his weight off his hindquarters. When he does, it's jackpot time. *Click,* he gets a big handful of goodies, and lots of enthusiastic praise.

FRONT-END LOADING

Once the horse is coming up straight to the trailer, you can offer him a target to touch. In this approach you're going to let the front end load the back end. Ask him to touch your whip. At first he'll probably just stretch his neck out and leave his front feet firmly planted in the safety zone. No problem. After a couple of successful touches he'll start to relax. Touching his nose to a target was probably one of the very first things he learned with the clicker. It's a comforting, very familiar exercise that gives him a lot of confidence. If you can get your horse up to the trailer, the target stick will take him the rest of the way.

Using the target stick also teaches the horse how to stay on the trailer. It's like teaching a sit-stay to a dog. By withholding the click slightly longer each time, your horse will be learning to wait. He won't get his treat if he doesn't stay on the trailer touching the target stick. That's a useful skill when it becomes time to do up the butt bar.

LOADING PEREGRINE-STYLE

With Peregrine I use both approaches, with a variation on the theme tailored to his particular needs. I put him in his bridle for loading. If he's having a "sticky" day, we work on shoulder-in and piaffe. The piaffe is his own special version of practicing basic leading. I'm saying the same thing to him: "Come forward from behind, but don't run through the front end." The higher equilibrium demanded of the piaffe and the lateral work keeps his stifles from locking, and focuses him more on me.

Once he's listening to me, I know I'll be able to ask him to step up into the trailer without worrying about him running out over his shoulder. When he can come up to the trailer in a perfect straight line in piaffe, I know he's ready to load. He's relaxed. He's thinking forward. He's straight in his body, and from that position, he'll be the most comfortable once he's on the trailer.

At that point I let him stand with his nose facing the trailer. I ask him to come forward from a gentle tap on his hip, and I also start to offer him a target to touch. The combination gets him on the trailer and keeps him on. I never close him up until he's been on and off several times. I want him solidly on the trailer, and that means stepping clear up to the front and eating in a relaxed normal manner. Any hesitation taking his treat means he's still afraid, and he's not ready to close in.

I wish I could say that working Peregrine this way has solved the problem forever, and I now have a horse who walks right onto the trailer every time I ask. It hasn't. Given his stifles, Peregrine may never learn to be totally comfortable with trailers. He has a legitimate reason to say, "I don't want to go on this thing."

I do sympathize, but when I need to transport him, he has to load. Usually a quick reminder of what is wanted is all I need, and the lure of the target stick reassures him once he's in the trailer. What has evolved over many trials is a humane, safe system that works.

So is this the only way to get a horse on a trailer? Absolutely not. It happens to be what I've chosen after years of experimenting with different approaches. The point is, you can piggyback the clicker onto most trailer-loading techniques. The goal is the same in all cases: to get the horse to step forward onto the trailer. When he does, in whatever way you are asking, *click!*, he gets a treat.

Add this to your toolbox, and I think you'll find that horses will load faster for you, and much more safely. The key is preparation. The time to clicker-train your horse is not five minutes before you're going to ask him to walk onto a trailer. Make the clicker part of his regular training program. Take time to work him from the ground. Teach him the cues he'll need, and you'll be delighted at how easy trailer loading can be.

CHAPTER TWENTY

Biting: Learning to Read the Language of Horses

One of my clients was very worried. Her new horse was starting to bite. He hadn't been at all mouthy when he was with his previous owner, but now he was grabbing at her clothes. The implication was that all this clicker training was teaching him bad habits. She'd had a horse with perfect manners, and now he was biting.

"Okay," I said. "Show me what he's doing."

We went into his stall together. I needed to see the behavior to know what kind of response she should make. She stood in front of his shoulders and started rubbing up and down on his withers. Her horse arched his neck in response. His lips started to wiggle. He stretched his neck around and nudged her shoulder.

"You see!" she said, stepping back from him in alarm. "He's biting."

I had to smile. This wasn't biting. This was social grooming: "You scratch my back, and I'll scratch yours." Watch two horses turned out together, and you'll see them engaged in this behavior. They'll stand side by side to give each other a vigorous massage (Fig. 46).

That's why, when you find your horse's itchy spot, he'll start to wiggle his lips and bite at the air. It's a reflex. He just can't get a good scratch without wanting to return the favor. My client was new to all this. She'd never watched horses just being horses. She was doing what I'd told her. I wanted her to spend time stroking and rubbing her horse, and the result was he was biting her!

The solution was a simple one. Just stand a little further back, out of range, and scratch away. Now we had a happy horse getting a back rub, and a happy owner.

This story brings up an important point. If you're a novice handler, take some time to learn about horses. Many times people have problems because they don't understand what is normal and natural for horses.

Fig. 46: These two horses are socially grooming each other. When you scratch a horse around his withers, he may respond by trying to groom you just as he would another horse. What appears to be biting is just your horse trying to scratch your back while you scratch his.

CLOSE ENCOUNTERS

Most of us understand that horses are prey animals. As such they have a strong flight response. That's why they spook and shy at things we wouldn't worry about. They live in herds, and are therefore very social and feel insecure and vulnerable when they are by themselves. These are all things most of us know. But one of the most important differences between humans and horses is something that is rarely talked about. Humans are contact animals, and horses are not.

Cats and dogs are contact animals, as well. That's part of why we enjoy them so much as pets. What is nicer than having your dog or your cat curled up beside you? I have three cats who love to sleep curled up together. Horses do not do this. Yes, they will socially groom one another, but that is usually the extent of their friendly physical contact. Spend some time watching a herd. You'll see horses standing close to one another, enjoying each other's company, but you won't see them actually coming into close physical contact.

Think about how horses respond when you first start handling them. Try to run your hand over their shoulder, and they'll jump away. Even a horse who basically likes people and trusts them may initially be skittish about being touched. This is something you have to teach them to enjoy.

Why am I spending so much time talking about this? Because I think it's important to understand this difference and what it means from the horses point of view. We need horses to accept contact. After all we're going to sit on them. We couldn't be much more intrusive than that. We need to ask permission, and not just force ourselves on the horse.

SACKING OUT

Think about sacking out. The first time I heard what that meant, I was told the horse was tied up tight so it couldn't escape while someone swung a feed sack at it. As long as the horse was struggling and fighting, the "trainer" kept chasing it with the sack. As soon as it gave up and accepted the contact, the "trainer" quit.

I now have a different image of sacking out, thanks to John Lyons: one in which you approach the horse gently with your hand. Just before the contact becomes uncomfortable for the horse, you take your hand away. If you think the horse is going to move away from you in three seconds, you take your hand away in two. The horse knows exactly what your intentions are. You only wanted to touch his forehead, and then you were going to walk away. In effect you are asking permission of the horse. You are saying, "This is all I want to do. Is it all right with you?" You are treating him with the same consideration you'd give a small child sitting in the dentist's chair. You aren't trying to bully him into anything.

Both forms of sacking out result in a horse you can physically touch. The difference is in the kind of relationship they build.

A GUEST IN THE HORSE'S "HOUSE"

People intrude on horses all the time and they don't even know it. Watch the next time you have a visitor in your barn. How do they walk up to the horses? The horse is taking a nap in its stall, or eating its hay, and what do they do? They walk up and start petting its face. The horse lays its ears flat back. "Not now," it's saying. "Who are you anyway?" And the people go right on petting it (Fig. 47). They wouldn't walk into a room full of strangers and start hugging them, and yet they'll do that with horses. We need to ask permission of the horse before we enter its space, and the horse needs to learn to give us that permission each and every time we ask for it.

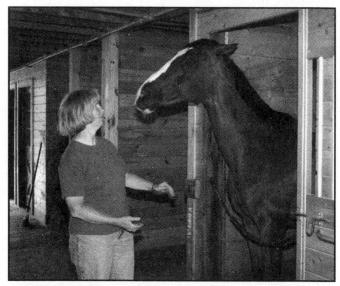

Fig. 47: An unwelcome guest? People intrude on horses all the time. Often they aren't even aware they're doing it. Peregrine just had a nap interrupted and he's showing his displeasure. He's not interested in having his face rubbed. He just wants to go back to sleep.

How do you ask permission? First, remember your manners. This is not a contact species. Don't stand in close to a horse unless you have a reason for being there. Don't overstay your welcome. Think about how you'd welcome a new neighbor. You'd pay a quick visit. You'd go in, you'd introduce yourself, you'd say a few words, and then you'd leave. You wouldn't sit down in the midst of all her unpacking and start chatting. You wouldn't start rearranging her living room furniture, or criticizing her choice of wall decorations. If you did, she might not invite you back again. Once you're good friends, you can drop by uninvited and stay for hours, but not now.

That's how you should think of your horse. You don't want to just barge in on him. You want to be invited. And you want to keep your visits pleasant so you'll be invited back.

FEAR VERSUS RESPECT

How do you do that? You begin by showing the horse exactly what you want. We've talked about sacking out with your hand. (See p. 55, The Clicker Saves a Life.) Once a horse is comfortable inviting you into his "house," you will have removed a major reason for both biting and kicking. Until then, he'll still feel as though he has to protect himself.

Aggression comes from a place of fear. I do not want my horse afraid of anything I do around him. If I tap him with a whip, I want him to move over because he understands the signal, not because he's afraid of the pain. Fear is a bad deal. It interferes with learning, and it's dangerous. If my horse is afraid of anything that I'm doing, I need to change my lesson right away to work directly on removing his concern.

Fear is different from respect. I want my horses to respect me. I am an authority figure. If I ask my horse to step aside, I expect him to move over without an argument. If I carry hay out to his paddock, I expect him to wait until I tell him he can have it. I do not need my horse to be afraid of me to have respect, any more than a child needs to be afraid of his parents to respect them.

An unbroke horse will move away from a driving aid out of fear. I have seen trainers use this fear in their training. Their horses may be responsive, but they never look as beautiful as the horses who have learned through understanding and respect rather than fear and intimidation.

I gain my horse's respect the same way I might gain yours: by being consistent and fair; by explaining thoroughly exactly what I want; by always setting you up for success, and never for failure. I gain respect through all the incremental steps that are detailed throughout these chapters.

EXPLORING THE WORLD

Horses don't just bite to protect themselves. A horse uses his mouth very much the way we use our hands. He explores the world with his lips. Stand in close to a horse, and he'll want to feel your jacket and nuzzle your shirt. If he finds a pocket, of course he's going to want to push his nose inside. It's only natural. People who park themselves directly in front of a horse are just setting themselves up for trouble. It's like putting a small child down in front of a cookie jar and expecting them not to open it.

It starts out so innocently. First the horse just nudges you a little. You think it's kind of cute. He's just being friendly and sweet. He pushes you a little harder, and maybe you swat him aside. He thinks this is great. You're inviting him to play. He grabs at your jacket the way he would another horse's halter, and suddenly you explode in anger. Now you're yelling at him and getting mad.

So what is the solution? Well, you could punish him for a problem you in effect created. Or you could remove the cookie jar by stepping back out of his space. If he tries to follow and crowd in next to you, you'll review his basic leading skills until he is standing quietly with the length of your lead rope between you. (See Ch. 10, Baby's First Steps: Early Leading Lessons, and Ch. 15, Ground Manners for the Older Horse.)

BUILDING GOOD MANNERS

A mouthy horse is a horse who doesn't have enough to do. If your horse is nipping at you, put his feet to work. Just like everything else, horses have to learn how to stand still and wait for us. Think of them like little kids. We don't expect a first grader to be able to sit focused on a task for as long as we would a fourth grader. Focus is a learned skill. If we want our horse to stand quietly without fussing we have to teach him how. It's a skill many of us overlook. We just expect our horse to be able to do it, especially if we've gotten used to older, well-mannered horses.

So how do you teach a horse not to be mouthy? You give him something to do. You put his feet in motion. You ask him to back up, to step sideways, to circle, to turn. When he responds correctly, you click him, and you do the last thing many of you would expect: you give him a treat. You reach into your pocket and you feed him some grain. Then you make a big fuss over him. You rub his face, you cradle his head. You play with his mouth. Mouthy, aggressive horses are often starved for attention. Give them what they're craving, and you will solve the problem. When you also use the clicker, they learn they have to earn the attention they so very much desire.

I know there will still be some people who will worry that all these treats will turn their horse into a biter. All I can say is, that has not been my experience. When the horses are first introduced to the system, yes, they will try to mug your pockets. That's part of the learning process, but it's a very short-term behavior. They will discover that going directly to the vending machine doesn't get them anything. Performance does. Leave your person alone, stop nudging him for food, follow his suggestions instead, and lo and behold he feeds you!

If you're consistent and only give your horse treats after you've clicked, you won't have a biting problem. You'll be "mugged" instead with behavior, and as far as I'm concerned, that's a good thing. I want my horse asking what he can do next, and eagerly trying to get the vending machine to work. I can choose to reinforce anything I want. Standing still is just as much a rewardable behavior as anything else. If that's what I want, that's what I'll shape.

I see more problems with nipping and nudging in horses who aren't clicker trained than in horses who are. These horses have no clear rules, no guidelines for when treats appear. They are operating on a variable reinforcement schedule that their owners have set up without ever being aware of it. At random times, carrots appear. The horse doesn't know when to expect a carrot, so he's constantly looking. Is it any wonder these horses become pests? Don't people act the same way? How many of you rattle the vending machine when your Coke doesn't come out fast enough?

I like to spoil my horse. That's part of the fun of having a horse. I fix Peregrine hot mashes in the winter. I sweep loose hay into his stall for a late night snack. I pick out his stall seven or eight times during the course of the day. I make sure he gets extra turnout time. I bring him carrots and peppermints. I bake him granola treats for special surprises. But when I feed him treats, I click him. I won't have Peregrine spoil my fun because I've let him get bad manners.

The clicker doesn't make mouthy horses. Quite the contrary, it teaches horses how to behave politely around food. With a clicker-trained horse you can have your pockets stuffed full of his favorite treats, and he won't be fussing at you trying to get you to feed him. What he will be doing is focusing on his work, and trying his best to please you.

CHAPTER TWENTY-ONE

Crossing the Line into Aggression

Fig. 48: Peregrine in flight.

CLOSE CALLS

When Peregrine was two he was turned out with an older Thoroughbred gelding. He and Touch got along fine together until we rotated them into a pasture the mares normally used. The older horse was sniffing manure piles when Peregrine joined him. Touch pinned his ears flat against his skull and went after Peregrine.

Anyone who owns horses has seen one horse grump at another. This was different. This wasn't just a threat. Peregrine spun on his heels and fled (Fig. 48). Touch charged after him with his neck stretched out, ready to grab Peregrine's flank.

They were in a huge nine-acre field with a long steady climb up to the top end. They reached the top of the field, and for one heart-stopping moment I couldn't see them. Then Peregrine came racing down the slope with Touch still dogging at his heels.

I stood at the open gate shouting to Peregrine. He didn't see me in time to turn. The two horses swept past me down into the lower section of the field. Touch never wavered in his attack. He was on Peregrine's flank every step of the way.

They made another circuit of the field, and swept down past me again. As Peregrine started his third climb up the hill, I could see he was tiring. He cut across the brow of the hill and galloped toward the open gate. It looked as if he was going to make it. I stood aside for him, but Touch put on a burst of speed and drove him past the gate.

They galloped through another half circuit of the field. Peregrine turned toward me again. He wasn't lined up with the gate, and Touch was outflanking him. Peregrine ran straight on and crashed through the fence. His chest hit the top rail and splintered the boards. Thank goodness for wood fencing. The boards shattered, but Peregrine didn't have a mark on him.

Touch broke off his attack as soon as Peregrine was out of the field. I have no idea what triggered such a violent outburst, but I do know how Peregrine felt. I have also been charged by a horse.

Fig. 49: Touch and Peregrine sharing a more peaceful moment.

LIFE FROM THE MOUSE'S POINT OF VIEW

My first experience with this other side of horses happened a year before Peregrine was born. The owner of the stable where I boarded had just bought a young Thoroughbred stallion from an auction. She couldn't say enough good things about him. He was a Bold Ruler son, very beautiful, a truly impressive-looking horse, but what really struck her was how calm and gentle he was.

Two days after she brought him home, I went into his stall to groom him. I was walking over to him with his halter when he charged. It happened so fast, I couldn't even react. He grabbed me by the hip, jerked me up off my feet, and held me dangling in his mouth like a cat with a mouse! There was no warning. No pinning of the ears, no swish of the tail. I thought of every story I'd ever heard about people getting killed in stalls. I went limp, just like a mouse does. If I'd put up a fight, who knows what he would have done. Instead he lost interest and just dropped me in the back corner of his stall.

I lay absolutely still and started hollering for help. The barn was usually full of people. This was the one time everyone was outside. I kept hollering, and finally someone came running to see what all the ruckus was about. I didn't move until the stallion was distracted in the opposite corner of his stall. As we learned more about him we discovered that this attack was no fluke. If he'd been sweet at the auction, I suspect it was because he had been drugged.

WHAT BASEBALL BATS DO TO HORSES

I had another horse charge me. I was giving a clinic, and he was the last horse in a day filled with difficult horses. Every one of the horses came in with major leading problems. They'd knock into you, run over the top of you, spook at nothing. Finally, this horse came out. He seemed almost pleasant by comparison. He was a little sticky, a little slow to respond, but nothing like those other horses.

I started to teach him to back up. He was doing great until we got near the wall. His feet began to stall out. That's normal, and it's part of the lesson. You want the horse to learn how to handle his haunches and swing himself around so he clears the wall. Most horses start to feel a little claustrophobic at this point. Out in the middle of the ring where they have lots of space they'll back up easily, but now their feet feel as if they're stuck in cement.

This horse didn't just feel stuck. He felt trapped. I tapped him on his front legs and asked him to back. Instead, he swung around and charged. It happened so fast no one watching could have done anything to stop him. He grabbed the collar of my jacket. If it hadn't been winter, he would have grabbed skin.

The owner told me afterward she'd rescued him from a man who used to beat him with a baseball bat. I wasn't the first person he'd attacked, and sadly,

I wasn't the last. I never saw the horse again, but I heard several months later that, after he went after someone else, his owner finally put him down.

CROSSING THE LINE INTO AGGRESSION

Experiences like that have taught me to take biting very seriously. When a horse charges, it happens so fast there is no time to react. John Lyons tells a story of a horse who went after him. He says someone could have talked to him all night and never convinced him that he wouldn't have time to react to a charging horse; but that horse didn't need all night. He only needed a couple of seconds. That's how long it took for him to charge twenty feet across the arena and knock Lyons to the ground.

When a horse charges, there is no time.

When a horse charges, something has gone seriously wrong. All the normal restraints that keep us safe are gone.

When I talk about aggressive horses I am not talking about horses who make ugly faces at dinner time, or who bite at air when you saddle them up. I am not talking about horses who nibble on your jacket, or lift a hind leg when you groom them. These are normal horses engaging in normal horse talk. That doesn't mean it's acceptable behavior, but ordinary training methods are usually enough to keep the behavior from escalating.

The horses I'm addressing in this section represent a very small percentage of the total horse population. They are horses who have crossed a critical line. Flight is no longer their first response. Attack is.

Very often these horses do not posture. They do not make threatening gestures. Their attacks come without warning. That's what makes them so very dangerous to deal with. One horse I have known for years was like a Vietnam veteran having flashbacks. He was a very sweet horse who seemed totally unable to control his sudden violent outbursts. I learned from him that the only safe way to handle these truly aggressive horses was at a snail's pace.

KICKING VERSUS BITING

I used to think that horses that kick were just as dangerous as horses that bite. Certainly a hard kick can crack bones, and even kill, but there is a difference. A horse that kicks is still a horse who is trying to get away. A horse that bites is attacking. I'll get in a round pen with a kicker. I won't with a horse that charges. I take

the Lyons story seriously. I don't need to be convinced that a horse is faster than I am. I already know that. Until you've worked with these horses you cannot imagine how totally vulnerable and fragile you really are. Just remember, when you have a horse at the end of a lead, or out in a round pen, he's also got you. If he comes after you, there is no time to stop him, and no one can help you.

ROOT CAUSES

People always assume that aggressive horses must have been abused. I'm sure this is sometimes the case, but it is not necessarily so. I've known aggressive horses who were simply spoiled. One Connemara mare I met briefly years ago was weaned as a two-year-old and then spent the next four years of her life by herself. Her owners were not experienced handlers and really did not know what to do with a young horse. No one ever said "no" to her—until she was sent out to be boarded. She was used to being the boss, and now here were people trying to tell her what to do. She was the only horse I've ever met who made no distinction between people and horses. She would squeal and strike at you just as she would at another horse.

She was sold to a twelve-year-old girl. After she kicked the child and broke her leg, she was sold once more, this time to a slaughterhouse.

I have known hundreds of horses. I can count on the fingers of one hand the number I have met who were truly aggressive. I really don't consider the Connemara mare to be in that category. She just needed to learn the rules for being around people. If she'd been sold to an experienced horse person instead of to a little girl, her story might have had a very different ending. Her original owners simply didn't know enough about horses to understand what an inappropriate match this really was.

ETHICS

This kind of situation raises many difficult ethical questions. What do you do with a horse that has crossed the line into aggression? Do you try to work with it? Do you sell it? And if so, what are the moral and legal responsibilities that you have toward the horse and his new owners?

Do you simply put the horse down? Or do you retire it out to pasture? What responsibility do you have to the vets and blacksmiths who still have to handle the horse?

These are not easy questions to answer. I am sure there will be people reading this who would say, "Why bother? There are so many nice horses out there. Why would you even think about working with horses like this?"

In my experience it's seldom that easy. From what I've seen there are no right or wrong answers. There are only choices, and none of them very pleasant ones.

Think about it. How much did you know about your horse before you bought him? Most people know very little. They may have only seen the horse a couple of times. Maybe the horse grumped at them in the stall, but lots of horses will do that. Maybe it pinned its ears when the saddle was tightened. That's not so unusual.

The early warning signs may well have been there, but the people just didn't recognize them. Now they have the horse home, and they're stuck. The people I know with aggressive horses had no idea what they were buying. They thought they were getting a perfectly nice horse, only to find themselves trapped in situation with no easy answers. Just look at their choices.

They could sell the horse. We've all heard of stories where someone sold a difficult horse they were struggling with. The horse connected with its next owner and went on to become a champion show horse. Stories like that do happen, but more often than not the horse just ends up getting passed along from one situation to the next. If you sell the horse, you could be condemning it to a lifetime of rough handling and abuse. Plus there's always the concern that it will seriously hurt somebody. The people I've met who own dangerous horses have them because somebody else wanted to pass on the responsibility. Now these new owners have some hard choices of their own.

The alternatives to passing the horse on are either to try to work with it, or to put it down yourself. These are not easy solutions. I've seen people create some remarkable changes in horses, and I've also seen how much dedication it takes. Not everyone is prepared to face the risks which working with an aggressive horse entails. There are lots of nice horses out there, horses who won't come after you if you make a mistake. The risks are high with aggressive horses, and the rewards can be slow in coming.

On the other hand, putting an otherwise healthy horse down is never easy. Whenever I raise this possibility with people, I always get back the same response. The horse may have come close to killing them. It may have charged them out in the paddock, or bucked them off on the trails, but there is a bond between them. They look beyond all the aggressive posturing and see a wonderful horse. That's the horse they thought they were buying. It's the horse they have fallen in love with. They can't even think about giving up and putting the horse down.

When an owner tells me that, I try to help in whatever way I can. That's what happened with a mare named Fig. Fig is a horse many people would have put in the ground, but her owner, Megan Mullody, wanted to give her a chance.

LESSONS IN CREATIVITY: A MARE NAMED FIG

Megan was caught in a situation that is all too common in the horse world. She had a difficult horse, and no place to work. Like many people, Megan kept her horses at home. She'd converted the interior of an old cow barn into horse stalls, fenced in an acre or two of rough land for pasture, and rode out on trails.

If she'd had an easygoing horse, her situation would have been fine. The problem was, the Thoroughbred mare she owned was dangerously aggressive. Both Megan and her mother were experienced horse people. Together they owned three other horses, and Megan's mother had spent several years working with a Thoroughbred trainer. These were not beginners out of their depth with a difficult horse. When they bought Fig, they simply had no idea what they were bringing home.

Fig's aggressiveness had escalated during the year they had owned her. She wasn't safe to lead. If you tried to take her somewhere she didn't want to go, she'd either plant her feet and refuse to move, or she'd drag you off in the opposite direction. If you tried to stop her, she'd wheel around and kick you.

She'd charge at anyone who walked past her stall. Fig didn't just snap at the air, or grab at your clothes. When she went after you, she meant business. She wouldn't stand tied, which made her almost impossible to groom. If you got behind her, she'd kick you. If you got in front of her, she'd bite you. She was aggressive with the two mares she was turned out with. The list of problems just went on and on. In fact, it didn't sound as if there was anything positive to say about her.

Megan had nowhere to work. She didn't have a riding ring, or even an open area of level ground. Her turnout paddocks were knee deep in mud from the spring rains. The only solid footing was a narrow driveway. What we really needed was a round pen with a good fence. Megan had nothing. When you lack good training spaces, you have to become creative.

Fig taught me many lessons in creativity. That's really why her story is important here. Most problems are easy to solve if you have the right tools. An afternoon spent in a round pen can work wonders. Schooling your trail horse in a level ring, or getting your ring horse out on the trails, is sometimes the perfect cure for the problems you're having.

But what happens when you have a difficult horse and no training facilities? You can read all the magazine articles you like, but when your only open work space is knee deep in mud, training becomes almost impossible. Add into that mix a dangerously aggressive horse, and it makes you want to run, not walk, from the situation.

PRINCIPLES AND TOOLS

The challenge Fig presented was to take the training principles and learn how to make them work in a situation where the usual tools weren't available. We really were starting with nothing. We had no place to work, and a horse who would charge if you got tough with her. Most horses who make ugly faces are simply bluffing. If you really insist that they get out of your space, they'll back down. For most horses pain is a motivator that works, and that's what's been used throughout the history of training.

Fig wasn't most horses. Fig wasn't bluffing. She was one of that handful of horses who really will come after you (Fig. 50). You have to be very good with traditional training methods to stay safe around these horses.

I prefer to look for alternatives. The instant I begin to wonder if a horse's ugly posturing is more than bluff, I need to change tactics and find another way. Megan had told me Fig would grab hold with her teeth. I didn't need a demonstration.

PROTECTED CONTACT

Conditioning Fig to the clicker seemed like a good place to start. I wanted a solid wall separating us for the first few sessions. This was the one place where we got lucky. Fig's stall gave us a training arena.

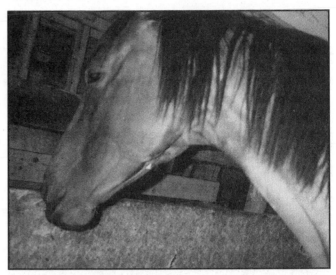
Fig. 50: Fig as I first met her.

Megan and her mother had converted the central aisle of an old dairy barn into horse stalls. The stalls were arranged so that you could walk all the way around the outside of Fig's box. The front and two sides were open half-walls, while the back was built more like cow stanchions, with vertical slats going all the way up to the ceiling. Fig could put her head out between the boards, but she couldn't swing it from side to side, and a horizontal cross bar made it almost impossible for her to lunge at us. It was like having her in a mini round pen. We had access to her from all sides, but at the same time we were behind protective cover.

Megan kept apologizing for the primitive nature of her barn. I thought it was perfect. We found a large plastic pill container to use as a target and began clicker training Fig.

Fig caught on in minutes. She was one of those horses where you start wondering if the whole thing is rigged. She just never missed. Megan and her mother were thrilled. It's always exciting to see a horse catch on and begin to respond intentionally to the clicker and the target. When it's a horse like Fig, who has been so shut down and defensive, it's especially thrilling.

Fig had to put her head out through the back wall to reach her target. As she touched the pill container, I reached up and brushed my hand very quickly over her neck. The vertical partitions blocked her from swinging her head to the side. The wall made it awkward for her, and safe for me.

The first time I flicked my hand over her neck she pulled back before I could click her. She hung back from her target. You could see her sorting through the dilemma. She wanted to touch it, but she didn't want to be near me. I waited, and finally she put her head back through and brushed her lips very gingerly against the target. She had made her choice.

I let her touch it a couple more times, before I reached up again. This time she paused long enough for me to click her. That one little step was the beginning piece that unlocked Fig's world (Fig. 51).

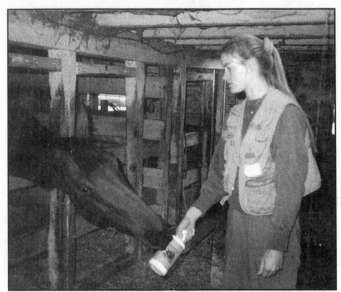

Fig. 51: Fig at her target, a plastic bottle in Megan's hand. We began Fig's training in her stall because, like many people who keep their horses at home, Megan did not have a safe training area to work in.

DIARY OF A DANGEROUS HORSE: GETTING OUT OF REFORM SCHOOL

I wish we'd had a video camera recording the progress we made with Fig. Every session contained major breakthroughs. The change in Fig during just our first session together was so overwhelming that I thought, here's a great case history to share with people. But her story kept unfolding. Every week there was another chapter that needed to be told. I could have written this entire book simply around her; and in a way I did. I started with Fig at roughly the same time I started writing the first five introductory chapters.

Fig didn't let us skip any steps. It was as though we had a huge canvas to fill in, and only a tiny paint brush to work with. With another horse we could have filled in the empty spaces with a few large paint strokes, but not Fig. She made us look at every step in detail. I put off writing about

her and instead concentrated on the rest of the book. What I discovered was, section by section, I was really telling her story. You already know how we trained Fig. Everything I've written applies to her.

I am using her story to show you how you can put all the principles and exercises together to create a major change in a horse. I am going to present this section in diary form, so you can get a real-time sense of how training progresses. I've found many people get frustrated when they don't see a miracle cure right away. They've gone to clinics where in the space of one afternoon they see a rank horse become sweet as a newborn puppy. What they fail to see are the thousands of hours that the clinician spent learning how to handle horses like this.

These same people often feel frustrated when they can't apply the work they've just seen directly to their horse. They go home feeling just as stuck as they did before the clinic.

This section is for all the people who train at home and have trouble finding a starting place. More than anything else, I want you to understand that you don't need a fancy horse and expensive equipment to get good training results. All you need is an understanding of the rules of shaping and an extra measure of patience.

As you read through this section, it may seem as though the training progresses at a snail's pace. Megan and I spent months working with Fig. Training isn't a race. I could have worked Fig through these steps by myself in less time, but that wasn't the point. I wanted Megan to become comfortable with her horse. I believe very much in the philosophy that says "Give a man a fish, and he eats for a day; teach him how to fish, and he can feed himself for a lifetime."

Megan and her mother were the ones who were going to have to handle Fig on a daily basis. I needed to make sure Megan understood the tools I was giving her. The best way to do that was to have Megan train Fig directly. I'd guide her through the steps, but she needed to be the one handling the horse. That way she could feel the changes in Fig as they were occurring. Training might progress at a snail's pace. That's something I was comfortable with because in the end you have a horse and rider who understand all the pieces and can work successfully together.

Here's how Fig's training proceeded:

Session one: Clicker training

We conditioned Fig to the clicker.

Session two: Sacking out

We built on the success of the previous session. Fig let us touch her neck, but got concerned and would retreat back into her stall if we tried to reach beyond her shoulder. We solidified her understanding of the clicker and the target, and introduced the cue word "touch."

Session three: Head lowering

Megan was trying to groom Fig when I got to the barn. She was in the stall with her, and Fig was snapping at her, threatening to bite every time Megan touched her with the brush.

Megan and her mother had noticed major changes in Fig through the week, which was why Megan was now willing to go into the stall with her. Fig's faces seemed to be more posturing than actual aggression. As long as we didn't overface her or get too demanding, it looked as though it was going to be safe for Megan to stay in the stall.

Our first priority was to get control of the head. Fig was constantly snapping at Megan's arm. I wanted to give Megan some tools to keep the teeth away from her.

I had Megan come out of the stall so I could explain what we were going to do. As soon as we left, Fig retreated to the back of her stall. When we came back into the barn a few minutes later, she turned her hindquarters to us and pinned her ears flat. Challenge number one was going to be catching her without getting kicked.

The target training provided us with the perfect answer. I stood at her stall door and rattled the pill container. Fig's ears perked forward. She looked over at us. She hesitated for half a second, then walked over and touched her target. Never have I been more convinced of the usefulness of clicker training than at that moment.

Our next step was to get a bridle on her. Fig fussed. She tossed her head, and clamped her teeth, but Megan managed to get the bit in her mouth and the headstall up over her ears.

The bridle was going to be our principle training tool. We were going to offer Fig a clear choice. She could stand quietly with her head down, or she could

have Megan's hand in her mouth. What do I mean by that? When you take the slack out of the reins, you're putting pressure on the bars of the horse's mouth. That's not necessarily painful, but it certainly is annoying. Think about how you feel when you visit the dentist. He doesn't have to be drilling for you to want his hand out of your mouth. That's pretty much how the horse feels about bits. You can get them to do amazing things for you just by showing them that correct responses will cause you to release contact on the reins.*

That was the bargain we were going to set up with Fig. She could go on posturing and trying to side-swipe Megan, or she could put her head down and stand quietly. The choice was hers, but, as long as she was acting up, Megan would keep contact on the rein. The instant Fig even thought about dropping her head, Megan would let go. We were going to sweeten the pot even further by adding the clicker and rewarding correct responses.

(Note: If you try this on your own horse, use a snaffle bit. A full cheek snaffle is ideal because it won't pull through the horse's mouth. Curb bits are not designed to work laterally like this, and should not be used for this kind of single-rein work.)

That was the principle, now for the practice. I had Megan stand by Fig's left shoulder. She picked up the inside left rein so there was no slack in it and held it steady against the base of Fig's shoulder.

The slope of the shoulder blade makes a handy shelf where you can anchor your hand. You don't want to get into a pulling contest with the horse. This exercise wasn't about trying to drag Fig's head down to the ground. Megan's instructions were to take the slack out of the rein and wait. If Fig tried to swing her head around to the side to grab at Megan, Megan could counter that move by running her hand vertically up Fig's neck. That would give her enough extra leverage to keep Fig's head from swinging around. As long as Fig resisted against the rein, Megan would continue to anchor her hand. The instant Fig offered to drop her head, Megan satisfied her half of the bargain by letting go (Fig. 52).

At first Megan didn't understand that she needed to keep tension on the line when she lifted her hand up. She was taking it up and forward. The result was an unintentional release of pressure. The message

---

*This is called "negative reinforcement." The horse learns and remembers a behavior that gets rid of something unpleasant, just as it would learn a behavior that earns something pleasant.

Fig received was, swinging your head around to bite is a great way to get Megan's hand out of your mouth. That was definitely not what we wanted to be saying.

With a little practice Megan got the hang of the exercise. She learned how to counter Fig's moves by keeping her hand steady. Fig couldn't swing around to bite at Megan without putting more pressure on her jaw. It's important to understand that Fig was doing this to herself. Megan wasn't pulling on the rein. She was just being a solid post. It was up to Fig whether she was going to pull on that post or release to it. Every time she softened and dropped her head, Megan let go of her end of the rein.

In that first session Fig would indeed drop her head, but she couldn't leave it down for more than an instant. That's normal. Dropping the head at this stage makes the horse feel vulnerable. They aren't yet ready to trust you. Each time Fig lifted her head, Megan took the slack out of the rein. Fig started to look like a yo-yo. Up, down; in the mouth, out of the mouth.

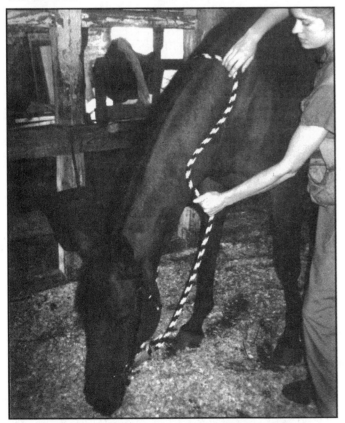

Fig. 52: We taught Fig to lower her head by putting pressure on the rein when her head went up, and releasing it when it dropped. With her head down she couldn't bite at us. The low head position helped her to relax.

Megan had enough to think about without also timing the clicker. That became my job. I started by clicking Fig whenever she dropped her head. Now she had an even better choice. Make faces and fuss, and Megan will have her hand in your mouth. Soften and drop your head, and not only will she let go of the rein, she'll give you a treat.

Switching over from a fixed to a variable reward schedule was easy. I simply began withholding the click a little longer each time, to encourage her to leave her head down. Fig struggled to contain herself. We could see she wanted the treat, but she just wasn't used to controlling her reactions. She had always grabbed first and asked questions later.

This was clearly hard for her. We worked in short, five-minute sessions with long breaks in between. We probably worked her six or seven times that day, spread out over a two-hour session. Our only goal was to ask her to drop her head. If we had asked for anything else, we would have totally overwhelmed her.

Session Four: Bridling, head lowering, and sacking out

Fig greeted us with her rear end just like the last time. Rattling the pill bottle brought her to the front of her stall where she let us put a halter on her. I wanted to continue our work on head lowering, but first I wanted to spend some time teaching her to accept the bridle. I wanted to teach Fig to put her own bridle on. Megan had taught her the verbal cue "Touch." I held the bit up and said "Touch." Fig held back. She wanted no part of this new game.

I held the pill bottle up behind the bit and repeated the cue. This time Fig reached forward and bumped the bit as she tried to touch the bottle. After a couple of repetitions I removed the pill bottle, and she came forward to touch the bit.

I started to withhold the click. Fig bumped the bit a little harder and opened her mouth. *Click!* This time she got a jackpot—grain instead of her usual carrots. Fig started to take more notice. She opened her mouth around the bit a second time. *Click!* I again gave her an extra handful of grain. A couple of repetitions later, and she was consistently taking hold of the bit.

That was the first step. The second half of this equation was getting the head stall up over her ears. I used the technique I've already described for bridling. (See Ch. 4, Everything Is Everything Else.) I asked Fig a series of questions. I lifted the bridle part way up her face and asked her if she could still keep her head down. If she did, *click!* She got a treat. I didn't care if she spit the bit out to eat her carrots. Starting over from square one just gave her more of an opportunity to learn what I wanted.

Even once I had the bridle on over her ears, I wasn't done. I slipped it on and off again three or four more times before I was satisfied. Then I had Megan repeat the whole process. By the time we were finished, Fig was practically putting her own bridle on. All this was done over her stall door. Neither of us had gone into the stall with her yet.

Now we continued with the head-lowering work of the previous session. Megan went into the stall with her and asked her to lower her head. Fig had clearly been processing her lessons. Her head went right down to her ankles and stayed there. There was no more yo-yoing up and down. She began to get that relaxed, dreamy-eyed look horses get when they finally understand the head-lowering lesson.

Again we upped our criteria. Megan sacked her out at the same time she continued to ask her to leave her head down, in this relaxed but vulnerable position. Megan began by running her hand over Fig's neck and shoulder.

Fig was fascinating to watch. Biting had become such a habit for her, she had trouble stopping herself. It was like trying to get a person to stop chewing their fingernails or saying "you know" all the time. It's so ingrained they don't even know they're doing it.

Fig had to really concentrate to control herself. She couldn't help but have flashes of her former behavior. When Megan's dog, Jake, ran over to clean up a dropped carrot, Fig lunged at him as she usually did. Several times she forgot herself and snapped at Megan. In between dodging Fig's teeth, Megan did a good job managing the bridle and the sacking out.

We added a soft brush to our criteria. Megan ran it over Fig's shoulder. Fig kicked. Megan didn't yell at her or make any attempt at correction. Instead she asked Fig to lower her head. When all four feet were on the ground, and Fig's head was down, Megan clicked.

Megan brushed Fig's withers. This time Fig controlled herself and got clicked right away. By the time we ended the session, Fig was standing quietly with her head down around her ankles, and Megan was brushing the length of her back.

I looked at my watch and discovered that we'd been working with Fig for almost two hours without a break! That's quite a change from the previous session, when she could barely go five minutes at a time.

Session five: Leading lessons—forward and back

As soon as we walked into the barn, Fig came up to the front of her stall to greet us. I held the bridle out for her. She put her mouth around the bit and dropped her head, waiting for me to lift up the headstall. She couldn't have told us any more clearly than that that she was ready to work.

Megan had made good progress during the week, getting Fig to drop her head and accept the soft brush. Fig was much more comfortable letting Megan stay with her in her stall, but she was still protective of her hindquarters. She wasn't snapping at Megan as much, but she was still having sudden, unpredictable flashes of anger. Megan was doing a good job controlling Fig's head, but Fig was still dragging her around the stall. It was time to connect the feet to the rest of the system.

We taught her first to back. As Fig started to walk forward, Megan pressed her fingertips into Fig's chest, just where the front leg joins the base of the neck. Fig ignored the pressure and kept walking. Megan persisted until Fig came to a stop on her own. *Click!* Megan instantly took her hand away and gave Fig a treat.

Megan again pressed her hand against Fig's chest. Fig's response to the pressure was to walk forward again. It was awkward, but Megan managed to keep track of the reins, and still hold her fingers pressed against Fig's chest. Fig dragged her around the stall, ignoring the pressure. When she finally stopped, she got a click and a treat, and Megan took her hand away.

After a few minutes of this, Fig stopped walking forward. Now it became a waiting game and a real test of patience.

The temptation at this point is to force the issue: to get the horse to back up by smacking her on the chest, or pulling on the reins, or simply pushing her back. The problem with force is it takes choice out of the equation. Fig could stand there ignoring Megan, or she could take a step back and get a treat. This was her opportunity to learn that she had other options besides resistance.

Fig up to this point had only one plan: "Hurt them first before they can hurt you." Megan waited, and Fig shifted her weight. She didn't actually take a step back, but I saw her shoulder soften ever so slightly under Megan's fingers. It was such a tiny shift I don't think Megan was even aware of it. I clicked, and Megan took her hand away. From that tiny beginning we shaped backing up.

What the left side knows, the right side still has to learn: Megan taught Fig first from the left side, then the right. Changing sides on Fig meant dodging her teeth. Fig threatened and made faces. I'm sure if we'd gotten tough with her, she'd have gone after Megan. As long as we didn't escalate, she didn't either.

Megan had to repeat the entire training process, on the right side. This is normal. Horses are very specific in their learning. Just because Fig understood the backup signal from the left side did not mean she had a clue when we transferred it over to her right side. Everything had to be repeated. The right side was actually harder than the left because this was Fig's stiff side.

Megan helped Fig learn on the right side by switching back occasionally to the left. The reinforcement that came with correct responses kept her working with us. Before long Fig was beginning to back up consistently from both sides.

If Fig started to drag Megan around the stall, Megan now had a safe way to say, "No, that's not what I want you to do." Fig responded to her because, for the first time in her life, she really understood what somebody wanted.

Our next big challenge was to teach her to go forward. The trigger for this was going to be reaching back and touching Fig on the hip. The first time Megan tried, Fig lashed out with her hind leg, pinned her ears flat and snapped at the air in front of her. Megan was quick to ask her to drop her head. Fig started to lunge forward, and the backup cue put an instant stop to that.

Megan asked twice more for Fig to come forward. Fig continued to kick out, but we did get a couple of tiny steps in the right direction. She clearly wasn't ready for more, so we left it at that, and ended the session instead with some simple requests for head lowering.

Session six: TTEAM work

When we walked into the barn, Fig was in the back of her stall, clearly in a grumpy mood. We shook the pill bottle, and she came right over to the front of her stall. When Megan held the bridle up for her, she took the bit right away and dropped her head down so Megan could slip the headstall over her ears. Fig might be feeling grumpy, but she was ready to work.

We reviewed the backup cue, which she responded well to on both sides. Megan then asked her to come forward. Fig surprised us all. She took a step forward! She didn't kick out once during that entire session. Megan added more layers to that first step. Within minutes she could ask Fig to come forward and walk around the entire stall, and then stop and back up whenever she asked. We were beginning to have some real control.

Fig had reached the stage where she would drop her head and leave it down for extended periods. Megan could position her anywhere she wanted in the stall, using the cues to back up or come forward. She was accepting some grooming and was comfortable letting Megan run her hand over her back and hindquarters. Now that she was reasonably safe to handle, the next step was to add some TTEAM body work into the mix.

TTEAM and clicker training are natural partners. Like clicker training, TTEAM is a very gentle way to work horses. The whole premise behind TTEAM is that fear and pain interfere with learning. At the heart of TTEAM is the Tellington Touch, a system of body work that opens channels of communication with the horse.

I knew from past experiences that TTEAM can have a profound impact on a horse. I wanted to use it with Fig, but first we had to be able to handle her safely. The clicker had gotten us to the point where we could now use the Tellington Touch.

The foundation of the Tellington Touch (TTouch) is a circular movement of the hand. The TTouch brings awareness to the body. It's like hooking up a central computer through little switches all over the horse's body.

To do the TTouch, imagine the face of a clock about the size of a wrist watch resting on your horse's body. Place your lightly curved fingers at six o'clock, and gently move the skin that's directly under your fingers around the clock for one and a quarter circles. The key here is to move the skin and not just slide over it.

Once you've completed your circle and a quarter, lift your fingers up off the horse and begin again. You can move your hand randomly over the horse's body, or you can work in parallel lines by making a circle and then sliding your hand over to begin the next circle. For best results you should balance yourself by making the circles with one hand, while your other hand rests comfortably somewhere else on the horse.

The pressure you use for the Tellington TTouch can be very light. To get a sense of what we used on Fig, rest your thumb against your cheek. Use the tip of your middle finger to make several circles on your eyelid. Press only as firmly as feels comfortable for you, then repeat these circles on your forearm. On a scale of one to ten this is about a three pressure. We used a range of pressure on Fig from about a one, the lightest possible touch on your eyelid, to a five or a six.

We did the circles with our fingertips, and also with the whole flat of our hands. Fig's eyes got soft and dreamy. Her whole demeanor changed. She was clearly enjoying this. Her muscles softened and relaxed. Her head drooped down even further. It was an astounding transformation from the hard-eyed, mean-tempered horse I first met. Little by little we were unlocking doors and opening up Fig's world.

Session seven: Foot care

Now that we had some basic tools, it was time to start focusing in on some of Fig's key issues. The most pressing problem we faced was foot care. Fig had had no routine daily foot care for almost a year. Trying to pick out her feet was simply too much of an ordeal for Megan to do on a regular basis. Every ten weeks or so the blacksmith managed somehow to get at least her front feet trimmed. With a lot of patience he could usually do her back feet. Megan had been lucky so far that Fig had never had an abscess or any other injury that required treatment.

Our first goal was simply to teach Fig to pick up her feet. Safety was, as always, our main concern. If Megan leaned down to ask for Fig's foot, she wouldn't be able to control her head. That would leave Fig free to swing around and bite her. I also didn't want Megan putting her head within range of Fig's hind legs. We had to get Fig's foot up without reaching down for it.

I had Megan ask Fig to back up. To take a step Fig had to first lift her foot. My job was to time the click so that we captured the exact moment when the foot came up off the ground. Megan was skeptical. She didn't see how this could possibly work, but she was a good sport and went along with the process.

At first Fig offered several steps of back up. She was moving so fast it was hard to mark the initial lift of the leg. In a sense we'd done our job too well, teaching her to move. Now that's all she wanted to do in response to the backup cue. Just standing still and lifting a foot was not an option she saw.

It took us, I'm guessing, about half an hour before she finally realized we didn't want all those extra steps back. All she had to do was stand still and lift her front foot to get a treat. That was easy enough. She was more than willing to do that.

Megan was starting to be a believer. Now when she pressed her fingers into Fig's chest, Fig responded by stopping, shifting her weight, and lifting her left foot a couple of inches off the ground. I started to withhold the click. Ten minutes later the foot was coming up to knee height.

Once Fig was adding that much height consistently, I instructed Megan to take a hold of the foot. I wanted her to keep it just for a second until she heard me click, and then she was to let go. Again, I was able to withhold the click a little longer each time, until Fig was picking up her foot from a cue on her chest, and letting Megan hold it for a count of about ten seconds.

We switched over to the right side, and discovered we were in for a much more difficult process. The right was the side Fig leaned down on. It was much harder for her to pick up her foot. We worked on that side just to the point where she would stand and shift her weight off her foot, and then left her at that for the day.

Session eight: Front feet

Fig had definitely figured out the previous lesson. Even before Megan had the bridle on her, she was lifting her left front foot up practically to her belly. Megan asked her to drop her head. Fig obliged, but she also lifted her foot.

We focused on the right side. Fig clearly understood what we wanted; it was just physically much more difficult for her on this side. We helped her by reaching part way down her leg to identify the foot we wanted.

By the end of the session Fig was consistently picking up both front feet in response to a chest cue. But even more than that, she was allowing Megan to clean them. For the first time in almost a year Fig was having her feet picked out.

Session nine: Hind feet

Fig came up to the front of her stall as soon as we walked in the barn. Even before we brought the bridle out, she was offering us her front feet. Her whole attitude had shifted. It was almost comical to watch her, with her head down and her left foot lifted up to her belly.

Our goal for this session was to get the hind feet up as well. Here, even more than on the front, safety was our main concern. When Fig kicked, she wasn't bluffing. Any method we used had to meet the following two criteria: Megan could not bend down, and she could not step past Fig's shoulder to ask for the hind foot.

We had used movement to get her front feet. We did the same thing now to get the hind feet. We had already taught Fig the cue we needed. Megan touched her on her hip and asked her to come forward. In the confines of the stall that meant Fig could really only circle in a tight bend around Megan. My job was to click her at the exact moment when her inside hind foot lifted to come forward.

Megan was a real doubting Thomas on this one. At first Fig simply walked Megan around the stall. She was so pushy it was hard to capture pieces we could build on. We went back and reviewed the front feet. That helped. When we asked again for the hind feet, Fig wasn't so eager to walk off. Instead she offered us a front foot. She stood with her foot dangling in mid air expecting me to click her.

I knew she couldn't hold her foot up forever, though she was certainly trying. Finally, she gave up, and put her foot down. Megan was ready for her. She had her hand on Fig's hip waiting to ask her to shift her weight over. Fig cocked her hind leg. *Click!* She got carrots and a handful of grain.

From that simple beginning we were soon able to get her to pick her hind foot up, just by pressing on her hip. The next step was to reach down and take a hold of the foot. Megan did this in stages. First she just ran her hand down Fig's hip. When Fig stood still and kept her hind foot cocked, she got clicked.

Megan eased her hand a little further down Fig's leg to her hock, *Click!* She got a treat. The next time she ran her hand all the way down to her ankle. Fig never once tried to kick. We got really bold. Megan asked her to lift up her foot. She stroked her hand down her leg and took a hold of the foot. She held it for just a second or two before releasing it. Fig got another major jackpot for that one.

Fig was enjoying herself, but Megan needed a break. This kind of work takes tremendous concentration on the part of the handler. You can't afford mistakes. Fig was showing wonderful self-control, but she would still flash back into sudden bursts of anger. We ended the session by asking her

to pick up her front feet, and left her with a big jackpot of carrots.

Session 10: Confirming the lessons

We continued to work on her hind legs. By the end of the session Megan could pick up and clean all four feet.

Session 11: Sound discs—putting an end to the biting

Fig was clearly beginning to relax and enjoy her training sessions. She understood what we were asking. She actively wanted the company. She wasn't afraid of Megan, nor was she trying to boss her around and be lead mare anymore. In many ways she was a different horse; but she was still side-swiping Megan with her teeth. We needed to find a way to put an end to the biting.

I still wasn't prepared to punish her for it. I don't think that would have helped us, and it might have gotten one of us hurt. The side-swiping had become more like a nervous tic than an aggressive act. The positive behaviors we had shaped were becoming security zones for her. Dropping her head created an immediate shift in her mental state. We had ways of saying to her, "relax, calm down." Now we also needed a way to say, directly, "Don't bite."

Once again I looked beyond traditional horse training to find the answer. A client had just shared with me a video from an English dog trainer, John Fisher. She liked his work, and thought I might enjoy seeing the tape. Much of it focused on general care. Since I don't have a dog of my own, that part didn't interest me, but there was one segment that really intrigued me. Fisher showed how he uses sound discs to eliminate unwanted behavior (see Ch. 25, Dogs and Cats).

Sound discs are simply a set of flat metal discs attached to a key ring. The dog he demonstrated them with was a big, bouncy fellow belonging to an elderly couple. The dog loved to greet his people by jumping up on them. His exuberance was the problem. They didn't have the strength to control him, and they were afraid he'd knock somebody down.

Fisher began by offering the dog several tidbits out of his hand. The dog wagged his tail happily as he gobbled them down. So far he was liking this game. Next Fisher put a tidbit down on the ground. As the dog went for it, Fisher snatched the food away and dropped the sound discs. They made a harsh clanging noise on the floor, but the dog was so focused on the food he didn't even flinch.

Fisher repeated this step several more times. He put the food down on the floor and snatched it away before the dog could get to it. Each time he dropped the sound disc just as he removed the food. By the third repetition the dog was noticeably hesitating. By the fifth he didn't even try to take the food.

Fisher offered him a tidbit out of his hand. Nothing Fisher had done had made the dog afraid of him. The dog went right over to him, wagging his tail. Fisher let him take the food, then he put another bit down on the floor. The dog hesitated, and then instead of grabbing for the treat, he went across the room and lay down next to his owners.

Well, this is interesting, I thought, but how do you use it? The next segment answered my question. Fisher invited the dog to come say hello to him. The dog came bounding over, wagging his tail exuberantly. Two strides away, Fisher dropped the sound disc. The dog skidded to a halt and retreated back to his people. At that time, I wasn't sure why it worked, but I was intrigued by the effect.*

There are times when I feel like the proverbial mad scientist. I wanted to experiment with the sound discs, but I didn't have any dogs handy. What I had were three cats who were scratching a newly upholstered couch. If the sound discs worked, this would be an interesting test.

I conditioned my cats to the sound discs in exactly the same way Fisher had shown on his tape. The results were the same. Within a very few repetitions, the cats were scooting from the room. The real test came the next time they tried to use the living room couch as a scratching post. I was in an adjoining room, but when I dropped the sound disc, the scratching stopped instantly.

Well, I thought, this is even more interesting, but would it work with horses? Fig seemed like the perfect candidate for my experiment. Megan had known me long enough not to laugh at my mad-scientist approach to training. There was just one problem with using the sound discs on Fig. Neither of us wanted to be the one to snatch a carrot away from her.

I solved this dilemma with a Rube Goldberg arrangement. I tied a string around a carrot. To make it even easier for Fig, we set the carrot up on a bale of shavings which we propped against her stall door.

As Fig reached for the carrot, I could whisk it away just by pulling on the string.

For a sound disc, I used a metal sweat scraper. It made a wonderfully awful high-pitched clanging noise as it hit the cement floor. If ever there was an aversive stimulus, it was the sound of that sweat scraper.

We had a good laugh at ourselves over this arrangement. I'm sure anyone looking in would have thought we had gone completely mad, but all I can say is it worked. Fig responded just like the dog on Fisher's tape. Within a very few repetitions she wasn't even trying to get the carrot.

Okay. That was Step One, but would it help with the biting? Megan went into Fig's stall and started to groom her. Fig was in a grumpy mood. She pinned her ears and took a swipe at Megan. I was waiting outside, a clicker in one hand and the sweat scraper in the other. The instant I saw her head begin to swing around, I flung the sweat scraper to the ground.

I would never have guessed it would have the effect it did on Fig. My concern about dealing directly with the biting had always been that it would cause her to become even more aggressive. At present her threats were all posturing, and we had worked hard to keep them that way.

When the sweat scraper hit the floor, Fig had her mouth open to grab at Megan's jacket. I watched her shudder to a stop. She dropped her head practically to the ground, and her whole body relaxed. It was an extraordinary reaction. Rather than making her more angry and aggressive, the sound disc had had the opposite effect. Fig became almost angelic. She couldn't do enough to please us. It was an astonishing transformation.

The effect lasted for maybe five minutes; then Fig forgot herself again. She reached around for Megan's coat. I was finding it very confusing having a clicker in one hand and a sweat scraper in the other. I almost clicked her for biting! Instead I again hurled the sweat scraper to the floor. Fig broke off her biting and dropped her head to the ground. Her entire expression was again transformed into peaceful calm.

I dropped the sweat scraper maybe three more times in that session. Fig started watching me for signals. If I even so much as wiggled the sweat

*Fisher's sound disks are a "conditioned negative reinforcer." The food disappearing is bad news; the sound means "bad news," just as a click means "good news." When the dog's behavior is marked with the sound, the dog does some other behavior instead. Ed.

scraper, that was enough to stop her. I could see that she was really trying to control herself. She had caught on incredibly fast to the connection. We were saying to her, "If you don't want to hear that awful clanging noise that makes carrots disappear, all you have to do is not bite." When you think how hard it is for people to break their nervous habits, you can appreciate the self-control Fig was showing us.

In the following session, I think I dropped the sweat scraper maybe three times in all. The session after that, only once. By the third session after this one, I just had to hold it. I never actually dropped it. If Fig started to forget herself, a warning shake was all I needed to stop her.

I continued to hold the sweat scraper for a couple more sessions, but I think I only had to drop it one more time. Fig still made ugly faces, but the lunging and side-swiping with her teeth were gone.

Am I recommending that we all start dropping sweat scrapers around our horses? I can just picture it now: a whole ring full of people fumbling around trying to work their horses with a clicker in one hand and a sweat scraper in the other! Talk about looking like a Thelwell cartoon.

So, no, I am not recommending that we all start whisking carrots out from under our horses. I've included it here because it's an interesting example. The sound disc let us break a deeply entrenched habitual pattern.

The people I learned horse training from would have had a different answer. They would have said, "Just get after her for it." I'm sure whoever originally trained Fig tried that approach, and discovered it didn't work. What they left us with was a horse you couldn't punish. Whatever they did, it guaranteed that getting tough was going to get somebody hurt. The sound discs offered us an alternative, and the bottom line was, it worked.

Session 12: Setting goals

By our twelfth session, Fig had come a long way in what was really just a very short time. Her basic stall manners were well in hand. She was a different horse from the mean-tempered, fire-breathing dragon I had first met. Megan could groom her. She could pick up her feet, and move her around in her stall. Fig was safe to be around.

Now it was time to start thinking about our ultimate goal: riding. Most of our time on this particular day was spent in a discussion of goal setting.

Two obvious projects popped out at once. One was leading, and the other was saddling. In order to ride her, we needed first to be able to get her out of that barn. At the moment that was a major challenge. Fig was used to a run-in, run-out situation with her turnout. Megan would open the back door of the barn, and Fig would walk out to the paddock by herself. If you put a lead on her she'd balk and plant her feet.

Saddling was the other priority. Megan hadn't tried to ride Fig in seven or eight months. Saddles tended to bring out the worst in Fig. Both lessons were important, but since it was raining on the day I saw her, we chose to start inside with the saddle.

As always we didn't start with our goal. Putting a saddle on is just another form of sacking out. Just as we did for bridling (see Chap 4., Everything Is Everything Else), we chunked the process down into tiny steps and began by asking Fig a series of questions.

"Will you stand still while I run my hand over all the places a saddle would go? Yes?" C/R.

"Will you stand still while I put this folded-up cloth over your back? your neck, your ears, your face? Yes?" C/R.

"Will you stand still while I flop this girth cover or this old towel over your back? Yes?" C/R.

Megan's tack cabinet provided us with a gold mine of things to flop on Fig's back. We used saddle pads, towels, girths, everything but the actual saddle. That we left for the next session.

Session 13: Saddling and leading

We did two things with Fig in this session. First we saddled her, and second we took her out of the barn.

Saddling brought out many of Fig's old reactions. Megan could put the saddle on her back, but as soon as she started to buckle the girth to the saddle, Fig started kicking violently. We weren't trying to do up the girth. Fig's old patterns were erupting just from the simple act of attaching the girth to the saddle.

I instructed Megan to ask Fig to pick up her front foot. Fig responded instantly. She lifted her foot so high she almost hit herself in the belly. The familiar behavior settled her. It was like handing a toddler a security blanket. Picking up her foot created a comfort zone for Fig. She dropped her head and let Megan finish buckling on the girth.

We asked Fig another series of questions to do up the girth.

"Can you stand still while we bring the girth under your belly? Yes?" C/R

"Can you stand still while the girth touches you under your belly? Yes?" C/R.

"Can you stand still while we put pressure on the girth? Yes?" C/R.

"Can you stand still while we buckle the girth to the lowest hole on the saddle billets? Yes?" C/R.

Megan continued to work her like this until she had the girth tightened all the way. Anytime Fig started to get anxious, Megan would ask her to pick up a front foot. Fig began offering us this behavior herself. She'd start to get tense, but instead of lunging at us, she'd lift her foot.

The transformation in her behavior was truly remarkable to watch. She'd gone from kicking the back wall of her stall and lunging at us, to standing calmly for saddling, within a matter of minutes. The clicker does so much more than simply teach behavior. The training had created a safety zone for Fig, where she could find refuge any time she felt overfaced.

In the second half of the session we put Fig's bridle on and took her out for a walk. Or at least that's what we attempted to do. Fig balked at the open door.

We went back to the very first thing we had taught her. I held her target out just an inch or two in front of her. Fig stretched her nose out to touch it and got clicked. I took a step back. Now she had to really reach for it. She took a tiny step forward and got clicked. In this snail's pace way we made it the ten feet or so to the front of the barn.

To get out, Fig had to make a sharp left-hand turn and step down through a people-sized doorway. Fig balked at the step. I held the target just barely beyond reach and waited. Fig stretched her nose out as far as she could. Her front feet were balanced on the edge of the sill, and her hind feet were rocked underneath her. That open doorway was as much of a challenge for her as stepping up into a trailer might be for another horse.

The training was the same. I knew she couldn't stand balanced like that forever. Eventually her hind legs would walk her front legs forward. Fig finally committed herself. She took one step down. I stepped back with the target and let the momentum bring her the rest of the way. Once she was in the lower section of the barn, all her balkiness disappeared. She led perfectly politely next to Megan.

Megan practiced getting Fig to stand still. The blacksmith was scheduled to come during the week, and we needed to make sure all her training would transfer out of her stall. We took Fig through a dress rehearsal.

Megan discovered she had taught her horse to ground tie, and she didn't even know it. Fig stood perfectly while we took turns picking up and cleaning her feet. If we had left out any steps for the blacksmith, she would tell us when he came.

Session 14: Graduation day—The blacksmith

This was the day all our prior work had been leading up to. Fig balked for a step or two as she came out of her stall. Her target cone brought her forward, and once she was in motion she followed Megan all the way out of the barn. We had explained the clicker to the blacksmith. He was willing to try anything that might help, even something as crazy-sounding as this.

Megan stood Fig up for him, and showed him the new trigger spots we'd established to ask for her feet. Fig was ready. She already had her left front foot dangling in mid air. To say he was impressed was an understatement. He was even more impressed when he got through all four feet without any trouble from Fig.

At the time I thought, well, this makes a good place to end Fig's story. Getting her feet done seemed like Graduation Day. Only Fig wasn't through teaching us things.

Shortly after Fig had her feet trimmed she had a five- or six-week break in her training. Megan had scratched her cornea, and her eye had become badly infected. She couldn't see well enough to work Fig. The next time I saw Fig, she was back to being a grump. She was making ugly faces and lunging at Megan's dog over the front of her stall. When Megan went in with her, she had to dodge her teeth. It looked as if we were right back to square one.

I didn't want to just repeat what we'd done before. Megan already knew how to do that on her own. I wanted to add some new pieces to the puzzle, so I proposed a change of tactics. We went back to working her from the outside of her stall, just as we had in the very beginning. Only now I was going to be more active in triggering the reactions I wanted. I was going to teach her round pen training in a ten-foot stall, and I was going to do it without ever stepping inside with her.

The first goal in round pen training is to get the horse to move its feet consistently in one direction. We found two long whips that let me reach Fig wherever she was in the stall. I shook one whip behind Fig and clicked her when she stepped forward away from it.

You have to be careful when you work in an enclosed situation like this. If Fig had felt trapped or overfaced, she might have tried to jump out of her stall. Timing is everything when a horse is confined. I wanted to be able to insist, with Fig, but I didn't want to frighten or frustrate her. Finding the right balance, knowing when to push for more, and when to back off, is part of the art of training. This is where patience and tact become more than just words.

Once I had Fig circling in her stall, I needed to be able to get her to change directions. She was moving to the right. As she came broadside to me, I switched the whip so it blocked her path. Fig stopped. She got clicked for that. I put the whip up in front of her again and waited. Fig responded by turning her head ever so slightly to the outside. *Click!* She got reinforced for that.

That's all I needed to shape an outside turn. I just kept reinforcing her for turning her head to the outside, away from the whip. Eventually she had her head curled around to the outside so much that her feet followed and took her through her first outside turn. Naturally she got a jackpot for that.

If Fig had started by turning her head to the inside of the stall, I would have begun with inside turns. Fig was giving us a marvelous demonstration of how shaping really works. All I needed to create inside and outside turns was to recognize that a slight turn of the head was a piece of behavior I could use. By selectively reinforcing head movement, I transformed it into an organized turn.

I repeated the same process to the left. In this direction, she wanted to turn back through the middle of the stall to track right again. I added a second whip to regulate this. I could keep one whip behind her to ask her to move forward, while the other controlled her nose. If she started to turn in, I could cross both whips across the center of the stall to block her path. It worked. She stopped with her nose facing the back wall where I was standing. I crossed the whips together in an X, closing off the inside of the stall, and waited.

Fig found the option that I had left open for her. She turned her head to the outside. Creating an alternative path is an important concept, no matter what training method you're using. You always have to leave the horse with at least one option. Trap a horse, and you'll have a wreck. This is what can happen to people under saddle who lock their legs onto the horse's sides at the same time they're hauling back on the reins. The horse has nowhere to go, so it explodes into a buck that sends the rider flying.

I had to be certain that I was leaving Fig with a clear option. I wanted to tell her firmly: "No. Not this way. Don't even think about running through me." It had been a long time since anyone had said "No" to her. If we were going to be successful, she also had to have a clear "Yes" answer.

Without all the preliminary work, this exercise might have ended in a wreck. Fig could have gotten frustrated and gone over the top of the stall. She might even have tried to charge us. The stall walls were not sturdy enough to stop her. Without all the steps we'd gone through in the spring, I would never have been able to ask her to work in such a confined space.

Horses have long memories. Fig might be back to her grumpy old ways, but she still remembered everything we had done with her. She had learned how to learn, and she understood in general terms what my signals meant. All I had to do was show her what her options were, and reinforce her for correct responses. When Fig turned her head to the outside, she found the open door I had left for her.

Shaping the inside turns took a little longer. The general concept I wanted Fig to understand was to move away from pressure. To get the inside turn, I placed the whips between the wall and her face. She'd been reinforced for outside turns, so naturally that's what she wanted to do, even though the whips were there blocking her.

When she barged through the whips, I didn't try to stop her. I simply reversed her, through an outside turn from the other direction, and asked again. Eventually she stopped, with her head slightly off the wall. She'd been trying to look to the outside, so this was a major improvement. Now, when I inserted the whips between her and the wall, she looked away from them, into the inside of the stall. She got a jackpot for that discovery.

The next time she didn't just look to the inside, she turned. The only problem was she ended up just circling back the same way she'd come. I still clicked her for the effort. I had part of what I wanted. I could shape the rest.

To get her to change directions I had to be able to follow through the turn by keeping the whips behind her as she came off the wall, and then pull them out of her way so she could cross in front of me. It was a tricky operation in such a small space, but she got the idea.

By the end of the session she had all the basic elements of round pen training. She understood that she was to move her feet when I asked, and to keep moving them until I either clicked her or asked for something else. She knew the difference between inside and outside turns. Even more important where Fig was concerned, she was no longer grumping at us.

In the next session we simply worked on more of the same. I wanted Fig to have a solid understanding of inside and outside turns before I turned her over to Megan.

The following week I taught Megan how to round-pen Fig. We had to go through some preliminary steps, such as having Megan "round-pen" me so she could get herself oriented. Fig was a little confused at first by Megan's mixed messages. This was actually a good thing. It helped her to learn to be a little more tolerant and patient (Fig. 53).

The main issue with Megan was getting her to be insistent enough in her requests. There comes a point in horse training when you need to be able to tell a horse to move, and not simply ask it. It's a line many people find very hard to cross, and it creates some real problems with the horses. It's what I call the pigeon effect.

The pigeon effect refers to a study I read about so many years ago now I don't even remember the source. A behavioral scientist taught some pigeons to peck at a bar to get food. When the pigeons were all fully trained and pecking strongly at the bar, he gave them all an electric shock. The pigeons stopped pecking.

"Well, that was interesting," he thought, "but, since they all stopped, maybe I didn't need to use such a strong shock." He got the pigeons pecking the bar again, and this time he lowered the intensity of the shock. If he used fifty units the first time, now he started with twenty. The pigeons went right on pecking. So he upped the intensity to thirty. The pigeons still pecked. He went up to

Fig. 53: Round pen training in a stall: We could teach Fig all the basics of round pen training, without ever going into the stall with her.

forty. No change. "Well," he thought, "I guess I got lucky the first time. I must have started with just the right amount."

He went back up to the original fifty units, and the pigeons went right on pecking. He tried sixty, seventy, eighty, ninety units, before the pigeons finally responded and stopped pecking. By starting with a low-intensity shock and building up slowly, he had desensitized the pigeons.

I tell this story whenever I see someone tap-tapping on a horse and getting no response. They aren't being fair to that horse. They are simply desensitizing their horse and teaching it to ignore them. They may be trying to be nice, but many times they are just setting it up for a beating.

The horse learns to tune them out. The result is an out-of-control, often dangerous horse. That's when a trainer gets called in. What he encounters is horse who will run right over the top of him, and so naturally he gets out a whip. The horse is numb to a light tap, so the trainer has to really lay into it to get any response.

Most trainers do not enjoy beating up horses, but if an owner has tuned a horse out and desensitized it to normal aids, sometimes they see no other choice. The only way they can get through to these horses is by shouting. In the horse's world, shouting means hitting harder. Of course, now we have another alternative. We can talk to the horse via the clicker.

Fig had learned what we wanted without our ever creating a confrontation. Now that we were shifting into another phase of her training, I didn't want Fig to learn she could just ignore Megan.

There's a stage in training where you wait patiently for the horse to figure things out, and there's a stage where you start demanding responses. We were beginning to treat Fig more like a normal horse. She'd reached the point where we could say to her, "This is what I want, and I want it now."

Megan needed to learn how to be assertive enough to send her that message. That's hard when you've had a long history with a horse like Fig. It took several sessions before Megan got comfortable with the idea that she could be insistent with Fig, and not have Fig challenge her back. That discovery was a major breakthrough for both of them. It created a wonderful shift in their relationship. Fig became almost cuddly. Her constant need to be the herd boss evaporated. She was finally becoming comfortable taking direction from her human handler.

So far we'd been playing a wonderful game with Fig—"101 Things You Can Do in a Stall"—and it was working. During the summer she had a mild colic, and the vet wanted her temperature taken twice a day for a week. We turned even this into a training session.

We asked Fig to target on her pill container. We positioned it so her head was in the back corner of her stall, and then we used the round pen training to ask her to move her hips over against the wall. She was now standing broadside to the wall. We could climb up on a hay bale and reach over the top board to handle her.

As always, the rules of shaping still applied. We didn't start with our goal, taking her temperature. First we sacked her out from this new position. Every time you shift position, you're changing the criteria. You can't just assume the horse is all right with this. Fig had her usual first reaction to anything new. She flattened her ears and swung away from us.

We turned this session into a three-person operation. Megan held Fig's target up for her. I used her round pen training to insist that she keep her hips lined up against the wall, while Megan's mother climbed up on a hay bale so she could lean over the wall and sack her out. Fig had a clear choice. She could swing away and have me to deal with, or she could hold herself against the wall while a person she knew and liked stroked her. When she chose self-control, she got clicked. Fig melted.

Once she realized what we wanted, she didn't need to be told to stay against the wall. She was more than willing to stand quietly for a TTEAM back rub. I joined Megan's mother on the hay bale. Within minutes we were both leaning out over Fig's back. It was a truly wonderful feeling to be so completely at ease around her, and to have her answering back with so much trust. I draped myself over her hips and stroked down her hind legs. It wasn't that long ago that she would have kicked at anything that touched her. Now she was peacefully enjoying the connection.

We eased the rectal thermometer in by slow stages. We didn't need twitches or tranquilizers to get the job done; just patience, and what seemed at times like a magical clicker.

Targeting solved another sticky problem for us. Fig didn't tie. On my first visit Megan had shown me the posts Fig had broken pulling back against a tie. Fig was learning to yield to pressure. We'd taught her to lower her head and take a step forward when she felt pressure from a lead. She was learning skills that would keep her from pulling back, but I knew that old patterns die hard, especially where Fig was concerned. As an added safety measure, we taught her to target something new.

Megan hung an old plastic curry comb in her stall. It was a simple matter to reinforce Fig for touching it. The round penning skills came in handy again. We gave Fig another choice. You can touch the target and get reinforced, or you will have to move your feet around the stall. Fig chose to touch the target.

When Megan was ready to try tying her again, she added the target. Before Fig could bump the end of her tie, Megan was instructing her to target. Fig's old feeling of being trapped vanished. She was too preoccupied with touching her target. She has never again pulled back against a tie.

The world outside

I was starting to run out of ideas for things you can do in a stall. It was time to venture outside. What we really needed was a round pen, so Megan built one. She blocked off the back corner of a paddock adjoining the barn. The entire area she enclosed was only about thirty feet square. The back of the barn formed one side of the pen, and board fencing formed the rest. Megan put up a temporary barrier across the open end of the pen. It was hardly what I would call an intimidating fence line. A hard bump from Fig would have knocked the whole thing down.

If we hadn't prepared Fig with all the stall work, we would never have succeeded with this makeshift round pen. It was simply too small and too flimsy to contain a horse like Fig. The first day we put her in it, we continued to work her from the outside of the fence, just as we had in her stall. It took a little adjusting to get used to the larger space, but we soon had her doing all her inside and outside turns in perfect synchrony with our cues. The training had transferred completely to a new setting.

It was time to stop treating Fig like a shark in a tank, and step inside the round pen with her (Figs. 54a, b, c). A lunge whip might have triggered some old memories, so instead we used a lariat. Megan went in with her. She reviewed all the round pen steps, beginning with the most basic one of getting Fig to move her feet. Fig couldn't resist making an occasional ugly face, but she never charged, and she never kicked.

We used the clicker to reinforce each new layer in the training. Megan taught her to target on the lariat, and she soon had Fig following her around the enclosure like a little puppy.

We did have one scare on our third session in the round pen. The blacksmith was coming again, and we were doing some preliminary work to get Fig ready for him. Megan asked Fig to stop by the far corner of the barn. Suddenly Fig leaped toward her, bucking and pitching and throwing her front legs up in the air. Megan dodged out of her way as Fig barreled past her.

A couple of outside turns later and Fig started to settle down. Megan asked her to halt again by the barn. Fig stopped, spun on her haunches, and plunged straight at Megan, only now I could see what was happening. She was being stung by yellow jackets! The blacksmith pulled in just in time to see Fig pitching around the pen. That wasn't exactly the picture we wanted him to see of her. Talk about bad timing.

Fig's run-in with the yellow jackets was really a confirmation of her training. In spite of her panic, she had still been able to listen to Megan. She didn't charge her or threaten her as she bolted out of the corner. And ten minutes after she was stung, she stood quietly and let the blacksmith trim her feet. In an odd way, the incident told us that Fig was becoming a reliable horse to be around.

With our success in the round pen I again thought, well, here's a tidy end to the story; but Fig just kept

Fig. 54a: It was time to stop treating Fig like a shark in a tank. Megan converted part of a paddock into her round pen. Megan is using the lariat to ask for more leg speed. The old Fig would have reacted aggressively to this kind of pressure. Here she has her ear riveted on Megan, and she is circling around her at a trot.

Fig. 54b: Megan is setting Fig up for an outside turn.

Fig. 54c: Fig leading at liberty. Megan is using the lariat as a target to get Fig to lead beside her.

on writing new chapters. The round pen opened the door to riding. We put Fig back into the round pen after the yellow-jacket incident. She was working so quietly we decided it was time to saddle her up. Megan tied the plastic curry comb to the fence and asked Fig to target. Fig stood completely at liberty while Megan tacked her up and got on (Fig. 55).

It may seem like we took a long time to get to the riding, but really that's all we'd ever done with her, right from her very first lesson when we taught her to touch a target. Teaching Fig to lower her head, to yield to pressure, to understand the cues to back up and step forward, to rebalance her weight so she could pick up her feet, to listen to signals asking for turns, these are all riding skills. It didn't matter that we had taught them to her in the confines of a stall, Fig knew what we wanted.

It was a thrill watching Megan ride her that first day in the round pen. Fig's head was down, and she was soft in the bridle. She listened to everything Megan asked of her. She turned, she stopped, she walked on. She never grumped, or balked, or tried to charge off. She was a horse you could have fun with and enjoy riding (Fig. 56).

Fig offered us more surprises as we went into the fall with her. The round pen became too wet to use, so we took her up into a grass field to work her. Megan discovered that this horse, who used to charge her with her ears pinned flat, now knew how to work politely on a lunge line. She also discovered that she could turn her completely loose, and Fig would work at liberty around her. We'd gone from a tiny stall to being able to round-pen Fig in an acre or two of open space.

Megan's mother summed it up best, as she was watching Megan teach Fig the beginnings of lateral work. "It's so wonderful," she said, "to see Fig get her life back."

At the time of this writing, I've known Fig for almost a year. The horse I first met is gone. In her place is a horse who loves to come out and work. The grumpy Fig has been replaced by a horse who likes to cuddle and rest her head in the cradle of your arms. The horse I first saw used to balk at going out of the barn, and drag Megan around on the end of a lead. Now she walks next to her like a little puppy. Megan wanted more than just a horse she could ride—she wanted a horse who could be her friend. With patience, perseverance, and the right tools, she got both (Fig. 57).

Fig. 55: Fig is standing at her target while Megan saddles her up.

Fig. 56: Megan's first ride on Fig as a clicker-trained horse.

Clicker training doesn't create miracles, though at times it seems that way. Fig's story is a wonderful example of how clicker training can work. We stopped worrying about the big picture, or our long-term goals. We didn't look at all the problems confronting us. Instead we simply asked, "What can we work on today? What little piece can we teach her that will take us one step ahead?" The steps seemed small at first, and the progress slow, but the process gained momentum. Fig now has a solid base of training to draw on, and she has mastered the most important part of that process. She has learned how to learn.

TRADITION AND MOTIVATION

It's easy to get locked into one way of doing things. Traditional methods are the foundation upon which we build sound training programs, but they should not keep us from experimenting and exploring new ideas. It is human nature to want to take thought beyond and not simply repeat the ideas of the past.

I enjoy dressage, the art of teaching horses to dance. Tradition is important to dressage riders. The classical methods set a standard of performance, and a means for achieving certain goals. For each generation of riders it is important that we have trainers who focus on the teachings of the earlier masters. I value their contribution. Dressage is like ballet. It's a living art form that needs to be passed on directly from person to person. You can't preserve it just by writing about it.

Dressage is also like ballet in that it keeps growing and changing. The great ballet choreographer, George Ballanchine, did not simply repeat the dance steps of the masters he had learned from. He took them beyond, into new forms of expression. We can do the same in the horse world. We can preserve the best of our classical traditions, and at the same time we can embrace new approaches to training. That is what the great riding masters did in the past, and it is what we can continue to do in the present.

Our horses need us to stay open and innovative. Their safety and well-being depend upon it. Horses have taught me that my toolbox is never big enough. Just when I think I've learned enough to handle most situations, a horse like Fig comes along to stretch my training in new directions.

Fig. 57: Megan wanted more than just a horse she could ride, she wanted a friend. With patience, perseverance, and the right tools, she got both. Megan's mother summed it up best: "It's so wonderful," she said, "to see Fig get her life back."

CHAPTER TWENTY-TWO

Playtime: The Power of Shaping and Variable Reinforcement Schedules

BUSTER CUBES

I'm almost embarrassed to say this, but I've learned more about variable reinforcement schedules from a plastic ball than I have from practically anything else. The ball in question is a Buster Cube.

A Buster Cube is a dog toy. It's a hard plastic ball shaped very much like a giant ice cube with a hole on one side into which you pour kibble. The dog rolls the Buster Cube around, and the kibble falls out at random intervals. I first heard about Buster Cubes through the e-mail clicker list. People kept saying how wonderful they were, especially for dogs that had to be left alone. I didn't think it was fair that dogs should have all the fun, so I bought one for Peregrine.

The cube is large enough and sturdy enough to withstand a fair amount of abuse from a horse, though I suppose if a horse stood directly on it, it would crack. The only problem I encountered converting it to a horse toy was finding the right treat to put in it. Chopped up carrots got stuck. Grain fell out easily enough, but Peregrine couldn't pick it out of the sawdust footing we have in the arena. What I finally settled on were sugar cubes.

Peregrine didn't understand at first that he could just roll the cube and sugar would come out. I had to teach him. That's where the clicker came into the game. He already knew about touching cones, so getting him to touch the Buster Cube was just a matter of holding it out in front of him and saying "Touch."

The next step was to have him track the cube to the ground. I followed the same steps I did when I originally shaped touching the cone. (See Ch. 2, Getting Started with the Clicker.)

To get him to roll it I simply withheld the click. He'd bump the Buster Cube, expecting to get a click and a treat. When nothing happened, he'd bump it harder. That got a click. It was an easy step to get him to push the Buster Cube hard enough to get it to roll.

That didn't guarantee a sugar cube would come out. I continued to click and reinforce him for good efforts. When the first sugar cube fell out of the hole he found it instantly. That got his attention. He gave the Buster Cube a hard push and another sugar cube fell into the sawdust. I didn't have to click him any more after that. The game was on. Within minutes that Buster Cube had taught my horse to push and kick it all over the arena.

THE POWER OF BEING UNPREDICTABLE

The beauty of the Buster Cube is that the horse never knows when the sugar is going to fall out. It's completely random. Sometimes a simple push is all it takes, and sometimes the sugar doesn't fall out until he's rolled it around for five minutes, and kicked it like a soccer ball.

What I learned from that cube is the value of surprise and randomness. The Buster Cube is built like a nautilus shell inside. It has chambers that trap the sugar cubes. As it rolls around, some of them tumble into the central hole and fall out. The cube doesn't reinforce specific behaviors. It doesn't differentiate between a hard knock and a feeble shove; but it can still get my horse to push it all over the ring. In many ways that little hunk of plastic is a better trainer than I am.

I learned some useful lessons watching Peregrine interact with the Buster Cube. That wasn't why I originally bought it. I was hoping it would break up the monotony of winter turnout. We keep grass in our paddocks by keeping the horses off of them in bad weather. That means through the mud season the only turnout is in the indoor arena. Normally, Peregrine simply goes out and takes a nap in the middle of the ring. It's not very stimulating for either his mind or his body. So that's why I bought him a Buster Cube. Now when he goes out he can chase after sugar cubes.

You never know when you start something where it's going to take you. I've used that simple trick of touching a cone for so many different things, and now I've even used it to let my horse "graze" during the winter (Fig. 58).

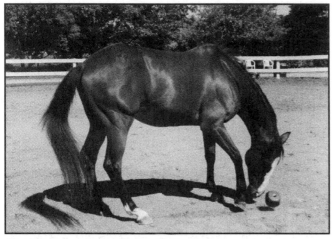

Fig. 58: Peregrine with his Buster Cube

GAMES PEOPLE PLAY: THE TRAINER'S GAME

Sooner or later I have all my clients play the Trainer's Game. It's something everyone who works with animals should experience. The trainer's game lets you experience training from the animal's point of view. I've watched hundreds of people go through it, and I've learned some very interesting things from the game.

I've seen how similar people are to the animals they train. They get frustrated and quit, just like their horses. They get stuck in patterns. They offer the same behavior over and over again even though it never gets reinforced. They do something you like, and then go off on the next trial and do something totally different. They produce the behavior you're after, without having a clue what they're doing. They do all this and yet, somehow, in the end, they always manage to end up "trained" in the behavior that's being shaped.

Through the Trainer's Game I've discovered that all these responses are a perfectly normal part of

learning. The more I play it, the more patient I become both with the horses and the people I'm trying to teach.

The rules are simple. You're going to pick a behavior to shape. It must be something that the other person would be comfortable doing. You're not going to choose something that would be embarrassing, dangerous, or physically difficult. The usual sorts of things are getting someone to walk in a circle, stand on one leg, walk backward, pick up a chair—simple behaviors like that. It's important that the person understand that the behavior is something a human can do. If they think you're trying to shape a horse behavior, you'll have trouble getting them to pick things up, or sit in a chair, or any of the other non-horsey things you may have chosen to shape.

You're going to treat your person like a dolphin in that you can't touch him. You can't mold the behavior or shape it by luring. Your only tool is the clicker and positive reinforcement. The instructions to your human subject are to move around at random. The more he moves, the more likely it is that he'll do something you can click. Each time he hears a click, he's to walk over to you for his "reward," usually a pat on the shoulder. (Horses get paid much better than humans do in this game.)

If the person gets stuck and starts asking questions, your only response should be to smile devilishly and say you don't speak horse. This is a chance for the person to experience training from the horse's perspective. He's going to discover that his horse isn't as stubborn, or as stupid, as he thought he was. Figuring humans out is not easy.

LIFE AS A "GUINEA PIG"

So what's it like to be a human in the trainer's game? Let's play it together. You're with a group of friends, and you're the first "guinea pig." You left the room earlier while they decided what they were going to get you to do. Now you've walked back in. You're not really sure what you're supposed to do, and you're feeling more than a little self-conscious.

Your "trainer" is sitting off to the side, and everyone has this expectant look of half-suppressed giggles. You walk a big circle round the room. Nothing happens. You wave your arms up and down and change directions. *Click!* Okay. You just did something. But what? You walk over to your "trainer" and she pats your shoulder. You go back into the center of the room and wave your arms. Nothing. You circle again. Nothing. You change directions. Nothing. You begin to feel anxious. What if you can't figure this out? How stupid are you going to look?

You turn around again. *Click!* Now you are truly puzzled. That doesn't seem like anything you were doing before. You get your pat and go back into the center. You try turning little circles. Nothing. You stop for a second.

"Click that! Click that!" you can hear your friends whispering to your "trainer."

You start circling again.

Click! Then you hear, "Whoops, too late."

Now what does that mean? You get your pat, and try something different. You go back to arm waving. Nothing. You try turning again. *Click!*

You get your pat, but you're still feeling totally confused. You stall out in the middle. *Click!*

"What do you want me to do?" you ask.

"I don't speak horse," responds your "trainer."

Okay, you read the directions. You knew that was coming, but this is really frustrating. Your "trainer" never seems to click the same thing twice. Maybe if you try to repeat exactly what you did the last time you were clicked, you can get a clue. You go back to where you were standing the last time. *Click!* Okay that's progress. Now what? You stand there a little longer. *Click!* and this time when you walk over to your handler you get an extra vigorous pat on the shoulder.

You go back into the middle and just stand there. "Is this what you want?"

"I don't speak horse."

This is really frustrating. You feel like screaming, or quitting, or both. Instead you take a step forward. *Click!* You get another vigorous pat. You go back to your starting point. You stand there waiting. Nothing happens so you take a step forward, then another step. *Click!* You get an extra vigorous pat and a "Good horse!" (accompanied by laughter from your other friends).

You retrace your steps, beginning at the same starting point and walking now four steps forward. Again you get a click. What is it they want? you keep wondering.

You repeat the pattern and this time you take six steps forward which brings you to the edge of a table. *Click!*

Is this what they wanted you to do? You test your theory by starting in the center of the room and walking directly over to the table. *Click!*

Okay. This is better. Only now what? You look down at the table. It's got the usual assortment of clutter on it: horse magazines, someone's hard hat, the telephone, a riding crop. Do they want you to pick up the crop? You reach for it. Nothing. You touch the magazines, the telephone, the hat. *Click!* That must be it. You collect your pat and go right back to the table. You pick up the hat. *Click!* and lots of laughter. This time you don't even bother getting your pat. You turn and look at the group. You know what it is. You pop the hat onto your head. Nothing. That wasn't it. In a sudden flash of inspiration you walk across the room and stick the hat on your "trainer's" head. Gales of laughter and major clicks! That was it!

"Okay," you say to the group. "I get it. My horse is a genius to figure out half the stuff I ask him to do. The next time he gets frustrated or stuck I'm going to be a lot more patient. I'm also going to get my revenge. Give me that clicker. It's my turn to be the trainer!" (Fig. 59).

Fig. 59: Playing the Trainer's Game: Our volunteer is being shaped to pick up the bucket, walk to the far end of the barn, fill the bucket with shavings, walk back to the other end of the barn, and dump it into a stall. We've got half the behavior. She's about to be clicked by our "trainer" for walking towards the stall. Note the horse in the background. The horses always seem to enjoy watching the people being clicker-trained.

LETTING GO OF GOALS

I've noticed that horses are often much better at playing the trainer's game than their human counterparts. They know how to learn, and to use the clues we give them to figure us out. Humans get stuck much more easily, and usually want to quit sooner. I think this is in part because they are worrying about "not getting it." They have a concept that there is some final goal that we're after, and if they don't reach that goal, they've failed. That creates a problem not just when they're playing the trainer's game, but when they're working with the horses as well.

I don't think horses operate like this. They aren't thinking, "There's some final product that I'm supposed to be learning and I'm just not getting it." When you have a clicker-trained horse, they're much more likely to be thinking, "This is fun. My person keeps clicking me. Every time I step over here, she gives me a treat. What a good deal."

I just don't see the frustration in clicker-trained horses that you see in their human counterparts. As far as the horse is concerned, at each step in the training it is being successful. There is no end product, no final goal. Those are human concepts. The horse can just relax and enjoy the treats it is earning.

I learned that, playing the trainer's game. It was my turn to be the subject, and my clients had decided to challenge me by getting me to goose step around them on a circle. I just relaxed and let go of any idea of figuring them out. If I was getting clicked, I was happy.

My human "trainer" went through all the normal range of emotions people go through trying to figure out how to create a complex pattern. She got anxious. She got frustrated. I felt none of those things. I simply enjoyed being clicked. I enjoyed walking on a circle since that so clearly pleased her. I enjoyed taking longer steps, and then lifting my feet higher and higher until I was prancing around the arena. It was, I admit, quite a sight, but it was worth it for the insights it gave me into the horse's mind.

I've played the Trainer's Game many times since then, and each time I do I learn something that makes me a better trainer. Goals do indeed drive the whole process forward, but at some point, as you move from the science into the art of training, their role changes. They become guideposts, not final destinations. Training becomes the framework within which you carry on a conversation with your horse. It is a process with no final product.

Think of a sculptor who is constantly molding and reworking his clay into the perfect sculpture. It's the feel of the material in his hands that he enjoys. It's the process of seeing the clay change and take on new forms that delights him. With horses, that's a process that never needs to come to an end.

I know many people view training as a chore, something that's in the way of their having fun. Obviously, I don't share this view. Training itself is a game, and one I very much enjoy.

Part IV

RIDING IN A STATE OF EXCELLENCE

CHAPTER TWENTY-THREE

Riding That Clicks

By now you should have a good idea of what the clicker is. It's an event marker, a tool that allows you to communicate more clearly with your horse. And it's a new way of looking at training.

When we were trying to come up with a title for the book, I asked each of my clients for suggestions. I got a number of good ideas. (The husband of one of my clients suggested "My Friend Clicker.") One client, Bob Viviano, stopped three times on his drive home from the barn. He kept thinking of more titles, and he wanted to write them all down before he forgot them. I liked his list, not because they worked as book titles, but because they formed a great description of a clicker-trained horse.

Here's a partial sampling:

A clicker-trained horse is a safe horse.

A clicker-trained horse is a happy horse.

A clicker-trained horse is a horse who listens.

A clicker-trained horse is a well-mannered horse.

Bob's horse, Crackers, has blossomed as a clicker horse. Crackers is a gorgeous, big-moving Appaloosa, but when I first saw him he was a stiff, nose-in-the-air, short-gaited, heavy-on-the-forehand, needs-a-crop-to-get-him-to-move horse. We started working together originally because of a jumping problem. At home Crackers was slow-moving, and tough to motivate, but at shows he galloped around the hunt courses, rushing all the fences. Bob wanted help regulating leg speed.

It should be no surprise that we went back to basics. We spent a year rebuilding the foundation, and in the process transformed Crackers into a stunningly beautiful horse. He's like a warm-blood in fancy dress.

My original mission with Crackers was to help him with his jumping, but as always you can never do one thing. Part of the process involved teaching Bob and Crackers lateral work. I had no idea what I was unleashing on the world when I did that. Bob has a passion for line dancing. His horse was learning some fancy footwork. Why not put the two together and teach Crackers to dance? With his clicker and a pocket full of grain he set to work to teach his horse the Electric Slide (Figs. 60, 61).

So I would add one other title to his list: "The clicker is about having fun."

IS SHE EVER GOING TO RIDE?

At this point in the book you may be saying, "This is great for Bob. I'm glad he's enjoying his horse, but when are you going to teach me how to ride with the clicker? After all, you've taught me how to hug my horse, how to lead my horse, how to load him in a trailer. You spent a whole chapter telling me how to put a bridle on, and another one teaching me how to get on. But when are we actually going to ride?"

My answer is, "I've done nothing else." Riding is simply training from the horse's back. The principles and techniques are no different just because you've put your foot in a stirrup and climbed aboard. Think about it. You're getting ready to mount, and your horse is dancing around you on the end of the lead. What do you do? You get him to move his feet. You ask him to turn and circle and step back and forth. Turn the problem into an opportunity to train, and pretty soon you'll have him light as a feather and standing still when you ask.

Your horse prances around and won't stand still under saddle. What do you do? You get him to move his feet. It's the same thing.

Fig. 60: They may not be ready for the Grand Ole Opry, but they're still having fun: Crackers and Bob giving the Double V Stables Summer Camp a lesson in country line dancing.

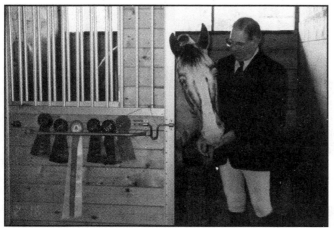

Fig. 61: And the winner is: Crackers and Bob! Can clicker-trained horses win in the show ring? Absolutely, and as clicker training becomes better known in the horse world, you'll see more and more horses doing just that.

A UNIVERSAL TOOL

There are so many different ways to ride, so many different styles. I enjoy dressage. I like to dance with my horse. But even in the dressage world there is no one way to ride, and certainly no one way to train. I know what works for me. But that doesn't mean it's the only approach. I see a lot of good riders out there, with great horses, and they aren't all doing the same thing.

What I want to emphasize here is, the clicker is a useful tool that can be applied to any and all styles of riding. The principles of shaping are fundamental to everything. The more you understand them, the better your results will be.

When people are struggling with their horses, it is usually because they have forgotten how important the foundation is. They are rushing the steps. They are asking for a finished product, but they never assembled the pieces. Many times they don't even have a clear idea of what they are trying to do. When I ask them how they tell their horse he's done something right, they have only a vague answer, or worse yet, no answer at all. They may have a seat like Velcro. They may be able to sit through the meanest buck, but they are still constantly struggling with their horses.

When I see someone with a horse that is working well, I see a patient rider: someone who has spent a lot of time teaching the basics, who has broken the training down into easy steps, who likes horses and respects their ability to learn, who wants the horse to be successful, and who has designed a program that allows the horse to learn at his own pace.

These are the real horsemen. They may not be the best "riders" out there. They may bounce out of the saddle at the trot. They may be struggling to find their balance at the canter. But they understand how to teach and communicate clear messages to their horses. This book is written for them.

So is that all I'm going to say about riding? Well, no. Actually, I've written another whole book that is specifically on riding and the clicker. That's not what I set out to do. Originally I wanted to make this all one book. I was afraid if I didn't include a riding section people might think the clicker was only for ground work. They might never transfer it to work under saddle. So I started writing about how I use the clicker, and that meant I had to talk about dressage and single-rein riding.

Once I started down that path, I knew I'd have to go the whole way and give a detailed description of the technique I use. I couldn't tell you how to incorporate the clicker into this kind of training without first explaining what it was. That meant I had to begin with basic theory. I had to explain my view that riding is a language. Once I did that I had to show you how to build the language out of pressure and releases. I had to explain what a give was, and how that lets you carry on a conversation with your horse.

This was a huge block of material to tackle, and I really wasn't sure how to go about it. Finally I just gave in and started writing. I wrote over sixty pages of text before I came up for air, and that was just the beginning. Once I began, it became like Topsy in the nursery rhyme. The material just kept growing. The solution was obvious. Create a second book: *Clicker Training for the Rider.*

"But," you're saying, "I don't want to wait for another book. I want to start riding my horse now. How do I begin?"

Riding with the clicker is easy, once your horse is responding to it from the ground. Simply climb on and ask your horse to walk off. When he's gone a few steps, click. You'll see his ears airplane around in surprise, and he may slam on the brakes.

Your horse will be confused. He's never been clicked under saddle before. What did he do? Where is the vending machine? How does he get to you?

Fig. 62a: You met Calvin in the section on trailering. Here we're using the clicker under saddle. He's softening beautifully into a lateral flexion, so . . .

Fig. 62b: Click! He's going to be rewarded for his efforts. Note his rider is giving him his treat on the side to which he was bent.

He may start turning or backing, trying to figure out how to reach his treat. Help him out. Draw his head around to the side with the rein and hand him his treat. Remember to reward him on the side to which he was bent. If you were working on the left rein, feed him from the left (Figs. 62a, b).

Some horses will just keep walking when you click. If you see no response at all, if the horse doesn't flick his ears or show any other signs that he heard your click, that probably means he doesn't really understand the clicker yet. You need to go back and do more ground work with him. Once you think he's really caught on to the game, you can try again.

With some horses it can help to have a friend assist you from the ground. Have her give you a pony ride. Get on your horse, but let her lead you around. Your friend is going to ask your horse for some of the same work you've taught him from the ground. Let her cue him to back, or to move his hips to the side. When he responds correctly, click him and have the ground person give him a treat. Gradually transfer everything over to the rider. Once your horse has made the connection with the rider's signals, you won't need your assistant any more.

Another variation on the theme is that the horse will noticeably startle when you click, but he won't stop. He's telling you with his ears that he heard the click and he understands what it means, but he thinks he has to keep going. He doesn't know that he can stop and get his treat. Use your regular riding cues to bring him to a halt. Draw his head to the side and give him a treat. After you've done this a couple of times, most horses will stop on their own after the click.

STOPPING

That raises an issue many riders will have with the clicker. They don't want their horse to stop. It's all right on the ground, but under saddle they've been taught the horse should keep going. Stopping to get a treat goes against everything they've learned.

This issue comes up most frequently with riders who are working the canter. Suppose you got interested in the clicker primarily because your horse has trouble picking up his leads. You're thinking this sounds like a useful addition to the toolbox. You'd like to have a clear way to tell your horse he's done well. So you've taught your horse to touch a cone, and you've done some preliminary ground work. He clearly understands the clicker. The first time you clicked him under saddle he did exactly as I described. His ears airplaned around, and he came to a stop.

You want to get right to work on your main problem, so you ask him to canter. He picks up the wrong lead the first couple of times, but, on the corner, he finally gets the right lead. You click him, and he slams on the brakes. You weren't prepared for such a sudden stop, and you end up wrapped around his ears.

At this point you're probably thinking: "This is no good. Once he's cantering, I want him to keep going. If I keep stopping him, how is he ever going to learn to stay in the canter?"

You're forgetting about variable reinforcement schedules. Think about how we shaped everything else we've worked on. When we asked our horses to back up, we were satisfied at first if they just shifted their weight. That shift in weight very quickly became a full step back, and then two or three steps, until finally you could back them any distance you wanted.

You're going to work the same way under saddle. When you ask the horse to pick up the correct lead, you're really focusing on the transition. Staying in the canter is another criterion. The rules of shaping tell us to focus on one criterion at a time.

Once you're horse is consistently picking up the correct lead, you can add a second criterion—staying in the canter. Instead of clicking him right away, you'll withhold the click for a stride or two. If he goes back to a trot, that's okay. Every time he breaks gait, he's just giving you another opportunity to work on transitions. The more you practice transitions, the better he'll get. When he finally gives you those extra couple of strides you were looking for, that's when you'll click him. He'll quickly learn that if he wants to get reinforced he has to stay in the canter.

Once he's consistently cantering on, you can add other criteria, such as head elevation, correct bend, changes of leg speed and direction. In this way, step by step, you can build a solid canter.

The key to using the clicker under saddle is to break down every exercise into tiny steps. Use the goal-setting section to help you design a lesson plan for your riding. The steps you put in will vary with each horse, and will depend very much on your riding background and level of experience. I know that if I'm having trouble getting my horse to do something, the problem is never in the layer of the training I'm working on. It is always because my horse is not understanding an underlying step. I need

to go back in the training and add in the pieces we missed along the way. For me the solution to teaching correct canter leads begins in the walk, and even before that with good ground work.

CHAPTER TWENTY-FOUR

Breaking Down Resistance: Three Problems, One Solution

I once heard a clinician state that riding was bad for horses. Her premise was that horses are basically built like suspension bridges, and we sit in the weakest part of the bridge. The result is that, over time, we break down the back. Her belief was that everyone who rides needs to accept the idea that, starting from day one in the saddle, they are crippling their horse.

My experience has been just the opposite. I am used to seeing the older horses I work with regain the flexibility in their joints that age and use were beginning to take away. It isn't riding that cripples horses. It's resistance.

John Lyons has three rules of training. The person can't get hurt. The horse can't get hurt. And the horse has to be calmer at the end of the lesson than it was at the beginning. I would add a fourth, though it is really just an extension of the other three. The horse must be sounder as a result of the riding than he was before. Good riding should not break down horses.

In 1994 Peregrine contracted Potomac horse fever. The long term effects of that almost put an end to his riding career. He spent most of 1996 confined to his stall with his feet wrapped in bandages. I had one of the top blacksmiths in the country helping us with him, but we just couldn't get him comfortable. As his confinement stretched into the fall, I watched his beautiful riding muscles waste away.

In November, a film crew from the BBC contacted me. They were doing a series on animal intelligence and were interested in clicker training. They wanted to come film what I was doing with the horses. On the day they came, Peregrine had been back at work for less than a week after a lay up of almost nine months. He had no muscle tone. He looked terrible.

All his beautiful topline had melted away with the stall rest. And yet, when the film crew came, he was able to go in the ring and work for over three hours! He never got tired. He never got grumpy. He put on a wonderful performance, much of it involving a very high level of collection. How could he do so much, when he'd done nothing but stand in a stall? Simple. He had no resistance.

RESISTANCE COMES FROM THREE SOURCES, PHYSICAL, MENTAL, AND EMOTIONAL.

Physical resistance

Peregrine embodies physical resistance. That's what his stifles created. To experience just a little of what it used to be like to be Peregrine, try this little experiment. Shake out your arm so your fingers, wrist, elbow, and shoulder are nice and loose. Now move your arm up and down. Do you feel how free and easy that is?

Next lock your elbow and shake your arm. There's a big difference, isn't there? When you stiffen your elbow, your whole arm locks up. You can barely move.

Now imagine what it must have been like to be Peregrine. When his stifles locked, it stiffened his spine, it locked up his shoulders, it clamped up his jaw. Every joint in his body was affected, and he had no control over when this happened. It wasn't something he did deliberately. It was a mechanical result of the way he carried his spine and pelvis, but it created resistance throughout his entire body.

Physical resistance is at the heart of many of our riding problems. It may not be as extreme or as obvious as it was with Peregrine, but it can still create problems for the horse.

Mental resistance

Another form of resistance is mental. The horse simply doesn't understand what it's being asked. Think about what that feels like. Remember the last time you were in a riding lesson, and you just didn't have a clue what your instructor was talking about? You wanted to please her. You were trying really hard, but you just couldn't get the right response from your horse.

We've all been there. Didn't you get stiff and resistant? The more your instructor pushed and tried to make you do the thing you're struggling with, the more rigid you became. I've certainly encountered this with clients I'm trying to teach. I'll find I've jumped ahead too many steps. Maybe it's the fourth time that day I've presented the same exercise, and I've left out some critical piece of the explanation. I'm assuming they already know what I want. Why aren't they getting this? It's clear to me. Why can't they see the pattern in their head? Why can't they feel the horse's response? Aargh! Resistance.

Does this sound familiar? We do it to our horses all the time. Haven't we all at some point wanted to scream at our horse for his seeming stupidity? You just feel like you're going to explode with frustration. "Why aren't you getting this?" you want to shout. "You were doing it yesterday!"

That may well be, but he may not have understood what he was doing well enough to recall it today. If you're not sure how that can happen, go play the trainer's game. (See p. 150, Games People Play.)

Emotional resistance

The third form of resistance is emotional. The horse understands the lesson. He's a wonderful athlete, sound, agile, full of energy. He's more than capable of giving you anything you want; but the ice is falling off the arena roof, or his best buddy just left the ring, or you just turned toward home, five miles out on the trail. Your horse is disintegrating into an explosive bundle of nerves. He's jumping out of his skin. You can barely sit him, and just a moment ago he was everybody's dream horse. You ask him to pay attention, and all you get is an explosive temper tantrum.

THREE ISSUES—ONE SOLUTION

By now it's probably a surprise to no one that the answer to each of these scenarios is the same thing: Chunk down your training, and apply the principles of shaping.

It doesn't matter whether your horse is having a physical collapse, a mental breakdown, or an emotional meltdown, the answer is the same. Chunk down your lesson. That's good news really, because these elements are usually so intimately connected it's hard to know what the root issue really is. Peregrine's physical problems created mental and emotional problems. I couldn't work on one without working on the other two, and I had to resolve all three elements before I could have a reliable riding horse.

What you discover when you take the time to break training down into small steps is that there are no limits. Whatever the lesson, whatever the difficulties, you can always break it down into smaller steps, and, if you need to, you can break those steps into smaller steps. Eventually, you will find the place where you can be successful, and you can build from there.

I know this because of the horses I have had as my teachers. Peregrine's mother was injured in a handling accident just before I bought her. I didn't know it at the time. She passed her prepurchase exam, but the spinal-cord damage she sustained left her with only very limited feeling in her hind legs. She couldn't tell where the ground was.

Conventional wisdom said I would never be able to ride her safely, but ride her I did. We went tiny step by tiny step, from a frightened horse who could barely stand, to the horse who introduced me to dressage. She was the first horse I ever taught to piaffe. We couldn't start with our goal. In fact, when we began all we had was a shattered dream and a horse who needed help just walking out of her stall.

We focused on whatever issues arose on any given day. If she stumbled and panicked stepping over the half inch sill of her stall door, that's what we worked on. If she couldn't walk over a ground pole, I put a rope on the ground. When even that was too much for her, I drew lines in the dirt. We just kept working away at whatever she needed, and gradually her balance improved.

So how do you begin? That's easy. Let the horse guide you. Recognize that a problem is not something bad. Your horse is not trying to embarrass you in front of all your friends. He doesn't hate you. He's not trying to get even. Horses don't think like that. Stiffness and resistance are just his way of telling you that he can't handle whatever it is you're asking him to do. It doesn't matter if he's done it successfully five hundred times before. Today he can't, and he needs you to chunk it down for him. Throughout the pages of this book you've been learning how to do just that.

Part V

NOAH'S ARK:
THE CLICKER IS NOT
JUST FOR HORSES

CHAPTER TWENTY FIVE

Dogs and Cats

Fig. 63: The clicker is not just for horses.

THE CLICKER IS NOT JUST FOR HORSES

The clicker is not just for horses. Let me repeat that. The clicker is not just for horses (Fig. 63).

Now that should seem obvious, but I discovered something very curious about clicker training. Many of the people using it seemed to have tunnel vision.

Most of my horse clients also own dogs. I was used to their rambunctious canines bounding out to greet me. Their owners would be shouting at them to get down, and the dogs would ignore them. Jumping on me was much more fun than listening to their owners.

I love dogs. I love their enthusiasm, and their zest for life. But when a dog comes charging across a muddy barnyard and leaps up at me before I'm even out of the car, I start thinking about training. I ask my clients if they had thought about clicker-training their dogs, and their reactions are always the same.

They look at me in surprise and say "Oh, does this work with dogs? Do you really think they'd learn it as well?"

Talk about irony. Here they were using the clicker with their horses and completely forgetting where it had come from. I first learned about clicker training by watching Karen Pryor and Gary Wilkes's dog training videos. Of course, this stuff works on dogs! And it also works on goldfish, and iguanas.

The clicker works. Period. If you have a pet hamster and you want to train it, the clicker works. If you have a goat or a chicken, the clicker works. All you have to do is take the principles outlined in this book and apply them to whatever animal it is you want to train. You may not be asking your parrot to accept a bridle, but the basic rules for shaping behavior will be the same no matter what the species is.

LI WU LEARNS TO STAND

Li Wu, my friend Pat Richute's Rottweiler, is a magical dog, one of life's angels. She's a happy, joyful, fun-loving spirit. Li Wu was the kind of puppy everyone fell in love with; she was so beautiful, so utterly charming. When she came wiggling up to you with her bright puppy smile, you couldn't help but laugh. As she grew older, her rambunctious, high-energy greetings became an issue. Not everyone was comfortable having a Rottweiler charge up to them. Pat was faced with the challenge of training her dog without crushing her joyful nature.

Many people are put off by rambunctious dogs, but I've learned from the horses to value energy. You have to have movement to train. That "flighty" Arabian spinning around the arena may actually be an easier horse to work with than the sluggish horse who doesn't want to move. You never, ever want to get mad at movement. That's the essential ingredient you need for all training, no matter what the method.

Li Wu's energy might have seemed like an obstacle, but it really made her very easy to work with. She offered so much behavior to choose from. Pat started with basic obedience. Teaching Li Wu to sit was easy. She taught it the way Gary Wilkes shows on his videos. She held a treat over Li Wu's head. As Li Wu looked up, her rear end went down. Without ever being touched, she was sitting. *Click!* She got a treat, and within a few repetitions, she was well on the way to understanding "Sit." Easy.

Fig. 64: With a little help from the clicker, Li Wu discovered how to balance in the "beg" position.

Pat used the clicker to reinforce "come" and to teach leading. Basic obedience work was a snap with a puppy like Li Wu, she was so eager to please. Pat gave Li Wu some new things to learn. She decided to teach her to "beg" by getting her to balance on her hindquarters.

She started the same way she did for the sit. She held a treat up over Li Wu's head. Li Wu plunked her bottom down on the floor. Pat held the treat a little higher. Li Wu stretched her neck up. *Click!* She got a treat. On the next trial Pat held it a little higher. Li Wu reached up with a front paw, lost her balance, and toppled over sideways.

Pat asked her to try again. Li Wu lifted her paw up, and Pat managed to click her before she lost her balance. On the next trial, she wasn't so lucky. Li Wu toppled sideways. Pat held the treat up again. Li Wu stared at it and very deliberately shifted her hips so her hindquarters were directly under her. This time when she lifted her front paw, she kept her balance. Without any prompting from Pat she had discovered what was needed in order to balance on her hind end. That's the real power and magic of the clicker (Fig. 64).

When Pat told me this story a couple of days later, I could still feel her excitement as she told me how Li Wu had figured out how to shift her hind end. It wasn't so much what Li Wu had done that made this story worth telling. Lots of people have taught their dogs to "beg." What makes this story important is the thrill Pat felt when she saw her dog solve the puzzle. That's what gets people hooked on clicker training.

MAGGIE

Pat's experience made me wish I had a dog to train, but not enough to actually want to own one. Getting up at dawn to walk a dog is not my idea of fun. But I like working with other people's dogs, and I am grateful to all my clients who have let me explore clicker training with their canine companions.

Maggie is one of the dogs I have worked with. Like Li Wu, Maggie is a rambunctious, nonstop bundle of high energy. She's a husky mix, a perfectly beautiful dog. She lives near the stable where I keep Peregrine, so I had seen her many times taking her young owner for walks. Maggie gave pulling on a lead a whole new meaning. I'm sure she could have hauled a fully loaded sled all by herself without any help from the rest of the team (Fig. 65).

Fig. 65: Maggie showing off her sled dog heritage.

I had my first real encounter with her when Kelly, her twelve-year-old owner, brought her to the barn for a 4-H obedience class. Maggie had a wonderful time dragging Kelly around the arena. It looked more like a lesson in water skiing than dog-walking. The instructor had to get the class organized. She couldn't give them the one-on-one assistance they needed. Kelly spent the next forty-five minutes in a losing battle trying to keep Maggie away from the other dogs. Finally, at the end of the evening the instructor took a young shepherd mix and Maggie aside for some individual work. She put prong collars on both of the dogs and instructed their owners on how to use them.

Prong collars for dogs are like chains on lead ropes for horses. They both use pain as a motivator, and, yes, they do give you quick control. In a group situation like this I can certainly understand why an instructor would choose to use them. I have to say I've used chain leads on horses, and I've found them to be very effective. I also know I've become a better trainer ever since I packed mine away in the bottom of my tack trunk.

That's how I feel about prong collars. They certainly do give you control in an emergency situation, but if you really want to learn about training, try packing them away in the same trunk as your chain lead and leverage bits.

I talked with the instructor after the class. She was very open to having me help with Maggie. As long as Maggie was lunging out at every dog who got close to her, she'd be disrupting the rest of the class. Over the weekend Kelly brought Maggie over

to the barn, and we began the process of teaching Maggie to associate the clicker with treats and behavior. We used a dressage whip as a target. I held it up above her nose and clicked her every time she bumped into it.

Maggie's attention was everywhere and nowhere in that first session. She was delighted with the treats—peanut butter on squishy white bread. She didn't wait to be offered. She jumped up on me, grabbing at my hands and pulling on my jacket. I was used to horses, who are generally much more polite about treats. It was a real exercise in discipline to ignore her needle sharp teeth raking across my knuckles.

At the end of the session, I helped Kelly lead her home. Maggie started into her sled-dog routine. I wasn't having it. If a thousand-pound horse can walk on the end of a lead without pulling, a seventy-pound dog certainly could.

I started off in a very deliberate pattern. I'd walk two steps, click, and halt like a post. I just planted myself in the ground. No matter how much Maggie pulled, I wasn't budging. It was no contest. I've held on to too many oversized equines to be pulled off my feet by a dog Maggie's size.

I took two more steps, clicked, and halted again. I kept repeating this pattern as we inched our way past the horse paddocks. Maggie kept pulling. I ignored her and kept my rhythm. Two steps, click, halt. Two steps, click, halt. She began to anticipate the stop. I could feel her pulling a little less. We got past the barn and the horses, and Maggie started to relax. She was actually waiting for me.

I lengthened her out to three steps. Four steps was too much for her. She just reverted right back to pulling. So we walked her home three steps at a time.

Kelly and I worked once more together before the next obedience class. It wasn't enough to prepare either one of them for an arena full of dogs, but we plunged in anyway. I spent the evening being a post. My job was to hold onto Maggie and keep her from lunging at the other dogs. Kelly's job was to do the actual training.

I'm not a dog trainer. You have to work with what you know, and that meant we treated Maggie like a horse. The rest of the class was working on getting their dog's attention. I chose a different starting point. We asked Maggie to move her feet.

The round pen training has taught me that attention may be the first thing you want, but it's the last thing you get. Asking Maggie to look at us in a ring full of other dogs seemed like an impossible task. With horses you begin by asking for movement, so that's what we did with Maggie. We played a simple game of come.

Gary Wilkes describes this game in his *Click and Treat* video. He calls it "Hansel and Gretel play Ping Pong." I started the game by first running backward. Maggie was only too delighted to chase after me. As she approached, I clicked and dropped a treat on the ground directly in front of her. She wolfed it down. I ran a few more steps back, clicked and dropped another treat.

Next I had Kelly call her and then run backward and drop a treat. I followed behind giving Maggie plenty of slack on her lead, but not so much that I couldn't reel her in instantly if she got distracted by another dog. Maggie thought our new game was great fun, and certainly worth leaving the other dogs for.

Now it was my turn to call Maggie. I ran backward and called her to me. Maggie turned and came bounding after me. Click, she got her bread crumb, or in this case, her peanut-butter-and-jelly sandwich.

We took turns back and forth for about five minutes or so, calling her to us. When she started focusing more on us than the other dogs, we found a quiet corner and started teaching her to sit. I held a treat over her head to lure her into position. Maggie plunked her bottom down and looked at us with total attention, for about two seconds. But that was long enough for me to click her and give her a treat. We worked on sits for just a few minutes, and then put her back into motion.

Maggie was a high-energy dog, with no ability to focus. She was like working with a young Thoroughbred. Get the feet in motion, give them lots to do, and the rest will come. By the end of the evening Maggie was sitting long enough for us to take a couple of steps back from her. She was holding the sit even when other dogs came fairly close to her. She would still drag you off without a moment's notice, but the rudiments of self-control were beginning to take shape.

The 4-H class ran only for four weeks, not long enough to make a lasting difference in Maggie. After the classes ended Kelly and I kept working together. I was enjoying being a surrogate dog owner. Over the weeks we began to see a definite change in Maggie. She was still an exuberant, joyful dog, but

Fig. 66: Maggie during a clicker training session.

she was also learning how to focus and control herself (Fig. 66).

She no longer grabbed at your hands for treats. She wasn't tugging at your sleeves trying to get you to play, or jumping up to grab at your jacket. She had learned how to hold a down-stay even when someone new walked into the room. Kelly bought a Gentle Leader, a form of head halter for dogs, which put an end to the pulling. Now she could go for walks without feeling as if she were water skiing. Maggie was learning to be a successful companion. Having the clicker in her life made her a much easier dog to be around.

Maggie and Li Wu clearly demonstrated that the clicker is a great tool for teaching basic pet obedience, but I'm sure the question many of you will be asking is—can you use it to win in the show ring? The answer is an emphatic yes. It's being done all the time. Clicker training is helping dogs win in the breed and the obedience rings. It's being used to train search and rescue dogs and service dogs of all kinds.

To begin training your own dog, I would suggest as a "must read" Karen Pryor's book *Don't Shoot the Dog* and Morgan Spector's *Clicker Training for Obedience: Shaping Top Performance Positively.* For videos and more ideas and resources, see Appendix C. As time goes on, more books will be written to guide you through every step of performance dog training. At the heart of them all will be the basic principles of shaping. Understand those, and you can train anything.

CATS

I think cats are easy to train. There, I said it. But then, I'm a cat person. I don't really care if my cats sit on the furniture or sun bathe on the kitchen counter. Most of the things people don't want their cats to do are, to me, just part of their charm.

Cats are such easy animals to have around. You don't have to housebreak them. They do that themselves. I suppose you could train your cat to walk on a leash, but it's not as important as it is for a dog or a horse. That said, let me share four pieces of training that will make living with your cat very much easier: targeting, variable reinforcement schedules, sound discs, and, of course, clicker training.

TARGETING

Cats naturally target. Anyone who has ever played with a cat knows this. Dangle a piece of string in front of your kitten, and it will chase it. You can use targeting to teach your cats to "heel" and to come when they're called.

Most cats will come when you call them. The only problem is they come in cat time. Anyone who has ever lived with a cat knows what I mean by that.

Dog people go to the back door to call in their dog, and they stand there expecting an immediate response. Cat people go to the back door, call their cat, and then go fix themselves a cup of tea. They know puss is on her way in. She's just coming in cat time, which is very different from people time. She heard you, and she is coming, but first she has to chase down that rustling leaf, leave a message for her neighbor, and make sure the chipmunks have been behaving. She has a dozen other little chores that have to be attended to before she can present herself at the back door. You can usually count on a lag time of at least fifteen minutes or so, just long enough for you to get your tea and settle down with a book in your favorite chair. That's exactly the moment when she'll arrive at the back door and begin meowing plaintively, demanding your immediate attention.

If you'd like to change the way this game is played, you can do it with a little target training. You don't have to turn this into a formal training session. Just pick your cat's favorite chase toy and get her in the habit of following it as you move around the house. (By the way, horse owners have a wonderful source for cat toys. The plastic strips that seal supplement

Fig. 67: Wendy the Wonder Cat, Catherine Crawmer's agility-trained cat.

containers make the best chase toys. Check out your Strongid C container next time you open one. It's just like opening a box of breakfast cereal. You get two great toys inside every lid.)

My target-trained cats follow me everywhere I go around the house, and they come instantly when they're called. It's very much like the target training you can do with dogs, only even easier. All you have to do is play with your kitten, and you'll be teaching it to heel and to come.

You can formalize this with the clicker. Simply hold the target up in front of your cat, and click each time she bats at it. Once your cat has learned to associate touching the target with treats, you can use the clicker to train specific behaviors. Catherine Crawmer began by teaching her clicker-trained cat to jump on a stool, and extended the behavior to include all the obstacles in a dog agility course. Her cat is featured in Karen Pryor's wonderful video, *Clicker Magic* (See Bibliography and Resources). If you don't believe cats can be trained, you need to watch this cat race over the course under Catherine's direction (Fig. 67).

VARIABLE REINFORCEMENT SCHEDULES

Cats are themselves wonderful trainers. I think in part that's why I appreciate them so much. I have always enjoyed watching good trainers train, and cats are certainly among the best. They are masters at organizing their households exactly as they like them. When I'm explaining variable reinforcement schedules for the first time to someone, I usually tell them about a lesson I learned from one of my cats.

This cat would start out the night curled up at the foot of my bed, taking his half out of the middle in classic cat style. Around one in the morning, he'd decide it was time to leave. He'd wake me up with his persistent scratching at the bedroom door. Now at one in the morning I am not the most solicitous owner, especially in January when the house is cold. My first response to his scratching was simply to shove a pillow over my ears and hope he'd give it up.

No such luck. He just kept on scratching. I would start to think maybe he really did need to go out. What if he had to get to his cat box? I'd resist for another minute or two, and then invariably I'd get up and let him out. The next night we'd repeat the same scenario. No matter how long I held out, he always outlasted me. He was a better trainer than I was. Without fail, I would eventually get up and let him out.

That was before I read Karen Pryor's *Don't Shoot the Dog* and learned about variable reinforcement schedules. What a classic example. The longer I held out, the more I guaranteed that he would keep on trying the next time.

That cat taught me a lot, and one of the most important lessons was that these principles are real. It's like gravity. Someone may argue it doesn't exist, but if you throw an apple up in the air, it is going to fall down. I wasn't thinking about variable reinforcement schedules, and certainly my cat wasn't either, but I had inadvertently taught him to scratch all night long.

How did I solve the problem? Well, when I added two kittens to the household, I put a cat box in my bedroom. Since I knew the older cat had access to the same box, I wasn't worried about his needing to go out. Now I could outlast his scratching, and, since unreinforced behaviors tend to diminish with time, he eventually learned that doors stay closed at night.

FISHER SOUND DISCS

Inevitably, when you are talking with someone about cats and training, the question of "how not to" comes up. How do I get my cat not to scratch the furniture; not to jump on the kitchen counter; not to climb the living-room curtains.

The standard answer that you will read in most cat training books is use a water gun. When the cat starts to scratch, you spritz him with a shot of water. I have to admit, I have tried this. I never thought I would use water on a cat, but when my kittens joined the household, I decided they were going to be strictly inside cats. That in itself wasn't a problem, until they decided their favorite scratching post was the newly reupholstered living room couch. To keep the peace in the house I filled a dose syringe with water and kept it at the ready.

A solid spritz on their shoulders did indeed send them scooting out of the room, but it had two major drawbacks. First, I had to be in the same room as the cat. And second, I needed to be a fairly decent shot. I usually just ended up getting water all over the good furniture, and the cat kept on scratching.

That's when I started experimenting with John Fisher's sound discs. (See Ch. 21, Crossing the Line into Aggression.) I had seen Fisher's video and was intrigued by the idea. I learn by experimenting. If an idea interests me, I play with it. I see what it does, and how the animals react. If I like it, I add it into the mix. If I don't care for the results, I just say, well, it may work for that person, but it's not a match with me.

The Fisher sound discs were intriguing. On the video John shows how to condition a dog to them using food. The discs become an aversive stimulus. You drop the disc, and the animal immediately stops whatever it was doing and leaves the area. On the tape he used the disc to stop a dog from jumping up on visitors, and another from running out a door.

I decided to try it with my cats. One of the kittens loved cookies, so I started with her. I broke off a tiny corner of a biscuit she was particularly fond of and offered it to her. She gobbled it right down and came back for more. I set the next crumb down on the floor. As she went for it, I dropped the sound disc and snatched the crumb away. The discs fell onto a flagstone floor so their effect was indeed startling. She jumped back several inches.

I offered her another crumb on the floor. She hesitated, and then tried to grab it. I dropped the discs and snatched up the food. She jumped back under a chair, but again approached the food when I set it down a third time. I dropped the sound discs, and she jumped back.

The next time I offered her the food from my hand. She took her crumb without showing any signs of fear. So far so good. I put another crumb on the floor. She hesitated. I waited. She hung back for another second or two, then tried to grab it. I dropped the sound discs, and she scooted from the room. Interesting.

I had a chance to test the sound discs a short time later. I was in the kitchen when I heard her scratching the living room couch. I stayed right where I was and dropped the sound discs. Instant silence. She came scooting past me and disappeared down the basement stairs.

Over the next few days I repeated this, and I discovered several things that I liked. First, the sound discs continued to work, even days after the initial conditioning. I was concerned that the effect might diminish with time, but, if anything, it seemed to intensify.

Second, the cats never showed any fear or resentment. When I dropped the discs, they would scoot out of the room, but they never ran away from me. The sound discs stopped the behavior, but I didn't see any adverse emotional reactions.

Third, and this was something I liked very much, I could use the sound discs to stop a behavior without getting angry myself. I wasn't yelling at the cat and telling it "No!"—I was simply dropping sound discs. I could do that without getting emotional.

Another interesting point—when I conditioned both kittens to the discs, I could say one cat's name, drop the discs, and only the cat I had spoken to would respond. The other cat might be in the same room with us, but it showed no reaction whatever to the sound.

So, did the cats stop scratching the furniture? Well, no. Do you remember the ninth method in Ch. 7, Nine Easy Steps to the Perfect Horse? Learn to live with it. Furniture scratching just didn't bother me enough to make me consistent. The cats eventually resumed their scratching, and I basically just accepted it. My cats, it turns out, really are better trainers than I am.

CLICKER TRAINING CATS

Are my cats clicker-trained? Yes, and it's proven to be much more fun and effective as a training tool

Fig. 68: Lucy: my clicker-trained cat.

than either water pistols or sound discs. I clicker-trained my youngest kitten, Lucy, when she started to be a pest at breakfast. She wanted to share my morning toast. I'm all for indulging my cats, but I know from experience that this was not a habit I wanted to encourage.

The first time Lucy started pestering me at breakfast I introduced the clicker. I taught her to sit. I did it the same way you do a dog. I baited her with a bit of food. Her little nose went up in the air, and her hind end sat down. *Click!* She got her treat.

Cats being cats, it took her a few minutes to eat it. She finished her crumb and started sniffing around my plate for more. I baited her with another piece of bread. She sat. I clicked. We repeated this twice more before she lost interest and jumped down. Over the next week, every time she came over to check out my breakfast I'd ask her to sit. We'd do three or four trials. I'd get my sit and she'd get her tidbit of bread. By the end of the week she was sitting consistently on a verbal command, and her attention was focused entirely on me, not my morning toast.

Food begging has never been a problem with her. If she wants a nibble of something I'm eating, instead of mugging my plate, she politely sits and waits. Once I reward her a time or two for a good sit, she's satisfied and goes away. Now that's behavior I can live with (Fig. 68).

CHAPTER TWENTY-SIX

The Rest of the Barnyard

GOATS

Goats, rabbits, ducks, and geese are all frequent barnyard companions for our horses, and they all can be clicker-trained. Goats in particular seem to me to be the perfect candidates for clicker training. They're active, curious, and highly food-motivated. The sad thing is, many of the goats I have met have been bored, frustrated animals that get into trouble whenever they're turned loose. Their owners simply do not give them enough to do.

I had my first goat-training experience not too long ago. I was working with an Arabian whose only companion was a goat. During our training sessions the owner tied Goaty out on the lawn to keep her out of the way. Goaty hated leaving her horse. She hated being taken away from all the fun. Her owner would grab her by the collar and literally drag her out to the tie. I watched this a time or two, thinking how much easier it would be just to clicker train her.

On my next visit, I had some extra time, so I taught Goaty to target on a whip. The goat thought this clicker-training stuff was a wonderful game. She was delighted to touch the whip. What else would we like her to do? Spin in a circle? Stand on her hind legs? She was much easier to train than her equine companion, who offered very little behavior by comparison.

The next week I began the session by asking the goat to follow my target out to her stake. It took about ten minutes that first day, but there was no wrestling, no tug of war, no dragging her out from the barn. She got an extra jackpot when she let me hook her collar to her tie, and I left her happily munching a handful of breakfast cereal.

Training isn't really about teaching animals fancy tricks. First and foremost, it's about making it easier, safer, and less stressful for people and animals to coexist. Yes, you can drag a goat out to a tie, but why would you want to? It's so much easier just to teach her to walk out to it on her own.

LLAMAS

I met my first llama back in 1984. I was helping Linda Tellington-Jones at a TTEAM clinic. We were just finishing up the weekend training when Linda was invited by one of the participants to come stay overnight with her and meet her herd of llamas. Linda had the time, so a batch of us piled into our cars and drove two hours south to the farm of Marty McGee. That was Marty's first introduction to TTEAM, and from that meeting she went on to become a TTEAM practitioner and to introduce Linda's alternative handling methods into the llama world.

I had never really been around llamas before. The first thing I discovered about them was that they look like overgrown stuffed toys that you just want to cuddle and hug. The second thing that I learned was that they hate to be touched.

Marty had several very stand-offish animals, one in particular that was a rescue case, a very nervous young male. Llamas hum when they're feeling stress. As we crowded into the small barn where the llamas were kept, we heard a lot of humming.

When Linda works with horses, it's like watching pure magic. They just melt in her presence. She can take a terrified, aggressive horse that is wheeling around on the end of a lead, trying to kick anything that comes within range; and within minutes it will be standing quietly with its head down, its eyes dreamy, a picture of total relaxation.

I sat perched up on a hay bale and watched while she introduced herself to the llama. I wouldn't have had a clue where to begin, but Linda seemed to know instinctively what to do. She eased her way past the llama's defenses. She simply flowed past its fears. The humming stopped. The llama relaxed. It let Linda touch her. It let her move her hands over its head and neck. Marty was astounded. Not only was this llama letting someone touch it, it was actually enjoying it!

Those were the first llamas I encountered. I've met others since. I find llamas to be fascinating and frustrating animals. Horses enjoy their human companions. They appreciate all the grooming and the attention. The llamas I was bumping up against didn't. If you reached out toward them, they would scamper away. They shared a different kind of relationship with their people, but one that could be deepened through clicker training.

Ron and Sue Ailsby understand this. They've been clicker training llamas with great success. Any animal that we keep as a domestic pet must tolerate a certain amount of handling. Ron and Sue have learned how to make that contact pleasant for the llama with the clicker.

In a post to the e-mail clicker list, Sue captured beautifully the real power of the clicker. She was talking about a training session where she was teaching the llamas to target on her hand. In order to be offered the food dish she was holding in her right hand, they had to first bump her left hand.

Sue wrote: "With many of these animals, this is the first voluntary touching of humans they have ever done. Other people have talked about the calm that descends on a dog when the universe becomes coherent—this happens with the llamas, as well.

"I have a five-year-old female I purchased last spring. I'm positive she had never considered humans to be coherent; all she could do was try to get away before something awful happened. At one point she stood between my two hands swinging her muzzle back and forth, wanting the food, but knowing she couldn't grab for it, not wanting to voluntarily touch my hand but knowing that was the only way to get to the oats . . . Finally, she made the correct decision, touched my hand, got the click, and started to swing back for the oats . . . but stopped in the middle and just stared at my face for a moment. Her ears were relaxed, her face was calm and sweet (the first time I had seen her face relaxed). She slowly reached forward and smelled my face (!!!) then went back to the dish and ate her oats. A magic moment! 'Grateful for the information, really.'"

Jim Logan is another llama breeder and trainer who uses clicker training. Jim has produced an excellent video, *Click and Reward*, on llama training. When I asked Jim to share some of his experiences with llamas, he sent me the following essay.

"We have come from over fifteen years of training llamas using traditional, correction-based training techniques. We were not an easy sell for clicker training! Skeptical? Very much so! The results on our llamas have been dramatic—after two years of clicker training llamas, we are 150% convinced this training method has real value. The mental attitude of our animals has dramatically changed, with our llamas actually wanting to be taught!

"The biggest difference that we see is how relaxed and happy the llamas are when we are using this type of training. They are totally focused on the task at hand. Instead of worrying about what 'We, The Humans' are going to do to them, or what we are going to 'Make Them Do,' they concentrate on what they were doing at the moment of the click.

"The benefits of using the clicker are enormous. We had been working for three days with a yearling male llama with the clicker, teaching him to stand for catching and haltering. The owner came up to take the llama home, and was playing around on our llama obstacle course. She approached a low wooden bridge on the ground and encouraged the young male to cross over it with her. At each approach, the llama would first refuse, then flail about wildly, jumping high into the air and off to the side, doing everything except for touching that bridge. After several attempts, I suggested using the clicker. One foot toward the bridge, *Click!* One foot up, *Click!* Walk across the bridge, easy as pie!

"The llama looked at us as if to say, 'Well, why didn't you just say so!!!!'

"The owner could not believe it! It was such a dramatic turnaround! The clicker is a clear, calming signal that truly reduces stress and fear in stressful and scary situations. It is something that the llama can really understand, comprehend, and apply to his life, everyday.

"We have used the clicker to teach everything from stand, catch, halter, lead, and load to obstacle work. The llamas have learned a variety of other behaviors too—pick up the trash and put it in the garbage, take off my hat, close or open the barn door, turn the arena lights on, go get your halter, stack up the grain bowls, etc. We can clearly see by their attitude that they are enthusiastic about these training sessions. The llamas not being worked at the moment pace along the fence, waiting their turn. When it is their turn, it is the norm to watch them buck and kick happily, going into the training area for their lesson. Try and get that kind of attitude with traditional training!

"We strongly encourage all llama owners to give clicker training a try. A few short sessions to introduce the clicker will go a long way to managing your llamas more quickly and easily. There will be less stress for you and for your llamas, and you will be able to achieve your training goals much faster than before."

One of the things I most appreciate about clicker training is how versatile a tool it is. While I was working on the final chapters of this book, one of my clients sent me two llamas to train. Jim's video gave me a starting point, or at least a place to head. The llamas he was working with all took food from the hand. I was starting with two skittish youngsters who scooted to the opposite end of their pen if you held out your hand.

I met these llamas for the first time during a clinic. People weren't going to see much clicker training if we couldn't get near these animals, so Friday night before the clinic started, I went out to the barn and sat in their pen with a bucket of grain on my lap. There were four weanlings in the group, and a year-and-a-half-old female. The older female was bold enough to come over and eat out of the bucket. That encouraged the weanlings. They started crowding in to eat. I clicked each time one of them reached his nose into the bucket for grain.

That's all I did Friday night. Saturday morning I went out early and sat with them again. This time I put my hand in the bucket. If they wanted grain, they'd have to touch my hand to get to it. Again, I clicked each time one of them reached into the bucket.

The older female led the way. She was willing to eat grain off my hand, but scooted back if I lifted my hand up out of the bucket. I'd increased my standards too fast. I lifted my hand more slowly, and within just a very few minutes she was taking grain directly from my hand. I was well on the way to having a clicker-trained llama.

Several hours later the clinic participants all crowded into the llama pen and continued the process I had begun. Once the weanlings were comfortable eating out of our hands, we taught them

to target on a closed fist. Instead of holding our hand out flat and offering them grain, we closed our hands. The llamas were expecting food. When they nosed our hands, click, we opened our hand and fed them. From that simple beginning we could teach the llamas to lead. By withholding the click, we could get the llamas to follow our hand around the pen (Fig 69).

Fig. 69: The llamas progressed from eating out of a bucket held on our laps, to taking food directly from the hand, to targeting on our hands for a click and a treat, to following a hand as we led them around their pen.

I wanted to be able to touch the llamas, but every time we reached toward them, they scooted away. They started humming, a sure sign that this was stressful. Okay, we needed more steps. I borrowed a basic idea from the horse training, and started sacking them out. I started with the older female. I walked toward her with my hand raised. She scooted to the far side of the pen. I kept walking toward her. No matter where she turned in the pen, I followed her, until I saw her glance over in my direction. The instant she did, I clicked, dropped my hand and turned away. She was too nervous to take food from me, but I could still give her something she wanted. It's not very flattering, but removing my presence was the one thing she found most reinforcing.

After I'd done this half a dozen times, she began to understand that she could stop my pursuit simply by looking at me. She starting looking at me sooner, and she wasn't just glancing in my direction. She was turning her whole head. The next time I turned away, she took a step toward me. I clicked again and held out my hand. She came forward and took the grain I was offering her.

In the next trial, she stopped almost instantly. Instead of turning away I just dropped my eyes and offered her the grain. She approached me again, and ate out of my hand. The next time she stood her ground and let me touch her back. *Click!* It was jackpot time.

We were beginning to assemble the pieces we'd need to handle these llamas. The next piece we wanted was haltering. Jim Logan's *Click and Reward* video showed us a simple way to do this. Jim taught his llamas to target on their halters.

Our llamas were already targeting on our hands. It was a simple matter to hold the halter up and have

them touch it instead. When they nosed the halter, click, they got a nibble of grain. In just a very few minutes we had all five llamas eagerly pushing their noses into the open loop of the halter.

When the clinic ended Sunday night, even the most timid of the weanlings was approaching people, following targets, accepting a halter, and allowing himself to be touched. One of the things I appreciate most about clicker training is that it gives you such a gentle way to establish a relationship with an animal. Two of the llamas went home with me after the clinic. I am very much just in the early stages of learning about llamas, but the one thing I have discovered is the clicker is a super way to train them. All the principles and exercises outlined in this book can be applied directly to them (Figs. 70, 71, 72).

Fig. 70: We used targeting to teach the llamas to come when called. While two of the handlers hide their target sticks, the third person presents her target and says "Come." This is a great exercise I borrowed straight from the clicker dog trainers.

Fig. 71: The result: clicker training makes catching the llamas easy. When I call them in, they come right up to the target stick and follow me in.

Fig. 72: Ever since I met my first llamas back in 1984, I've wanted to hug a llama. Now, thanks to a little "clicker magic," I have llamas who hug me back.

COWS

Burt Smith in Hawaii has come up with a novel application for clicker training. He isn't trying to train a single individual. He works with an entire herd. Burt serves as the Extension Specialist in Pasture and Livestock Management for the University of Hawaii at Manoa.

In 1987 Burt began behavioral studies on cattle and other herd animals. He was attempting to solve some of the problems that were developing with the adoption of intensive grazing programs, in which animals had to be frequently moved from one pasture to another. These studies led to the development of low-stress herding techniques. The basic rationale for low-stress herding is simple. The more slowly the animal moves away from a herder, the less stress the animal experiences. The lower the stress, the greater the meat or milk production; the greater the production, the higher the net economic return.

Training takes this idea one step further. The handler is no longer sending the herd away from him. Instead he becomes the herd leader and the animals simply follow him. According to Burt, "Proper training, using positive reinforcement, is capable of removing almost all psychological stress, and even allows for a tolerance of mild physical stress. Such training quickly changes the role of the herder from predator, to object of curiosity, to trainer, to leader."

Burt describes his method for doing this: "The first step in training is to condition the animal to a signal that means food is coming. I've found that a New Zealand dog whistle works best, as it carries well for over a mile. So far, it is just like training a dog or a horse; find a reward they will work for and then condition a signal to that reward. Actually everything's pretty much the same, it's just that you have to go about it in a slightly different fashion. The first such difference is that you get one, or at most two, training sessions per day, depending on how frequently you move your cattle to fresh paddocks. Unlike giving a dog a piece of hot dog as a reward, when you open a fresh paddock for a herd of hungry cattle, their reward goes on and on until they finish their grazing bout.

"Another little problem is dealing with the individuals' and the herds' respective flight zone. Unlike pets and most pleasure horses, virtually all livestock have a flight distance with respect to humans. On some Western ranches this zone is measured in furlongs, and on others in feet. So when a potential trainer waltzes out there, the first order of business is often reducing this flight zone down to acceptable levels of fifteen to thirty feet. This doesn't happen in a day, but it can within a week or so if the proper techniques are followed.

"'Whatever you are doing—you are doing it too fast!' That's a major law of quiet herding. Cow speed is 2.5 mph or slower. Anything moving faster than the group bothers them. Simply moving at a slow walk, and stopping whenever they become nervous or start to run, goes a long way in calming down a herd of animals.

"Reducing the flight zone can be accomplished at the same time the animals are being conditioned to the secondary reinforcer. But you have to remember, until you demonstrate differently, you are a predator. A thing to be respected, if not feared."

All this is sound advice for those of us working around horses. If anyone is struggling with a horse that is hard to catch, you may find some useful hints in Burt's work with cattle. So how do you begin?

"If the animals are used to being moved to fresh pastures frequently, so much the better. If not, a bit of herding may be in order to bring them up to the gate. As the lead animals pass through the gate, sound the signal. Continue to do this for several days running. Then simply arrive at the area, go to the gate, and sound the signal. You are looking for motion toward you (and the gate) by any individual somewhere near the front of the group. As soon as you have that, start backing up, attempting to draw them toward you. This may take several sessions, depending upon past experiences of the herd. The important thing is to get them to walk through the gate to fresh forage. Periodically, sound the signal, as different animals pass through and put their heads down to take a bite.

"At this point, if your goal was simply to get them to come when you sound a signal, you have essentially accomplished your objective. It will take a few more times to set the signal firmly in their minds, and you may wish to work a little more on getting the stragglers to come a little quicker, but for all practical purposes the behavior is well on its way to being learned.

"To become a leader requires a little more effort. It is not actually necessary, but to avoid confusion you should adopt a second signal that will come to mean 'follow me.' For example, a long blast could mean: 'come the gate is open,' whereas two short blasts could mean: 'come, follow me.'

"If you are drawing them through the gate, you have already begun the leader training. The next step is to begin to guide them to some part of the new paddock where the forage is the very best and stop there. Wait until they appear to be following you pretty well, which, if you're good at picking out good eating spots, may be only a few days. If you're a hopeless connoisseur of grass, try going to where the grass has a blue-green tint, or where there is a lot of clover or other legumes (some grass is known by the company it keeps). At this point call them to some place along the fence, not at the gate. As they approach you, draw them toward and through the gate and to the best dinner in the place. Gradually extend your position away from the gate until they are following you some distance.

"At this point you might try some large sweeping maneuvers around the old paddock before moving into the new. Eventually they'll follow you almost anywhere. The acid test comes when you attempt to lead them into a catch pen or corral. In general, catch pens and corrals bring out bad memories, so you may experience some reluctance. This can be overcome by leading them through the pen or corral a few times simply to get to a fresh paddock on the other side. If they absolutely refuse to come into the corral, don't force the issue. Put something they like such as a salt or molasses block just inside the corral gate, and leave the corral gate open. Come back tomorrow and try again."

Burt ends his discussion with the following two comments:

"If you know what you're doing, the total time will be under twenty-one days of training sessions. If you don't know what you're doing but are teachable, it may require three to four weeks. If you're unteachable, then you have a job for life.

"I don't know where the end point of herd training is, or even if there is an end point. I do know that a herd that follows a trainer/herder to a location arrives there a lot quicker, a lot fresher, and is ready to go to work as soon as they get there, putting on weight, making milk or fiber, more than one that had to be driven. As an ex-open-range cowboy I also know the fatigue and bone weariness that results from driving cattle even short distances. How much easier, faster, and simpler it is for all concerned to simply lead them."

As someone who has experienced the frustrating job of moving horses around that don't want to be caught, I can whole-heartedly agree.

CHAPTER TWENTY-SEVEN

The All-Species Clicker Class

Fig. 73: No matter what the species is, the basic rules for shaping are the same. This was the llamas' first "All-Species Clicker Class." They were joining more experienced clicker-trained animals.

We clicker trainers have a lot to learn from each other. I appreciate every opportunity I get to work with other species, and to learn from other trainers. We are all so creative. Each one of us provides a unique perspective that stretches us beyond where we currently are. That's why we started the All-Species Clicker Class at the barn where I keep Peregrine. It's an informal group. We meet Friday nights, and we share our training experiences and expertise from different fields. Our four-footed participants so far have included horses, dogs, a goat, and, of course, the llamas.

Here's an account from our very first meeting, which I posted to the e-mail clicker list.

"Friday night we had the first meeting of the 'All-Species Clicker Class.' In attendance were three horses, one dog, and a goat, plus their owners and four spectators/helpers. Everyone except the goat was already clicker-trained. The horses included

Magnat, an Arabian who was handled by his blind owner; Crackers, an Appaloosa, who is learning to line dance using the clicker; and Robin, a twenty-three-month-old Cleveland Bay cross who is the newest member of my equine family.

"The dog, Penny, belongs to one of my riding students. They've been doing obedience work together, and this fall they added clicker training into the mix. The goat was being handled by a teenager who owns a very rambunctious husky mix. I've been helping her with her dog, and she's become a very good clicker trainer. She had the most difficult job of the night, holding onto Oakie. If you think a dog can pull, you've obviously never gone water skiing behind a goat.

"Our mission is first and foremost to have fun, and second to work on the skills all these different animals would need if we were to enter them into a dog obedience class. My personal goal is to go beyond thinking like a horse trainer. I want to stretch the boundaries of what and how we normally teach horses. For starters I invited my dog training friends to come and share what they know, and to train their dogs alongside the horses.

"We sent the goat off to the side to be conditioned to the clicker, while the rest of us worked on heeling patterns. We used our helpers as traffic cones and worked on figure-eight patterns. Penny, our canine representative, worked off leash, but for this first session we kept the horses on leads. We also worked on extended stays (ground tying for the horses), and then moved onto retrieves (Fig. 74).

"Penny won the bravery award for the night. At one point she was heading for her dumbbell, when Robin saw it. He wanted to pick it up, too, and made a face at Penny. Penny is a very timid dog, but when her person asked her again, she went ahead and retrieved her dumbbell.

"Magnat and Crackers did an excellent job of picking up their horse dumbbells, and Robin got to show off his retrieving skills by chasing down a plastic cone. I can throw it out twenty or thirty feet, and he'll retrieve it. He has trouble holding onto it. When he comes trotting back to me, it swings so much he tends to drop it. We've been experimenting with horse dumbbells, but so far we haven't made anything that will hold up to his youthful enthusiasm.

"Crackers took a break to play with his Buster Cube, and then we finished off the night with a little equine line dancing exhibition. I put Robin through the pattern for the first time which includes lateral work and some quick changes of direction, and found he could do it with ease. How wonderful to be so young and limber."

CLIMBING MOUNT EVEREST

I'm sure there are people who will read this and think we've gone over the edge. They'll be saying, "Aren't you carrying this clicker training stuff at little too far? I can understand why you might want to train with dogs around, but why would you want to teach a horse to retrieve a dumbbell?" The answer is the same one people give for climbing Mount Everest: because it's there. If you can teach a dog to pick up a dumbbell, why not teach a horse?

If nothing else, these games are making our horses much harder to spook. They proved their worth to me when I took Robin out for one of our first long walks together. We had to pass a teenager shooting

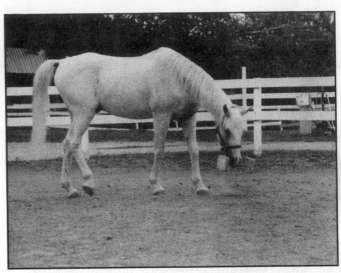

Fig. 74: Magnat, the Arabian, retrieves his dumbbell.

basketball hoops. I saw Robin hesitate for about half a second, and then he walked right by. He understood about balls. That kid couldn't scare him.

Treating our horses like overgrown golden retrievers makes training fun for all of us. That's especially important for Robin. While he's learning to stay focused on me in the midst of chaos, he gets to play with cones and chase after dumbbells. I couldn't ask for a better training situation for any horse than our "All Species Clicker Class." Think of the distractions he's learning to work with.

But even more basic than that is the attitude it creates in the animals we're working with. One of the hallmarks of clicker-trained animals is they love to learn.

WHERE DO WE GO FROM HERE?

Clicker training began with dolphins doing simple tricks in swimming pools. Now, thirty years later, the technology has evolved to the point where dolphins are performing complex tasks out in the ocean for their trainers.

We're at the stage, with horses and other domestic pets, where these trainers were thirty years ago. We're just beginning to figure out how to get simple behaviors from our animals. As more of us start to experiment with clicker training, and really learn how to use it, I think we're going to be astounded at how much our animals can really do. One of the most exciting elements of clicker training is that we are all pioneers in this together. None of us knows just how far this new technology will take us. When I watch good trainers train, no matter what species they're working with, I learn more about what is possible, and I learn how to stretch the boundaries of my own training skills.

Clicker training is truly the leading edge of modern animal training. It's exciting to think about what training will be like in ten years as we expand on this new technology. As more and more people discover clicker training and begin experimenting with their own animals, I think we are going to see an explosion of creative ideas. We're going to see what is really possible, and it's going to take us way beyond our current patterns of thinking. That's the challenge I want to put out there. Have fun with all of this. I know I am (Fig. 75).

Fig. 75: Training becomes a joy when it lets you play with your horse.

Appendices

Appendixes

APPENDIX A:

When Is a Training Problem Not a Training Problem? Checking Saddle Fit

THICK VERSUS THIN: SADDLE PADS AND BITS

Why do some horses hate being tacked up? Why do they resist the bridle and dance around for the saddle? One obvious reason may be pain. You may not have a training problem at all. If your horse clamps his teeth shut every time he sees a bridle, have a vet check his teeth. Make sure he checks the entire tooth row, including the back molars. Those molars can be hard to reach, but hooks back there can make a huge difference in how readily your horse accepts a bit.

If your horse is still fussing, even after you've had his teeth floated, take a look at his bit. How thick is it? We often think of fat bits as being very gentle. We've been told a thin bit is like having a piece of wire cutting into your tongue. In reality, neither extreme may be very comfortable for your horse. The thicker bit may be simply too big for his mouth. If his teeth don't come very far out of the gum line, he may not be able to close his mouth comfortably. It's like having a fat wad of chewing gum you can't spit out. After a few minutes it can be really annoying.

Thicker isn't always better holds true for saddle pads as well. We want our horse to be comfortable. We know that a nice, thick cushion feels good to us, so it stands to reason our horse will like it, too. So we buy the thickest, softest pad in the tack store. None of those thin quilts are good enough for our horse. The problem is that the thick pad may actually end up making your horse sore.

To understand how this works, look carefully at the shape of your saddle. Put it on a saddle rack with your favorite thick pad. The back half of the saddle is fairly flat. It's designed to sit evenly on the broad expanse of the horse's loins. The front half needs to mold around the horse's withers. What that means for your horse is that you have added one layer of thickness behind, and two in front.

If you're not following that, look carefully at the front of the saddle. The pad folds down on either side of his withers. It's only a single pad, but you've added one layer of material between his right shoulder and the saddle, and another between his left shoulder and the saddle. This means you've raised the saddle up more in front than you have behind.

This can do several things. With the added thickness, you may actually be pinching his withers. One way to check for this is to put the saddle on your horse and test the amount of bounce it has. Put your index finger under the back of the cantle and lift. A well-fitted saddle will not lift up off the horse's back. A saddle that's fitting poorly over the withers will bounce up easily. When you add a thick pad, you can actually turn a well-fitted saddle into one that bounces.

CORRECT POSITIONING OF THE SADDLE

Correct placement on the horse's back is very important. You want the saddle to sit behind the shoulder blade, not on it. A saddle that's too far forward won't be level, and it can create a lot of pain, rubbing against the cartilage at the tip of the shoulder blade.

To learn where to put your saddle, take the edge of your hand and run it back along your horse's shoulder. You'll feel a point where your hand will drop down behind the shoulder. That's where most English saddles should sit. Now, take your saddle and do the same thing. Start with it too far forward, and slide it back until you feel it drop into place behind the shoulder.

IS THE SADDLE LEVEL?

Even with your saddle correctly positioned on your horse's back, a thick pad can still make it unlevel.

If the front end is higher than the cantle, the rider will be sitting way out of balance. He'll be posting out of a hole, with his feet shooting out in front of him. Every time he lands, he'll be banging his horse in the back. It won't take long for your horse to say he's had enough!

FITTING THE SHOULDERS

A saddle should mirror the contours of the horse's shoulder. Look at the saddle from the front as it sits on the horse. A good way to judge fit here is to hold two whips against the horse. Line the first one up with the horse's shoulder, and the other one with the saddle. They should be roughly parallel with one another.

You can also feel under the saddle to check for uneven or excessive pressure. Be certain to check both sides of your horse. A saddle that fits well over one shoulder may pinch on the other side. And while you're checking for symmetry, be certain to look carefully at the saddle itself, from the front and the rear. A crooked saddle isn't going to help either you or your horse.

Check also for a broken tree. Hold the front of the saddle pressed against your side, and apply pressure to the cantle. If the tree is broken, you'll feel the saddle bend in the middle. A broken tree can seriously injure your horse's back, and should not be used. There is no remedy for a broken tree other than a new saddle.

CHECK FOR PRESSURE POINTS

Be certain to check the amount of clearance the saddle has over the horse's spine. With a rider up, you should be able to fit two to three fingers between the horse's back and the saddle.

A thick pad can change the fit and create pressure sores. Put your saddle on your horse without any pad. Check the amount of clearance you have, then feel for uneven pressure along the horse's back. Reach up under the saddle flap. If it fits well, you should feel no gap anywhere along the weight-bearing surface of the padding.

Now add a thin quilt and check for gaps. Next try your thick pad. Chances are, you may now feel a substantial gap right in the middle of the saddle, where most of the rider's weight is concentrated.

Rather than distributing pressure evenly across the horse's back, the pad is actually concentrating it against the withers and the loins.

You were trying to make your horse as comfortable as possible, and instead you made his back sore. You bought a nice, thick bit for the same reason, and now he hates bridling.

Okay, so now you've got a saddle that fits, you've changed your bit, and you had the vet float his teeth. He's got no excuses, and he's still being a jerk every time you tack him up. Why? Because he's still expecting it to hurt. So now it's time to go back to training, to chunk down each piece in the sequence until he tells you he's comfortable.

APPENDIX B

Tongue Clicks

This may seem like an odd subject to be including in a book, but I've found a lot of people have trouble clicking. They cluck. They squeak. They chirp. But none of these are quite right, so they give up. That's a bad deal, so we're going to have a lesson in tongue clicking. If you already know how to do it, you can skip this section. For the rest of you, your attention please. Class is now in session.

First, a word of encouragement. When I first started with the clicker, I couldn't make a tongue-click, either. I was so glad I had a little plastic box to help me out. I still use the clicker whenever I start a horse. It's such a distinct sound, I think the horses notice it sooner and learn the game faster than they do with a tongue click.

Once they're listening to the mechanical clicker, they have no trouble transferring to a new sound source. I had one eager beaver who tried stopping whenever his joints clicked! Once they're tuned in, even a clumsy click will serve the purpose. (By the way, if your horse should start thinking that every stray sound is a click meant for him, just ignore him. If you don't respond, he'll very quickly learn which is the real click that produces goodies.)

When I first started, I didn't work at learning how to make a tongue click. It just happened. At first I could barely get the sound out. Now I can sit on the mounting block in our arena and stop a horse a hundred feet away. Talk about power! It's a great advantage in a lesson to be able to bring someone else's horse to a screeching halt. If they aren't rewarding their horse often enough, I can do something about it!

HOW TO CLICK

Now on to the actual how-to section. These instructions come from the e-mail clicker list. My

thanks go out to Vanna Campbell for sharing her very detailed and accurate description.

1. Put the tip of your tongue up on the gum ridge just behind your front teeth as if you were going to say the letter t as in "touch."

2. Allow the tip to flatten against the gum ridge as you move the back of your tongue up, as if you are simultaneously trying to say a k as in king.

3. As you get the contact in the back of your mouth, the tongue tip may slide back a little, until it is just behind the ridge it started out on. This is fine.

4. You should now have a little air trapped in a pocket between your tongue and the roof of your mouth.

5. You know the pocket is completely sealed (a complete seal is important) if you can feel contact all the way around your tongue. It is kind of hard to tell what is going on in one's mouth, but if you move your tongue slightly from side to side, it helps to create sensations you can interpret. If it feels like it is only touching in the front, it is, and you don't have a seal.

6. Once you have a little pocket of air sealed up, suck. By this, I mean pretend you are trying to suck soda through a straw. It is hard to do this, because your tongue is in the wrong place for normal soda sucking, but you will know you have it right when the sensation of your tongue touching the roof of your mouth gets firmer and clearer. Also your tongue will start to feel like it is tense, or like it is making an effort.

7. Try gently to open your jaw a lot wider, which will pull down on your tongue. You will know you have the right position, with a complete seal,

if your tongue resists moving away from the roof of your mouth. After a while you will just know you have a complete seal, and you won't have to test it this way anymore.

8. With your tongue in position, and your mouth only slightly open, suck harder and harder on the little pocket of trapped air.

9. At some point you won't be able to suck any harder, which is when you pull down the back of your tongue. The tip of your tongue can stay in contact with the front of the mouth, and in fact, it is easier to learn to do this click if it does. Once you get good at it, it won't matter what the tip does.

10. The sound you produce can be anything from a very clean, sharp, snapping click (which is what you want), to a very sloppy, scratchy, juicy click (more or less like the get-moving-horse click people do on one side of their mouths).

11. If you have a non-optimal click, the best cure is to just keep doing it. The usual progression is to have a lot of different things happen, and suddenly, a good one crops up. You go—What did I do? And it is not clear, but you keep on clicking, and a few more good ones come, and eventually they are all good, and you still don't know exactly what you are doing (but by that time it doesn't matter).

Vanna added to her instructions the following postscript: "Having said all this, I should tell you that just trying, without having any idea of what you are supposed to be doing, also works. All the boys in my seventh-grade class seemed to learn to do this great, loud click, and I am sure they did not use the above recipe. They were just highly motivated to keep at it until they could click."

GLOSSARY

PART I: HORSE-RELATED TERMS

Abscess: A localized collection of pus, often seen in the horse's feet. Since the hard wall of the hoof cannot expand, the buildup of pus causes extreme pain.

Aid: Any of the signals used by the rider to give instructions to the horse. Artificial aids include whips, spurs, and martingales. Natural aids include the rider's seat, hands, and legs.

Appaloosa: A Western horse, originally bred by the Nez Perce Indians, and known for its spotted coat patterns.

Arabian: A desert breed from the Middle East known for its great beauty and stamina. Arabians are the foundation breed for most other breeds of horses.

Bit: Part of the bridle; a metal mouthpiece which is used to control and direct the horse.

Bridle: The harness fitted about a horse's head, consisting of a headstall, bit, and reins, used to control and direct the horse.

Canter: One of the three basic gaits of the horse. The canter is a three-beat gait, a slow gallop.

Cavalletti: A series of small wooden jumps used in the basic training of a riding horse in order to improve its balance and strengthen its muscles.

Chambons: One of the many leverage devices used in lunging to teach a horse to round its topline.

Cleveland Bay: An English breed developed primarily as a carriage horse. Cleveland Bays are today considered an endangered breed with less than five hundred purebreds left in the world.

Colic: Sharp abdominal pains often caused by an obstruction in the digestive tract. Since horses cannot vomit, colic is a red-alert, call-the-vet-immediately situation.

Collection: In collection the horse shifts its balance backward and carries more weight in its hindquarters. Its body becomes rounder and more elevated, as it engages its hindquarters and lifts its back.

Cribbing: An annoying barn vice in which the horse clamps its front teeth onto a piece of wood and sucks air into its stomach. The behavior is said to release endorphins and is therefore self-reinforcing. Some cribbers swallow so much air that they upset their digestions and trigger bouts of colic.

Curb bit: Any bit, whether jointed or not, that uses leverage by means of a shank to which the reins are attached.

Draw Reins: Leather straps running from the girth through the bit and back to the rider's hands. Draw reins are leverage devices used for control and to mold a horse's topline.

Dressage: (1.) The art of training horses to perform in a balanced, supple, relaxed, obedient, but energetic manner. (2.) "Trained beyond the ordinary:" John Lyons.

Engagement: A movement in which the horse shifts his weight towards his hindquarters, lowers his hip joints, and brings his hind legs further underneath his body.

Gait: The manner of traveling. The horse has three basic gaits: walk, trot, and canter. In addition some breeds show other natural gaits including the pace and running walk.

Girth: A band, usually made of leather, cotton webbing, or nylon, passed under the belly of the horse and attaching to the saddle to hold it in place.

Green horse: A horse which is working under saddle but is not yet fully trained; an inexperienced horse.

Ground tying: The equine version of the canine "sit-stay." The horse stands in one spot, without being tied or held, until told to do something else.

Half halt: A redistribution of weight toward the hindquarters; used in riding to rebalance and steady the horse.

Haflinger: A small mountain horse originally from Austria.

Halter: A head piece made of leather, rope, or nylon that is used to lead or tie the horse.

Hand: A unit of length equal to four inches, used to express the height of a horse as measured at the withers. The fractions are given in inches. For example, a horse which is 15:2 hands is 15 x 4 inches + 2 inches, or 62 inches tall at the withers.

Haunches: The hindquarters of a horse.

Headstall: The main part of the bridle; it holds the bit and passes behind the horse's ears and across the poll from one side of the head to the other.

High School Dressage: the classical art of equitation.

Hock: The largest joint in the horse's hind leg, at the level of the knee in the fore leg.

Icelandic horse: A strong, sturdy, pony-sized breed from Iceland, known for its spectacular flying pace.

Lateral Work: Any movement in which the horse's hind leg does not step in the same track as the front foot on the same side. Lateral movements include haunches-in, shoulder-in, half pass, leg yields, and sidepass.

Laminitis: An inflammation of the sensitive laminae of the foot, the structures which attach the bone of the foot to the hoof wall. Laminitis is a painful and life-threatening condition.

Lateral flexion: Bending the horse to the side.

Liberty work: Working the horse from the ground without any leads or restraints of any kind attached to horse.

Lunging: The horse is asked to circle at a walk, trot, and canter around the handler, usually at the end of a twenty-foot line.

Martingale: A leather strap or straps running from the saddle or harness girth to the horse's head, that prevents the horse from raising its head too high.

Morgan: A small- to medium-sized American breed originally developed in Vermont.

Mount: To get up on the horse's back.

Near side: The horse's left side. It is usual to lead and mount the horse from this side.

On the bit: A willingness to respond to the slightest change in the rider's hand. The horse is well balanced and in self-carriage.

Piaffe: A classical high school movement, the epitome of collection. The horse appears to trot in place.

Poll: The area immediately behind the horse's ears.

Potomac horse fever: A life-threatening disease. Symptoms of high fever, loss of appetite, and diarrhea often lead to severe and even fatal laminitis.

Rein back: To make a horse step backward.

Quarter Horse: A stocky Western breed known for its powerful hindquarters, speed and versatility. Developed for working cattle, Quarter horses are popular today for all forms of riding.

Round pen training: Training a horse at liberty in a fenced-in enclosure, usually a sixty-foot diameter round pen.

Self-carriage: The horse holds himself in good balance without any restraint from equipment or rider.

Shoulder-in: A lateral movement in which the horse's outside shoulder comes in off the outside track, and the horse is bent away from the direction of movement.

Side reins: Leather straps running from the bit and attaching either to the saddle or a surcingle or belt. They are used to encourage the horse to flex its topline in order to bring it onto the bit.

Snaffle bit: Any bit in which the reins attach directly to the rings of the bit. A bit in which the reins attach via shanks is a curb bit.

Spanish walk: The equine version of the military "goose step;" a walk with a moment of suspension where the front leg lifts and fully extends. Done correctly the hind legs should remain deeply engaged.

Spooking: A term for the horse's swerving away suddenly from an obstacle or sound; shying.

Stifles: The joint above the hocks in the horse's hind leg. Structurally the stifle joint is the horse's knee, but it is higher up in the leg than our human knee.

Sweat scraper: A curved metal blade used to remove water or sweat from a horse's coat.

Thoroughbred: An English breed originally bred for racing, and now used widely as a sport horse.

Topline: The shape of the horse's upper body from his nose to his tail. The topline indicates how the horse is using its body.

Trot: A two-beat diagonal gait; one of the three basic gaits of the horse.

Walk: A four-beat gait, one of the three basic gaits of the horse.

Withers: The part of the spine that rises up between the horse's shoulder blades.

Wobbler Syndrome: Any of several conditions in which injury to the spinal cord has resulted in a loss of sensation in the hind quarters. The horse has difficulty feeling where its feet are and wobbles from side to side trying to maintain its balance.

PART II: CLICKER TRAINING TERMS

Bridging stimulus: A stimulus, usually a sound, that "bridges" the time gap between performance of a behavior and the receiving of a reward. Another term for secondary reinforcer.

Click: The sound produced either by a mechanical clicker or the tongue, used as a secondary reinforcer.

Clicker-trained: Refers to animals that have been conditioned to a click as a secondary reinforcer.

Cue: A discriminative stimulus preceding an operant or learned behavior, indicating the availability of reinforcement for that particular behavior; thus, in practice, a signal to execute a particular behavior.

Molding: Physically moving the subject into the position you want.

Motivator: An event or object capable of reinforcing behavior. Motivators can be either positive or negative, but they must make sense to the animal. For example, you might alter your behavior to pick up a twenty-dollar bill off the ground. A toddler might ignore the same slip of paper, but go after your dog's favorite chew toy lying next to it.

Negative Reinforcer: Any unpleasant event or stimulus that can be halted or avoided by changing one's behavior.

Operant Conditioning: Operant refers to the operator, that is, the subject performing the behavior, not the trainer. In operant conditioning, the subject learns to offer deliberately those behaviors that have been previously reinforced. When positive reinforcement is emphasized over negative reinforcers and punishment operant conditioning becomes a highly effective and pleasant way for an animal to learn.

Primary reinforcer: any event or stimulus which the subject wants innately, without learning, such as food. Presenting a primary reinforcer in conjunction with a behavioral event increases the likelihood of a behavior occurring again. Primary reinforcers that have been linked with a bridging signal or a secondary reinforcer become powerful training tools.

Punishment: An unpleasant or painful stimulus that stops a behavior as it is occurring. Because the behavior stops, at least temporarily, punishment is reinforcing to the punisher. Punishment however cannot prevent behavior from recurring.

Schedules of reinforcement
Fixed schedule: In a fixed schedule of reinforcement the reward is offered on a predictable basis, based on the number of repetitions of a behavior. In clicker training the fixed schedule is usually on a one-to-one ratio, i.e. give the behavior, get a treat. Fixed schedules usually occur in the early stages of training when the animal is first learning a particular behavior.

Variable schedule: In a variable schedule of reinforcement, the trainer reinforces some but not all occurrences of the behavior. Variable schedules may be used selectively (a *differential* schedule of reinforcement) to select for improved examples of the behavior, or randomly, to reinforce a well-established behavior unpredictably to maintain a high level of performance. Variable reinforcement schedules coupled with secondary reinforcers push behavior towards excellence.

Reward: Something which is gained after a particular act. Rewards are not synonymous with reinforcement, because they do not necessarily occur in conjunction with the behavior. Thus they may or may not influence future behavior, as reinforcers do by definition.

Secondary or conditioned reinforcer: An initially meaningless signal which is paired with the primary reinforcer, and eventually precedes it in a reward sequence. This is the bridging signal or "right answer cue". It tells the animal that the behavior it just did is desirable and will lead to a reward.

Shaping: Shaping, also called successive approximation, consists of reinforcing any small tendency to perform in a desired way, and then, in small increments, selecting for reinforcement slightly stronger movements or behavior, until the goal of a more complex behavior is reached.

Targeting: A shaping procedure in which the subject learns to touch, orient to, go to, or follow the movements of an arbitrarily selected object. Targeting is a shaping "shortcut" that facilitates many other training goals, such as trailer loading.

Bibliography and Resources

BOOKS

Burmaster, Corally, Ed., 1995, 1996. *The Clicker Journal Collection, Vol. I,* 1995; *Vol. II,* 1996. The Clicker Journal, 20146 Gleedsville Rd., Leesburg, VA 20175.

Lyons, John and Sinclair Browning, 1991. *Lyons On Horses.* Doubleday.

Pryor, Karen, 1995. *Don't Shoot The Dog! The New Art Of Teaching And Training.* Bantam Books.

___,1990. *Lads Before The Wind: Diary Of A Dolphin Trainer.* Sunshine Books.

Smith, Burt, 1998. *Moving 'Em: A Guide To Low Stress Animal Handling.* Graziers Hui.

Tellington-Jones, Linda and Ursula Bruns, 1988. *The Tellington-Jones Equine Awareness Method.* Breakthrough Publications, Inc.

VIDEOS

Logan, Jim. *Click and Reward Training For Llamas.* Snow Ridge Llamas, Rt. 3 Box 78, Chattaroy, WA 99003; 1-888-332-5425; e-mail: snowridgel@aol.com.

Lyons, John. *Leading and Loading Safely.* John Lyons Symposiums, Inc.

___. *Round Pen Reasoning.* John Lyons Symposiums, Inc.

___. *John Lyons Symposium Series I,* 6 tapes. John Lyons Symposiums, Inc.

___. *John Lyons Symposium Series II: Controlling the Mind and Body Of Your Horse,* 7 tapes. John Lyons Symposiums, Inc.

Parelli, Pat. *The Natural Horsemanship Video Course.* Parelli Natural Horsemanship Center.

VIDEOS *(continued)*

___. *The Seven Games Of Natural Horsemanship.* Parelli Natural Horsemanship Center.

Pryor, Karen. *Clicker Magic!* video and clicker. Sunshine Books.

___. *If I Could Talk to the Animals.* Sunshine Books.

___. *Shaping: Building Behavior Step By Step.* Sunshine Books.

___. *Sit! Clap! Furbish! Putting Behavior On Cue.* Sunshine Books.

___. *Super Training: Vols. 1 and 2.* Sunshine Books.

Tellington-Jones, Linda, *TTEAM Learning Exercises I and II.* TTEAM and Animal Ambassadors International, Sante Fe, NM.

Wilkes, Gary. *Click and Treat Training Kit,* video, booklet, and clicker. www.clickandtreat.com, 1 (800) 456-9526.

___. *On Target!* www.clickandtreat.com, 1 (800) 456-9526.

PRODUCTS

Buster Cubes
Legacy By Mail
P.O. Box 794
Kula, HI 96790
1-888-871-0623
Email: lgcymail@maui.net
www.legacy-by-mail.com

Clickers
Sunshine Books
49 River Street, Suite 3
Waltham, MA 02453-8345
Email: sales@clickertraining.com
www.clickertraining.com

PRODUCTS *(continued)*

Gentle Leader – Head Halter for Dogs
Direct Book Service
701 B Poplar Street
Wenatchee WA 98807
1-800-776-2665
www.dogandcatbooks.com

John Fisher Sound Disks, books, video
Direct Book Service
701 B Poplar Street
Wenatchee WA 98807
1-800-776-2665
www.dogandcatbooks.com

USEFUL ADDRESSES

The Clicker Journal
Corally Burmaster, Editor
20146 Gleedsville Rd.
Leesburg, VA 20175

Alexandra Kurland
110 Salisbury Rd.
Delmar, NY 12054
Email: kurlanda@crisny.org
www.crisny.org/users/kurlanda

John Lyons Symposiums Inc.
PO Box 479
Parachute, CO 81635
970-285-9797

John Lyons' Perfect Horse Magazine
Subscription Services
P.O. Box 420234
Palm Coast, FL 32142
800-829-2521

Pat Parelli
PNHMS Center
Box 5950
Pagosa Springs, CO 81147
801-864-2325

USEFUL ADDRESSES *(continued)*

Karen Pryor
Sunshine Books, Inc.
49 River Street, Suite 3
Waltham, MA 02453-8345
781-398-0754
email: pryor@clickertraining.com

TTEAM
Animal Ambassadors International
PO Box 3793
Sante Fe, NM 87501-0793
505-455-2945
email: TTEAMUSA@aol.com

Gary Wilkes
Wilkesgm@aol.com
www.clickandtreat.com
1-800-456-9526

Afterword

COMING ATTRACTIONS

The hardest part of writing this book was deciding what to leave out. I started working on it in the spring of 1996. By the time I had finished the final chapter, I had written well over 700 pages. We had to take something out. The riding section was the first to go. That filled a second book just in itself, but it still left this one overstuffed. Next came a nuts-and-bolts section on round pen training, and another wonderful section on trick training, and finally one on behavior chains. That means if there's something in this first book you wish I'd covered in more detail, the chances are I already have. You just have to wait for the next installment. If you want to know more about riding, or liberty training, or how to teach your horse to lie down, it's all going to be in there, along with some more wonderful horses and their clicker training success stories.

MY THANKS

Books like this are always the product of many people's efforts. I wish to thank all of my clients, past and present. Without your willingness to be guinea pigs, I could never have written this book. I especially want to thank all of you who shared your horses and dogs in the pages of this book. Thank you to Jeanette Rotundo and Indy; Lucia Vieiro Coleman and Dancing With The Sun; Joan Adams and Spirit; Mary Ann Nicpon and Monty; Mary Arena and Tibra; Pat Richute, Spock, and Li Wu; Sheila Kellee and Babe; Amy Cable and Mozart; Lindsey Green and Calvin; Ann Edie and Magnat; Bob Viviano and Crackers; Kathy Santola and Oliver; Laura Sommers and Penny; Kelly Vadney and Maggie; and Ginny Romero and Carey.

My special thanks go to Ceci Henderson of Penfrydd Farm for sharing her llamas with me; to

Burt Smith, Jim Logan, and Sue Ailsby, for sharing their clicker expertise; to Janet Seles of Green Mountain Icelandic Horse Farm; and to Catherine Crawmer and Wendy the Wonder Cat. I also want to thank Gary Wilkes and his wonderful dog, Megan. It was watching the joy with which Megan worked that really inspired me to explore clicker training.

I want to thank my teachers: Bettina Drummond—I would be an ordinary trainer if I had not seen her extraordinary work; Linda Tellington-Jones, who taught me to follow my antennae; and John Lyons, who gave structure to my training, and taught me that the horse doesn't know when it doesn't count.

I want to give special thanks to Karen Pryor, first for writing *Don't Shoot The Dog,* and second for offering me this opportunity to share clicker training with the horse community. Her work is changing the way all animals are trained.

I want to thank all my photographers: Cecilia Burns, Pat Richute, Laura Sommers, Marie Triller, and Mary Arena—I really appreciated how you always had time in your schedule to come and take pictures; Lucia Vieira Coleman—what a good sport you were to lend me your camera. Thanks also to Mundi Smithers, for proofreading the original clicker articles. Her excellent suggestions helped to focus those articles and create the foundation for the rest of the book.

My special thanks go to Lynn Dente, and her husband Chuck, owners of Double V Stable. Thank you for the excellent care you give Peregrine and Robin. You've made the barn a home for them. Thank you also for being so open to the clicker training. My thanks also go to all the boarders at Double V Stable. Your willingness to accept something new under your roof has been much appreciated.

I especially want to thank my father for taking me for my first pony ride at the age of three. This is all your doing. Thank you also for the generous use of your computer, and for only grumbling a little at all the hours I monopolized it. Thanks also to my mother for keeping my father occupied and out of the house so I could use the computer.

This list would not be complete without thanking Lucy, my computer cat, for keeping me company through all the hundreds of hours it took to write this book. And finally, I want to thank my two greatest teachers, Pippin and Peregrine.

About The Author

Alexandra Kurland earned her B.S. degree from Cornell University, where she specialized in animal behavior. In the 1980s she studied with Linda Tellington-Jones and became a TTEAM Practitioner. The other major influence on her riding at that time came from the high school dressage trainer, Bettina Drummond. In the early 1990s she added John Lyons' training into the mix to develop her own teaching program, "Riding In a State of Excellence." In 1993 she learned about clicker training and began to apply its principles to horses. Since 1996 she has been writing extensively about her experiences with clicker uses. Her home base is in upstate New York. She can be reached via her web site at: www.crisny.org/users/kurlanda. She is the author of three children's books, The Kenyon Bear Books, and she shares her life with her cats and her horses.

Index

Coming in
1999

Clicker Training for Horses: the Video

Clicker Training for the Rider
by Alexandra Kurland

www.clickertraining.com

Visit our website for publication dates and more clicker training books, videos, information and news

New products and events are also announced in Karen Pryor's free

Don't Shoot the Dog! News

To subscribe, send you name and address to:
Sunshine Books
49 River Street, Suite 3
Waltham, MA 02453

1-800-47-CLICK
781-398-0754
newsletter@clickertraining.com